Class and Property in Marx's Economic Thought

T0270847

This book presents the capitalist system as a function of the interaction of the three basic classes in the capitalist social formation. Through this, it shows how the corresponding conflicts and clashes of interests between those classes – industrial capitalists, wage labourers and landed proprietors – are unavoidable for understanding contemporary economic structures.

Analysing these economic structures in relation to the forms of property ownership, as well as the typical processes of production connected with them, the author points out how Karl Marx's theory of the capitalist social formation is closely connected with the emergence and existence of a national money market. At the same time, the book places a special emphasis on Marx's theory of ground rent and modern landed property, an aspect misinterpreted by many authors; and through an evaluation of the most important Marxian categories regarding the analysis of the world market and its development, further emphasis is placed on the concept of differences in labour intensity between nations. This evaluation illustrates how the main categories of capital, wage labour and landed property acquire a completely different internal relation in poor countries compared to Western capitalist societies.

Class and Property in Marx's Economic Thought aims at exposing a method for analysing contemporary capitalism through focusing on the basic relations of population groups in the capitalist social formation. It will be of interest to students and researchers within the field of economics, as well as other social sciences.

Jørgen Sandemose is Professor Emeritus at the University of Oslo, Norway, where he was made *Magister Artium* in philosophy (with a dissertation on concept formation in Hegel and Marx) in 1973, supported by a full candidatus magisterii exam from 1971. In addition to his academic career, he has worked for fifteen years in the chemico-metallic industry and has held positions of trust in local and national Norwegian trade unions.

In 1975 he published the monograph *Ricardo, Marx og Sraffa* (published in separate editions in Denmark, Norway and Sweden), where he exposed Sraffian mistakes related to Marx's theory of the *numéraire* and the "transformation problem". In English, he has published essays on the relation between Sraffa and Wittgenstein and on Marx's method in economic science.

Routledge Frontiers of Political Economy

Class and Property in Marx's Economic Thought
Exploring the Basis for Capitalism

Jørgen Sandemose

Routledge
Taylor & Francis Group

LONDON AND NEW YORK

First published 2018 by Routledge

2 Park Square, Milton Park, Abingdon, Oxfordshire OX14 4RN
52 Vanderbilt Avenue, New York, NY 10017

Routledge is an imprint of the Taylor & Francis Group, an informa business

First issued in paperback 2020

British Library Cataloguing-in-Publication Data
A catalogue record for this book is available from the British Library

Library of Congress Cataloging-in-Publication Data
Names: Sandemose, Jørgen, author.
Title: Class and property in Marx's economic thought:
exploring the basis for capitalism / Jorgen Sandemose.
Description: Abingdon, Oxon; New York, NY: Routledge, 2018. |
Series: Routledge frontiers of political economy; 242 | Includes
bibliographical references and index.
Identifiers: LCCN 2018002758 (print) | LCCN 2018005545 (ebook) |
ISBN 9781351006989 | ISBN 9781138543331 (hardback: alk. paper)
Subjects: LCSH: Marxian economics. | Social classes. |
Property. | Capitalism.
Classification: LCC HB97.5 (ebook) | LCC HB97.5.S246 2018 (print) |
DDC 335.4/12–dc23
LC record available at https://lccn.loc.gov/2018002758

ISBN: 978-1-138-54333-1 (hbk)
ISBN: 978-0-367-59017-8 (pbk)

Typeset in Times New Roman
by Sunrise Setting Ltd, Brixham, UK

Contents

Acknowledgements

Chapters 1 and 2 contain a restated version of the article "Overganger [Transitions]", which appeared in the Danish journal *Kurasje*, 1977. It was part of the syllabus in modern philosophy at the University of Oslo for some years. One of the themes taken up in the analysis of Marx's "reproduction schemes" in this chapter (on gold production) I have analysed more briefly in an article in the New York journal *Science and Society*.[1]

Chapter 5 is a revised version of my article "The Motley World of International Values: Modes of Production on the World Market", in *Theoretical Economic Letters*, 2015.

I thank the editors for permissions, and the Department of Philosophy, Classics, History of Art and Ideas (IFIKK) at the University of Oslo for financial support. First and foremost, I here repeat my gratitude to Guenther Sandleben for inspirational criticism, especially in our discussions on ground rent theory and the structure of the world market. Furthermore, thanks go to Per Frode Ariansen, Jari Bakken and Kjell Bjørgeengen for invaluable technical assistance. The latter has also made a thorough review of logic, composition and syntax, leaving me solely responsible for all extant errors.

Note

1 In the original translation into English of Chapters 1 and 2 (made for didactic purposes), the edition of Progress Publishers of *Capital* I–III was used. I have chosen to do so again here. In Chapters 3–5, quotes from *Capital* I follow the Penguin edition of 1976. It should be noted that all quotations from other original works of Marx are translated by myself. Also, taking into consideration my extensive use of *Capital* III, it should be remarked that I find no important difference whatsoever, regardless of theme, between this Engels-edited text and the original texts of Marx, published in the new *MEGA*, II/3.3 and II/4.2.

Introduction

This work tries to make a difference. The author aims at exposing a method for analysing contemporary capitalism and seeks to fulfil this task through focusing on the basic relations of population groups in the capitalist social formation – their work and property statuses, their types of revenue and their contrasting objective interests related to the existence of that society.

This means that in the following pages the reader will find no special weight laid on pure monetary phenomena, not even on "finance capital", the alleged entity which stands in focus for so much radical critique of the capitalist system today. Nor will one find any endorsement of the mainstream form of anti-capitalist Marxisant ideology.[1] In this work, no acceptance is allowed for the kind of abolition of Marx's theory of money and prices so prominent – not to say dominant and compulsory – in contemporary "leftist" opposition. Nor will one find the usual active ignoring of Marx's basic theory of modern landed property, with its immense significance for the main classes of bourgeois society.[2]

For the author, capital in its form of means of finance is a function of the general *capitalist money market*. I try to show how this concept was generated in Karl Marx's work as a synthesis of the antagonisms between the three *classes* which make up the inner structure of bourgeois society. One has to go inside this basic dynamic to find the real causes for the present (and ever present) critical situation of the capitalist mode of production on the world scale. No kind of action by specific financial institutions can count as more than an auxiliary means for the original structure in its striving to survive the pressures contradicting it from within, from the traditional industrial working classes and from the working populations in non-capitalist countries. Precisely the same can be said of all bourgeois *political* activity: society is not built on it, although kept in place by it, and real changes can only appear when driven by movements in class relations. In both examples, it becomes evident that no meaningful considerate action can be taken on the surface of society without real knowledge of its ground and basis.

This, however, does not contradict the possibility that the capitalist money market has a historical function whose importance surpasses even the relative force and autonomy ascribed to "financial capital" in Marxisant views. For while in capitalist developed countries, the money market appears as the *immediate* function of class structures, things are completely different elsewhere. On the world market, the money market turns into a force measuring itself against alien classes, strata incompatible with capital as such: patrimonial property structures, work systems based on the contract form alone ("formal subsumption of labour under capital"), etc., as we know them in "third" world industrial and agricultural systems. In its "action" against such forms, capital changes their appearances, potentially in a way it cannot – per definition – effect on its home front.

Such changes have been observed in the wake of capitalist colonialism, imperialism and "globalism". At no point, however, can it be contended that the money market in question has been involved in operations that has led any national or ethnic entity along the path of capitalist development to a reproduction of the original relations of wage labour, capital and landed property. That is to say: real capitalist countries belong to what we traditionally call "the Western world", and geographically they have not changed their total extension since the onset of capital-driven imperialism towards the end of the nineteenth century. Prevalent ideas of a "world system" of capitalist nations all over the globe are untenable – a uniformist product of a radical will to criticism, devoid of the potency to face the real challenges that are sunk in the contemporary slough.

The text unfolds in five chapters. In the first two, I offer a strictly theoretical exposition of the three main classes (i.e. the main property relations) in the classical capitalist society, namely wage labour, industrial capital and modern landed property, and how they were conceived by Marx in his attempt to show the inner coherence or "organic whole" of the system.[3] This description of the "anatomy" (Marx's expression) of modern Western society also implicitly shows the obsolete content of modern radical views of "pure capitalism". In the third and in the fourth chapters, I focus on the structure of Marx's theory of modern landownership and consequently of modern ground rent, which – unbeknown to many – he regards as the panopticon for both the money market and bourgois society at large. I try to fulfil this task with a close scrutiny of the most important of the radical Marxisant attempts to employ Marx's theory of land rent in contemporary discussions. Here, serious confusion and logical flaws are unveiled, and the drastic consequences of the common Marxisant adaptation of Walrasian theory of values and prices are indicated. The fifth chapter, in spite of the weight of presenting a theory of the movement on the world market on its own account, makes use of a polemical form of exposition. It adopts Marx's theory of the *intensity* of labour as value-producing, which is as good as overlooked in "radical" quarters, to show his theory of international commodity exchange, which I contend should be taken as the basis of any theory of the monetary dynamics on the world market, not to speak of possible "financialization". Here, as in the national capitalist economies, there should be no question of confusing the "genetic" basis of the money market with financial superstructures. The theory relating to differences in labour intensity is then employed to analyse the kind of unity the three categories of wage labour, capital and landed property that could be achieved in countries not dominated by any developed capitalist production. This comes all the more naturally, since the extant bourgeois paradigm of international trade depends on these categories, taken as so-called "factors of production".

This brings me to my final main point, which concerns the relation of this book with the last chapter of *Capital*: "The classes". As has been noted by countless readers, and made the object of speculation by a few, the chapter is not a chapter (it breaks off after only three pages). Whatever the reasons for the break-off, there is, at the very least, no reason to suppose that Marx doubted the core content of this concluding chapter. Nowhere in the ninety-five chapters (counted according to the German edition) preceeding it, is there any indication of half-heartedness in this respect, let alone the curious idea that Marx was on the verge of changing his fundamental ideas.

"The Classes" is (in all probability) designed as the last chapter in the last section (VII) of the third volume of *Capital*. This section, titled "Revenues and their sources", concentrates on illusions generated by capitalist production and is a kind of *Methodenlehre*, showing *how* the quotidian consciousness can develop into mediated, scientific knowledge by penetrating those illusions. The section's introductory chapter (48) is about "The trinity formula", which is good reason to believe that Marx meant the tripartite structure of the capitalist social formation to have determining qualities for the spread of bourgeois ("false", of course) consciousness.

The contemporary bourgeois viewpoint of given "factors of production", namely "labour", "capital" and "land", was well developed in Marx's time. It is the target of the criticism in chapter 48. It is only to be expected, then, that his final chapter (52) will return to "the creative Ground" (Marx's expression) of these fetishized forms, i.e. to an exploration of the three main classes and their concurrence.

In other words, what we should expect is a restatement, renewal or consolidation of the points on the "action" between the three forms of property: private landowning, the capital monopoly and the worker's "absolute poverty".[4] That "action" is most conspicuously handled in the *Grundrisse* and is later partially brought into the volumes of *Capital*.

Since section VII focuses on the "categories" as they *appear* in the *consciousness* of class-individuals, it is to be expected that Marx, among other things, meant to focus on their reflection as politically active class members. That would, in his case, imply a general mediation of the struggle for liberation of the working class.

This is not the least important reason for the composition of this book – focusing on the abstract depiction of politico-economic categories as well as on empirical relations and their place in modern discussions. It is condescending to think that conscious members of the modern working class are not aware of the necessity of a firm, consistent theoretical ground for political action. Nor should it be believed that a theoretical edifice which is inconsistent can possibly reflect the world as it is. Through its perennial, obsolete search for a consistent value theory, mainstream Marxisant thinking seems to have come to a dead end both in theory and practice. Revolutionary subjects scarcely fail to notice this.

Notes

1   The term "Marxisant" should be used to denote aspects of all kinds of commentaries on Marxian writings or of authors with a leaning towards Marx's theories. It is a happy formulation, which cures one of the temptation to denote non-Marxist individuals as Marxist solely because they claim a sympathy for the Marxian corpus. However, the

word is usually employed with an ironic undertone. So it may appear even in this work, but that is a contingent fact.

2   It is presupposed that the reader already has a general overview of Marxian categories and method, as it has been a more viable option to go fairly directly into extant discussions, to underline the need for developing a real actual "Marxism" far removed from imitations. Still, the concrete themes of the book do contain elements regarding the nature of the commodity, its exchange and circulation (especially Chapter 5), accumulation and wage structure (especially Chapter 1), relations to elder or other extant modes of production (all five chapters), the organic composition of capital (especially Chapter 5), Marxian values and prices (Chapters 2–5), etc., etc. On the whole, it should be possible for the reader to reconstruct a more general view of the Marxian edifice based on such a zigzag reading.

3   In all capitalist countries, there are large population segments which fall more or less outside the group of "character masks" that form the three-class core here depicted. That goes for segments connected to merchant capital, finance, civil services, industry officials, etc. Perhaps the most conspicuous exemplar is the petty bourgeoisie, privately owning means of production and to a certain extent hiring manual wage labour. However, the social way of life and political-economic position of any such group is determined by constellations reducible to core relations between industrial capital, productive wage labour and landed property.

4   For this term, see especially the *Grundrisse* (Marx 1993, 295; 1953, 202, and for the term "action" (Marx 1993, 275; 1953, 186)).

1   Structure and transitions of capital

1.1 Introductory remarks

We shall concentrate on Marx's *Capital* as a whole, with the aim of investigating the structure of that work, in the shape in which it has been left us in Marx's own edition of Volume I (1867) and Friedrich Engels' edition of Volumes II and III (1885, 1894). However, as will soon become clear, the main idea is that Marx's work is also a form of empirical construction, portraying the concrete, but general, shapes and structures of the capitalistic features which dominate Western economy and its world market.

The fact that Marx did not live to work out the final composition of either of the two last volumes of *Capital* probably accounts for the lack of explicit comments from him on the logical structure of the work in general. While there is no reason to doubt that Engels' editorial work relating to Marx's manuscripts was properly and thoroughly done, it goes without saying that he may not have elaborated points concerning the architecture and final structure of the work in the way Marx would have. This chapter tries to identify places in Marx's texts that may be considered essential for an attempt to reconstruct some of his ideas in this respect. This involves reinterpretations of the texts and also an attempt to reconstruct the content of one analysis that is missing from the manuscripts.

It seems that *Capital* is structured according to a plan designed by Marx in the years 1861–1866.[1] This plan replaced the one that he originally leaned on when writing the well-known manuscript *Grundrisse*.[2] In this plan, as can be concluded from the *Grundrisse* itself (Marx 1993, 275–279; 1953, 186–190). Marx made intensive use of the concept *Übergang,* most often translated as *transition*. What he meant to describe with it were the relations prevailing between the three main categories of his work, as it then was being planned: capital, wage labour and landed property. These were also meant to be the titles of the three first, and basic, books.[3]

I will try to show that the "transitions" treated there should be looked upon as moments of the very structure that produces the distinction between two "aspects" of exposition – that is, that they were adapted to the later work and integrated into it. If this is correct, it may be taken as strengthening the thesis that Marx's dropping of the first plan had to do with his real progress concerning the level of scientific analysis. At the same time, this progress was not of the kind that could in any way overthrow the methodological results that Marx must have reached through his work with the *Grundrisse* – at least not in so far as these had to do with the process of capitalist *production*.

This view implies that in the finished work from 1867 on Marx managed to retain his original theory of the transitions between the said categories, each of which also represents a social class, and to combine it with new insights, despite the fact that his views on the nature of essential categories like *circulation* and *competition* of capital had clearly changed in the meantime.

However, my primary aim in this chapter is to contribute to class analysis of capitalist social formation in general as well as of any specific capitalist society. The fundamental structure of the main classes and their interrelation is a subject of primary importance for such an analysis. This means that the chapter in a certain sense is formed abstractly, depicting the general characteristics of that society.

The rest of this chapter is divided into three sections. In the first, the point of the investigation is sketched as a problem of identifying the subjects (classes, class members) whose consciousness must be presumed to be material in carrying the exposition forward. In the second, Marx's analysis of the relation between use value and exchange value on the macro level, elaborated during his work on the first plan, is used to demonstrate the existence of two such different subjects in *Capital*. In the next section as well as in the following one, it is shown that as long as the exposition is tied to a level where prices of capitalistically produced commodities correspond to value magnitudes (i.e. are *value-prices*, meaning that each commodity is sold according to a rule dependent directly on the labour time expended in its production), the wage form and therewith the specific (and false, i.e. exploited) consciousness of the working class forms the subject in question.

In the next section, it is shown how conditions mature for the new subjective form, the one belonging to the individual capitalist as well as the capitalist class. It is claimed that the transition to this form is effectuated by an immanently necessary passage between simple reproduction and accumulation present in Marx's texts. To clarify this, it has been necessary to make a thorough analysis of certain aspects of the Marxian "reproduction schemes". (Details are to be found in the appendices to the chapter.) In the fifth section, conclusions relating to the structure of *Capital* are presented together with an evaluation of the relevance of that structure for Marx's overall view of history.

1.2 On the concept of transition

Let us start with a look at the third volume of *Capital*. Here the content of Volume I, "The Process of Production of Capital", is melded with the content of Volume II, "The Process of Circulation of Capital", into (an exposition of) "The Process of Capitalist Production as a Whole". In Volume III, Marx introduces concepts like "cost price", "profits", "rate of profits" – that is, categories which reflect the factual experience of the capitalist. Most important of all, we meet the category "production price", which takes over the role of "value" ("exchange value") as the centre of gravity of the expense of labour time at which any commodity is now sold and bought. This is as it should be. For Volume III investigates *appearances*, so that what is being described and analysed, are relations "in reality (i.e. in the world of phenomena)", as Marx puts it (1966, 47). The important fact is that we now have to do with a *world* of appearances, an *Erscheinungswelt*, as it is called in the German original (1968c, 57). Of course, appearances are thematic also in Volumes I and II. But there they are explained in relation to a background that is not at all present for the consciousness of the capitalist. In Volume III, they have to come into consideration as categories furnishing a completed *whole* of capitalist experience.

Nevertheless, the opening of the analysis of "The Capitalist Process as a Whole" presents us with an exposition which includes a subjective form that has not been developed with sufficient transparency in the preceding volumes. We should expect a comprehensive work like *Capital* to tell us why it is *necessarily* so that the form of analysis seen in Volumes I and II must pass over into an analysis mediated through magnitudes of production prices (Volume III). In Volume I in particular, Marx shows how the common consciousness of bourgeois society is fetishized through the existence of commodity and value production. He shows how the very source of value is hidden from everyday consciousness and has to be found and explored by scientific consciousness. But if that is so, it would also mean that an investigation based on the existence of value-prices should by itself show us the dividing line between the two levels of analysis. It would be only reasonable to suppose that we should meet some point where the exposition, so to speak, is broken up, and where it is shown that the *immediate* structure of value analysis itself has to be sublated (*aufgehoben*).

Marx might well be accused of vicious circularity, since his argument is dependent upon the existence of the form of consciousness typical of the capitalist – that is, of the economic "character mask", the possible conditions for which he is supposed to point out and explain. Such a criticism would naturally be extended to Marx's construction of the concept of the socially average rate of profits and of the production price.[4]

We should expect this "pointing out", if it exists at all, to turn up somewhere in the closing of Volume II, since that is what immediately precedes the exposition of phenomena tied to prices of production, i.e. average prices systematically deviating from value magnitudes. Volume II concludes with an analysis of the reproduction of the commodity-form of the *total* productive capital of a nation or a society (that is, the Marxian "reproduction schemes"). This should be significant for a subsequent investigation of "The Process of Capitalist Production as a Whole", which, in turn, should reactualize the discussion on the average rate of industrial profits, for it is this rate that results from the *sum total* of social capital and that transforms commodity values to production prices. That is, it is a function of the *totality* of the value of labour power, the value created by that power and the value upheld by it.

However, before we set out to look for such a possible "pointing out", let us make a more general methodological consideration of the problem of "transitions" in Marx's main work. Hopefully, the remarks above make it sufficiently clear that a kind of "immanent" passage is needed between the two last volumes of *Capital*. But what about the relation between the first two volumes – in other words, between analysis of production and circulation respectively?

Evidently, we need to look at how Marx de facto rounded off Volume I, for he composed the entirety of this part of the work on his own.

The closing chapter (33) is called "The Modern Theory of Colonisation". Through a critical exposition of E. G. Wakefield's theory of colonial land tenure, Marx describes the situation for industrial capitalists when there is no system of private property of land and soil. In that case, capital has no "economic" guarantee that the members of the working class will stay on in production.[5] On the contrary, they will flee from it, to become settlers and free farmers.[6]

The reason for rounding off Volume I in this way is to be found in Marx's *original* plan from 1857–1858, in spite of its important differences from the second. Here he points to how capital evolves into a social totality through subsuming other social expressions under itself. He calls this a system which is organic in nature but points out how it will lose its organic particularities when confronting new territory outside itself. Its representatives – the capitalists – then discover that the landed foundation of their system, modern landownership, where capitalization of ground rent makes the soil an expensive resource, has disappeared. Workers therefore have the possibility of fleeing from capitalist coercion, a possibility the British government sought to block through adopting Wakefield's legal proposals, e.g. in Australia (Marx 1993, 278; 1953, 187). Such a process Marx takes to be a "transition" from capital to landed property, and when it is realized primarily by an upward trend in the price of soil, this is because the price takes the form of capitalized rent and consequently will rise as the interest rate and the rate of the ground rent tend to fall *pari passu* with the general rate of profits.[7] That is, the accumulation of capital itself does not only effect an expropriation of immediate producers from the soil (landed property): it also guarantees a long-term high price of land, thereby constructing a permanent obstacle for proletarians who might wish to return to the soil establishing themselves as farmers.[8]

Marx wants to make this important point in the first volume of *Capital*. However, since chapters 22–33, relating to simple and extended reproduction, analyse accumulation in abstraction from phenomena of circulation, he cannot make the argument concerning the price of soil in *concreto* (the categories of the rate of profit and ground rent are missing). Therefore, for the time being, he is satisfied with showing how capital in the colonies, where it does not dominate society and consequently cannot regulate the price of soil in an economic way, strives to introduce a high price of land abruptly and politically. The main point is that capitalist production cannot be taken to represent a *totality* before one has also shown the necessary and prior exclusion of immediate producers from landed property.[9]

However preliminarily, it can safely be said at this point that the composition of the first volume of *Capital* indicates that Marx was conscious of the fact that the immediate process of production must be exposed as a kind of circuit, where capital in the last instance functions as a *self*-reproducing totality, or, as it shines through his draft plan of 1857–1858, generates wage labour and therefore its own basis when it produces ground rent.[10]

Evidently, to regard capital as a *self*-producing entity means regarding it as a subject. Since a subject necessarily is an individual of some sort, capital as a subject has to be seen as *the capitalist*, a human being carrying the character mask of capital. Indeed, the fact that the economic categories take the form of individual subjectivity is inherent in the Marxian concept of "transition". Actually, the preliminary draft in the *Grundrisse* shows us that Marx, after analysing the abstract world of appearances in capitalist production, would have brought the exposition of the category of "capital" to a close with a treatment of "the capitalist",[11] which was meant to lead to the analysis of "landed property". Similarly, a reading of the main draft shows that modern landed property is not introduced before it is possible to show that capital is something that "produces *itself*". The implication is that the "transition" from capital to landed property, or the "action" of capital on this property form, should be exposed as *conscious* action initiated by members of the capitalist class – which includes the possibility of bourgeois nationalization of land (Marx 1993, 279; 1953, 190). In a parallel way, Marx stresses that the pressure of capital on landed property leads the landowner to take independent, class-conscious action against workers (Marx 1993, 277; 1953, 187). Also, this "action" of capital is to be understood as a negation of capital's own presuppositions and consequently as its negation of itself. Marx goes on to say that this self-negation is nothing other than *"wage labour"*, which implies that subjects have a conscious *wish* for independence (Marx 1993, 279; 1953, 190). It is in this way of absolute negativity and conceptual self-negation that capital posits and manifests itself as the centre of a system which, through and through, gets its positive existence from social contradictions and exploitation of labour.

The Marxian concept of "transition" in the *Grundrisse* draft plan can then be characterized as follows: it indicates *general, basic* and *typical* forms of confrontation between main ("categorical") economic interests, viewed as objective social phenomena of which the participating subjects are *conscious*, at least in the sense that, through those phenomena, they identify themselves as members of distinct classes. As such, a "transition" is a *regular* form of interaction between classes in the capitalist social formation, superdetermined, as Marx points out, by "capital", which operates as an active *medius terminus* between the other two main categories. The result, then, is a "syllogism", where everything that is is *created*, "everything posited is thus also a presupposition", something which "is the case with every organic system" (Marx 1993, 278; 1953, 189). The closing of the first volume of *Capital* represents a transition inside such an organic system. It coincides with the transition of capital into wage labour, as it is illustrated in the *Grundrisse* draft plan. Consequently, it points to the real possibility of making the specific consciousness of wage labour, or of the working class, the motor that interconnects the phenomena of the production sphere analysed up to this closing point.[12] The illusions typical of the workers' class position are sufficient to obtain the result. The specific illusions of the capitalist are to be developed out of contradictions that arise from this basis.

However, it is not clear that the transition in question leads to any definite point in the exposition that follows. Some authors have taken for granted that Marx had to construct a transition between the first two volumes of *Capital*.[13] But, as we shall see, there scarcely is any *raison d'être* for such an operation, the structure of *Capital* being as it is.

At this point, however, a reservation. As late as 1865, Marx still had a different plan in mind to round off Volume I. His intention was to present as a final section the text "Results of the immediate process of production", which was edited separately in (the "new") *MEGA* (Marx 1969). In this draft he expressly says that he wants to use the subsection "Commodities as products of capital" as an *Übergang* to the "second book" (Marx 1969, 3, 4). However, it is not at all clear if the term is taken to imply the methodological context in which *Übergang* generally stands in the *Grundrisse*. In any case, this subsection analyses the commodity *not* as an individual entity but as an exemplar of a mass of similar products resulting from mass production in one determinate time span. Thematically, such an investigation transitions smoothly to the second volume, which (in its eventual shape) starts with the circuits of capital, albeit that the circuit of commodity capital is only the third to be analysed.

It should also be noted that the examples Marx gives of capitalist commodity production in this subsection are taken to a large extent from capitalist agriculture, as regards both the product types and the production process.[14] It is as if he was searching for a closing effect relating to agriculture that could in some way make up for the absence of the expropriation theme hinted at in the chapter on Wakefield that eventually was used. Perhaps it is also worth noting that his examples are equally fit for countries where feudal landlords have expropriated much of the soil (as in England and Italy), where the land is colonized by farmers or where it is owned by peasants in traditional fashion. The theme in question is capitalist agriculture, which in principle is of course compatible with all these forms.

However, it is difficult to figure out the reasons and implications of all this when it comes to Marx's methodological viewpoints in the months immediately preceding the publication of the first volume of *Capital*. Possibly, the discussions (which are known to have taken place) concerning the opening chapter on the commodity may have led Marx to change his mind. Taking back the planned last chapter on the commodity as an entity owned by capitalist mass producers may have been part of a mental compromise which included a change in the prospective first chapter – to mention just one possibility among many. All we can say for sure is that the first volume, ending with Wakefield, is as Marx would have had it.

So let us now have a closer look at the concept of circulation – not in the form of simple commodity circulation, but its extended version, the concept of *circulation of capital* – i.e. the theme of Volume II.

1.3 On the concept of measure

In the *Grundrisse*, there is a paragraph entitled (by Marx himself) "Transition from the process of production of capital into the process of circulation" (Marx 1993,

401–423; 1953, 305–325). It ought to be clear, though, that when Marx uses this title in 1857–1858, it is not possible to transfer its meaning directly to the relation between the said processes as they are separately described in the first two volumes of *Capital*. The reason lies primarily in the fact that the "process of circulation" is partly defined differently. In the main draft plan from 1857–1858, the terms are not even to be found; in the preliminary plan, "circulation of capitals" is mentioned, which is placed under a main heading covering some of the themes that later were treated in the analysis of the total social reproduction (and partly in chapter 49 of the third volume of *Capital*). That the concept of *circulation* is still undetermined to Marx himself seems to be confirmed by a point in the draft plan of 1859 (to which we have not yet referred) composed of references to the paragraphs of the finished text of the *Grundrisse*. Here he writes of a text several pages long that "belongs to section II, competition of capitals".[15] He clearly wants to tear them out of any specific unity with any *circulation*. This means that the text in question is much more strongly related to the problematics concerning the category of *profits* and its genesis – that is, to determinations belonging to the transition to the themes of the later Volume III of *Capital* – than with any "transition" between the subsequent Volumes I and II. This point of view is strengthened by the fact that the same text has an obvious affinity with themes related to what was presented later as Marx's "reproduction schemes". Two separate points are of importance here: firstly, Marx shows how the aggregate magnitude of consumption represents a barrier (*Schranke*) to capitalist production (Marx 1993, 404–405; 1953, 308–309); secondly, he notes how the totality of society's capital meets another barrier as soon as it increases its production of use values and consequently begins to feel the need for "surplus money" (Marx 1993, 407; 1953, 310) to circulate them.

In the draft plan of 1857, we can see Marx investigating the movement of prices as if this were something that belonged to the core definition of circulation (Marx 1993, 264; 1953, 175). This is an example of the same confusion as in *Capital*. As is clear from other passages in the *Grundrisse*, Marx was well aware that it is *competition*, not circulation per se, which is immediately combined with the "movement of prices".

A closer examination reveals that this tendency to identify two quite different concepts has to do with Marx's treatment of his category of "capital in general [*Kapital im allgemeinen*]". His counter concept here is, as is well known, "the many capitals [*Die vielen Kapitalien*]".[16] This last was for Marx just another phrase for the basis of *competition*, while with the first he meant the inner concept of capital, whose external expression were the phenomena of this competition.

In the passages in question, Marx underlines that capital (in the guise of "the many capitals") is "as much the constant positing as the sublation of *proportionate production*", i.e. of any "equilibrium state" in the economy. That is to say, the exposition of it as "capital in general" is an abstraction from its real oscillating movements.

Marx sums up his analysis of the valorization of capital to this point, underlining that he has treated "the individual moments" of capital as mutually indifferent; furthermore, "that they determine each other internally and seek for each other externally" and that there is present an "inner necessity of moments which belong together, and their indifferent, independent existence towards one another"(Marx 1993, 414; 1953, 317–18). The "moments" in question are precisely materials, instruments and labour power. Their existence is now used by Marx as a foundation for a concept of a plurality of capitals in the sphere of circulation. Briefly, his point seems to be that the special differences inside capital in general, i.e. between the components of the basket of wage goods, the instruments and the materials, gives us the scheme for contradictions and differences that we will meet later ("later" in a logical sense) in the guise of circulation of elements of capitals and of competition between capitals in the sphere of circulation taken in a general sense. As we shall see, this way of thinking produces striking results, especially as regards the analysis of "fixed" and "circulating" (better: "fluent", to avoid misunderstandings) capital – the names for the value expressions of instruments and materials respectively.

The point, then, seems to be that Marx, finding that the tensions of competition must be shown to originate inside "capital in general", is forced to locate them in the relation between the material elements of productive capital, as they present themselves as separate value entities. The concept of "the many capitals" of course implies a plurality of capitals *grounded* in this same division inside "capital in general", and consequently such a plurality stands forward as producers of materials, of instruments and of the components of the basket of wage goods.[17]   In these guises, they will later be shown to *compete*, since competition is the interaction between independent capitals. In developing these relations, Marx did not make a sufficiently clear distinction between "circulation" and "competition". That was to come later, in his works on the manuscripts of 1861–1863.

Let us now hold on to the *first* of the two above-mentioned points (the aggregate consumption seen as a barrier) and ask about its relevance for the analysis of capital circulation in what became Volume II of *Capital*.

Clearly, the concept of consumption as a barrier is not treated at all prior to the reproduction schemes, in the third and last part of Volume II. It is at this point that Marx passes over from the "merely formal manner of presentation" (1961, 394), where it is simply *presupposed* that the use values produced can also be consumed, to the investigation of the confrontation of capital with a seemingly given level of individual and productive consumption.

Further, it is important to note that Marx characterizes this barrier by saying that

> [u]se value in itself does not have the *measurelessness* of value as such. Given objects can be consumed as objects of needs only up to a certain level.
>
> (Marx 1993, 405)

The category of *degree*, which in this way belongs to use value, set up against the "measurelessness" of value, produces a new "measure" for the value of capital,[18] a measure which is precisely what we call the category of *profits*, which, as we shall see, results from the analysis of the total social reproduction of capital. Taken as exchange value *in general*, value measures itself in a use value, whereby it shows itself as an end in itself, made independent to exactly the degree that use value is made independent as a measure (as is especially the case with gold). But as soon as we talk about an exchange value in the form of *capital*, new determinations are added to the use value that functions as a measure. These new determinations are analysed later in Marx's reproduction schemes, where the status of use value as use value for the first time is investigated as something dependent on a consumption that is socially limited. In the *Grundrisse*, Marx expands his analysis by underlining that any person engaged in these exchanges accepts the definition of this use-value measure as a quality posited by total social consumption. He goes on, contrasting this with the form of barrier which is present in the simple circulation of commodities, i.e. by exchange value in general.[19] Here, the barrier is present simply by way of the fact that the commodity exists with a specific natural composition that has to be "translated" to the general form of exchange value. Now, however, conditions are different, for the factor that measures its supply is present in its own material composition. Its change into the universal form (value) can only happen in a given, limited quantity. This measure does not lie in the amount of objectified labour time but is generated by its *use* by others (Marx 1993, 406; 1953, 310).

In the total social perspective – that is, on the level on which we are now operating – the use value is use value only inside the quantitative limits that reflect the *need* (effective demand) for it. This implies a corresponding modification of that "use value" in which it is correct to say that the value now measures itself. This in its turn means that the concept of the socially necessary (value-producing) labour time has to be adjusted: material things produced in excess of the total need do not have any value – that is, they represent wasted labour time and are not even use values.[20]

As regards productive capital, it consists of *present* use values in the form of means of labour, raw materials and auxiliary materials. (The use value of labour power, namely living labour, is a negating activity and not something "present".)

Now, to anticipate for a moment, we know that the rate of profit implies that the surplus value is measured against the sum total of the capital advanced, not only against its "variable" part.[21] In this relation, a mystification is generated, to the effect that the use values, here the means of production, are in themselves value-producing. Evidently, this kind of representation is qualitatively more hardened than the kind of fetishism one finds in the simple circulation of commodities. Further, it is important to point out that when a recently produced surplus is thus apparently *measured* in relation to the "present" use values, then this is an appearance characterized by the fact that these "present" use values have in advance, *qua* present, been esteemed as measurable in virtue of their "natural composition".

In this way capital, taken in the form it will achieve in the analysis of reproduction in Volume II, by itself produces the new form of consciousness that corresponds to the category of profits. Formally speaking, it is only in this way that we are presented with a *third* volume of *Capital*, whose theme might be called, as Marx himself tends to do, *Kapital als Maß*, i.e. "capital as measure". In the *Grundrisse*, Marx actually speaks of the concentration of capital (which he still considers a theme to be exposed as a consequence of "the *competition of capitals*") as the "quantitative distinction of capital as at the same time qualitative, as *measure* of its size and influence". This would seem to result in an exposition that finds its natural starting point in what Marx calls "capital measured by itself. Profit" (Marx 1993, 264; 1953, 175).

What Marx seems to be implying is that we have to do with a Hegelian *Reflexion-in-sich,* or intro-reflection – that is, the subject thinking itself as an entity mediated through entities outside itself. Such a subject looks upon itself not simply as a starting point of reflection but also as a result of that reflection. If there is a "self" present, it means the presence of a *subject*, hidden up to this point – a subject holding the development together, thinking through categories such as "profits".[22] Marx says in the *Grundrisse* that if we look at capital as an intro-reflected relation of production, then we are looking precisely at the capitalist: "Capital is essentially a capitalist"; "Capital in its being-for-self is the *capitalist* [*das für sich seiende Kapital ist der* Kapitalist]" (Marx 1993, 303; 1953, 210–211).

That capital's *measurable* relation to itself can really be considered a relation of reflection has a double reason. Let us first look at its formal aspects and then at the material ones.

Firstly, given the tradition in which Marx is operating, the category of *measure* is to be understood as a quantity that has met barriers that have transformed it into a quality. Here, "value" is this quantity, which as such is *maßlos*, "boundless", "measureless". That is, it is originally a non-quality, for the point is that the individual qualitative entities, the different use values, insofar as they are translated without a problem into the general form, can be taken as disappearing into the quantity (namely value) of the simple circulation. But such an ideal movement turns into the meanest abstraction as soon as it becomes clear how the "value" in question meets the barriers of consumption. Value, then, reflects itself in relation to these barriers. However, that is *not* to say that it passes into a quality *in general*. On the contrary, "measure" is just a modified quantity, and as such it may once again sublate quality as such (that is, be reflected back on to itself). We know that in quite abstract terms, Hegel described this movement in his Logic of Being, where the stage prior to the transition into the Logic of Essence is the category of "measure", developed out of "quantity", which in its turn showed up as the truth of "quality". That a category like "measure" develops out of "quantity" was for Friedrich Engels an outstanding example of the transition of quantity into quality, as he stressed in his work on dialectics "in nature" (Engels 1970, 348) In the last paragraph of "Measure", Hegel develops the concept of the *Maßlose* ("the Boundless") in a way that fits very well with Marx's later construction, as we see it here, of the capitalist as a subject conscious of his profit.[23] The movement of capital appears as the dynamics of a measureless entity, since value tends to be indifferent to its qualitative material. Still, value is clearly limited by some force, not least because it is itself a result of certain abstractions from which it cannot escape indefinitely. Its limits come to the fore at the point where a material entity is no longer the object of consumption.

Secondly, the material reason is conspicuous. The reproduction schemes present us with a use value that at least potentially is to be understood as something that has a measure and standard not only in labour time (and *a fortiori* in the material measuring rod of gold) but also in its own "natural composition". This situation originates in the fact that it is the total social economic pattern that is now being investigated. As we have seen, it is only in this connection that it becomes necessary to understand individual as well as productive consumption as barriers. The product value that expresses the use value to be investigated is the whole gross material social product. As Marx puts it:

> [The] merely formal manner of presentation is no longer adequate in the study of the total social capital and of the value of its products. The reconversion of one portion of the value of the product into capital and the passing of another portion into the individual consumption of the capitalist as well as the working class form a movement within the value of the product itself in which the result of the aggregate capital finds expression; and this movement is not only a replacement of value, but also a replacement in material and is therefore as much bound up with the relative proportions of the value-components of the total social product as with their use-value, their material shape.
>
> (Marx 1961, 394)

At this stage of the exposition, then, the capital under consideration is bound to stand in a relation to *itself* (as value as well as materially). There is nothing outside of it with which it can make an exchange, for as long as we are looking at the aggregate consumption as a barrier, it is necessarily the totality of capital under consideration.

This last point is the chief material reason why we have before us a situation of intro-reflection: capital must be on the move, but here it can move only in relation to itself. Still, this is a real ground only for a *potential* relation. The fact that we *really* have before us a *concretum* enabling us to construct the form of "profit" does not, of course, grant that such a form will actually be produced. For that to happen, it must be shown that the new measurable relation in which the use value is now posited implies that it is impossible for capital to reproduce itself in the conditions given up to this point.

However, before we turn to that theme, it should be noted that *if* it is the new measure relation of the use value that is the formal condition of the existence of the rate of profits, then the "original" profit-form, as it catches the eye in the exposition of "the total process of capitalist production", cannot be the profit or the rate of profit of an individual capital as such, as it in fact seems to be in the third volume of *Capital*. On the contrary, the transition must lead us directly to the social average rate of profits, since in this case it is the total social capital that is effecting "profit" as a qualitative phenomenon. Only as such a *total* capital can capital be exposed as intro-reflection and consequently potentially as profit.

1.4 Wage labour as a formal subject

We shall now return to themes of the first volume of *Capital*, to investigate the still open question as to whether there might be found some kind of "transition" to the second volume. In fact, we have now located a theoretical nodal point that might give us such a transition: the idea that there is a transition from the production process, steering development of a set of "many capitals" that could meet in the sphere of circulation. But that was the *Grundrisse*. As regards *Capital*, we cannot even be sure that there is such a thing as a *sphere* of circulation in Volume II.

Let us have another look at production in its immediacy. We left the investigation in the preceding section alluding to a presumed circuit in Marx's exposition of the immediate process of production. But to the extent that such a circuit is to be understood as a result of a self-reproducing totality, it is naturally quite abstract. This follows immediately from the fact that the exclusion of workers is not shown *concretely* – that is, through the category of rent. The modern landowner, one of the two essential "character masks" confronting the working class, is not present in the first volume, because his form of revenue is not there. In precisely the same way, neither is the individual capitalist present in a truly concreteway, since his specific revenue is also missing: as we know, the form "profit" is a theme only for the third volume. His actions as described in the first volume (and second) will become fully transparent only through the exposition in the third.

Only one of the three modern forms of revenue is presented in the first volume (and second), namely the *wage*. This category, however, is just as concrete as profit or rent, and it duly belongs to the world of appearances – to the social web of illusions – since its existence implies that the value of labour power is mystified into a category of "labour price". The German term *Arbeitslohn*, the word translated into "wage", is nothing other than such an illusion, spreading the impression that the worker gets reward for his toil and not merely for his capacity, his "pure possibility", to toil.

Albeit that the theme is nowhere explicitly discussed by Marx, it is possible to point out two main reasons for such a special treatment of the wage form, making it an adequate basis for an investigation through the *value* aspect.

Firstly, the money which is paid for the labour power constitutes a *price*, but it is not, and can never be, a price of production (or a derivation thereof). The "price aspect" of Volume III, however, merits its name precisely because it departs from the level of immediate value magnitudes (Volumes I and II), inasmuch as the products of capital are no longer susceptible to being sold at prices oscillating around their values but, rather, at prices of production, due to the intervention of the average rate of profit. The commodity labour power, on the other hand, cannot possibly be a product of capital.

Secondly, irrespective of the question as to whether the commodity product is analysed on the level of values or on the level of prices, the magnitude of the part consisting of wages equals the sum of variable capital. This sum is paid to the workers irrespective of any changes in the proportions between the parts of the product value which taken together reflect its price. In no way can this element

(if we can call it that) of the price *or* value of a commodity change as a result of
the intervention of the rate of profit (a thesis which is decisive for the illusion of a
Marxian "transformation problem").[24] This is all the more clear in view of the fact
that labour power is paid *post factum*, so that the quantity of money that in a reproduction movement buys workers' means of consumption has been determined
before the prices of those means are set in the subsequent period of production.
Consequently, the variable capital does *not*, in contradistinction to constant capital,
transfer its own value to the product. The worker is paid independently of his
work, and evidently so, since labour cannot have a value at all. The quantitative
relations inside the net product are set independently of the last production
process. Marx expresses it as follows:

> One portion of th[e] new value merely replaces the advanced variable
> capital [. . .] or the price of the labour-power employed. But this advanced cap-
> ital-value does not in any way go into the creation of the new value. So far as
> the advance of capital is concerned, labour-power counts as a *value*. But in the
> process of production it acts as the *creator* of value. The place of the value of
> the labour-power that obtains within the advanced capital is taken in the actu-
> ally *functioning* productive capital by living value-creating labour-power itself.
> (Marx 1966, 29)

Thus variable capital is a possible "independent variable" in economic analysis of
given products, as opposed to other elements in the product value. But this fact is
directly dependent on the value-producing function of the wage worker, which is
completely independent of any capitalist price structure. Consequently it is, para-
doxically, justifiable to abstract from such price structures when investigating
capitalist production. Here lies perhaps the primary reason for the separation in
Capital of a level concentrating on analysis of "value-prices" and a level on prices
of production. But, of course, such a methodological reflection could not occur to
Marx before he had investigated the structure of the price of production, since it is
this that forces upon the commodity world a regular change in the price expressions of the different parts of product values.

   Marx's decision to adopt a new draft plan may therefore be connected with the
"deduction" of the existence of a structure of prices of production, a theme that is
barely touched upon in the *Grundrisse*.[25] He may have felt the need for a new
principle of exposition, one that did not rule out an exposition of the "categories"
of the original plan but placed it in a changed context.[26] In fact, if the reasoning
above is justified, one has to accept that the consciousness of the wage worker is
an important fact as regards the coherence of the exposition in the first two
volumes of *Capital*.[27] But the possibility of treating that consciousness as an independent entity comes from the analysis of the "categories", where, as we have
seen, the will of "wage labour" to posit itself as "independent" of *both* capital and
landed property comes to the fore.[28]

   Marx rounds off the first volume with an exposition of some necessary presuppositions of capitalist production as a whole. In chapters 26–32, in the part called

"Primitive Accumulation", certain predominantly *historical* conditions (enclosures, laws against the poor, state intervention in the "labour market", etc.) are discussed. In chapter 33, a *contemporary* condition is shown: the high price of soil, taken as a means to keep the proletariat in place. All these chapters address extra-economic coercion, not least on part of the state.

And, of course, these chapters stand out from the rest of Volume I inasmuch as the foregoing exposition – among other things – is dedicated to showing that the capitalist system has the power to reproduce itself by *economic* means. The extra-economic power is alien to it, and ideally is to be seen as a *precondition*.

That the system has the power of "peaceful reproduction" (up to the point where it is decisively threatened by the "inner enemy", the proletariat which it has itself produced) is brought out clearly in Volume III by the exposition of population-wide fetishized and ideological thought forms. As Marx implies, the continued existence of capitalist production is dependent upon popular prejudice. When this point can be made in Volume I, the reason lies precisely in the exposition of the *wage*, which, so to speak, mediates between the abstractness of the immediate value-analysis and the concreteness of the analysis based immediately on production prices.

Further, this also means that the wage worker and his mystified form of revenue "is . . . the guarantee that labour power, permanently and without extra-economic coercion, will reproduce itself in commodity-form".[29] The presence of such a subjugated consciousness guarantees the consistency of the whole exposition in Volume I (and for that matter also of the exposition based on value-prices in Volume II).

The subject in question must also be called a *formal* subject, for, as we know, it is a characteristic of wage labour that its executors, the wage workers *qua* property-less are standing in a pure, abstracted *form* relation to the means of production. This position changes only in the concrete process of production, as we shall see once more shortly. It is only the capitalist who forms an *immediate* unity with those means and constitutes a real and concrete subject – as long as we are following the premises of the *capitalist* mode of production.

Consequently, to the extent that capital, at the end of Volume I, returns to the production of wage labour, it is in reality wage labour that goes back into itself, mediated precisely through the wage. As soon as we see things this way, we are in a good position critically to comment on a well-known thesis by Marx at the beginning of the third volume: "Because at one pole the price of labour-power assumes the transmuted form of wages, surplus-value appears at the opposite pole in the transmuted form of profit".[30] The thesis would seem to imply both that the exposition of the wage is a prerequisite for the exposition of profits (and consequently of any rate of profits) and that there is a relation of formal causality between wage-form and profit-form, the former in some way causing the latter.[31]

It is rather curious to meet this kind of thinking in Volume III, since Marx, as we know, has already implied (introducing the model of reproduction) that in certain ways the exposition in Volume I had a formal character that must now be sublated.

However, there are certain points in Marx's exposition in Volume I that still might vindicate his thesis. They are to be found in the first chapter in the section on accumulation – to wit, chapter 23, entitled "Simple Reproduction". Here, Marx demonstrates the function of wage labour in holding together any process of capitalist reproduction, be it in simple or extended form. In the centre of his analysis of the reproduction of capital, he investigates the simple reproduction of the wage form itself. The point is that the wage is a revenue and consequently must be defined as a (variable) sum of money which periodically but continuously falls to the worker. This continuity, and in the last instance even the category of the wage itself, is *real* only against the background of an exposition of the self-reproduction of the system.

This simple reproduction Marx sees as mediated by the fact that the worker is paid *post factum* and consequently is continuously coerced to renew his contract with a capitalist to keep himself alive. Still, there an illusion to the effect that the variable capital is a magnitude originally "advanced" from capital. This is an illusion that can be dissolved through analysis, as we shall see. However, it is of great significance that the capitalist originally – in this text – is presented as a money-owner whose wealth does not originate in any exploitation of wage workers. We shall return to this fact, to consider the simple reproduction inside the reproduction schemes and its possible parallelism with the simple reproduction described in Volume I. Furthermore, we shall look at the same issue in combination with a renewed analysis of the need for additional equivalents connected with a general increase in the volume of production – a theme that Marx, as we have noted, touched upon in the *Grundrisse*.

Now to the analysis of simple reproduction in Volume I. Marx writes:

> Variable capital, it is true, only then loses its character of a value advanced out of the capitalist's funds, when we view the process of capitalist production in the flow of its constant renewal. But that process must have had a beginning of some kind. From our present standpoint it therefore seems likely that the capitalist, once upon a time, *became possessed of money, by some accumulation that took place independently of the unpaid labour of others*, and that this was, therefore, how he was enabled to frequent the market as a buyer of labour-power. However this may be, the mere continuity of the process, the simple reproduction, brings about some other wonderful changes, which affect not only the variable, but the total capital.
>
> (Marx 1965, 569, italics added)

Marx goes on, presenting the following example: if capital of the said kind from the outset is considered as a source of a revenue of 10,000 pounds, yielding 2,000 pounds (produced surplus value) a year, then its equivalent will be consumed individually at the end of a period of five years. (Since simple reproduction is presupposed, no surplus value is invested.) This simply means that what one calls the "original" capital has disappeared (been consumed). It is nothing but an illusion that makes the capitalist think that what he consumes is not the original capital but the net value product. It does not make any difference that he still has with him a capital of unchanged magnitude, consisting materially of means of production, for

> [w]hat we have to do with here, is not the material elements, but the value, of that capital. When a person gets through all his property, by taking upon himself debts equal to the value of that property, it is clear that his property represents nothing but the sum total of his debts. And so it is with the capitalist; when he has consumed the equivalent of his original capital, the value of his present capital represents nothing but the total amount of the surplus-value appropriated by him without payment. Not a single atom of the value of his old capital continues to exist.
>
> (Marx 1965, 570)

In this way, it is shown that the pure and simple existence of the process includes the reproduction of an antagonistic (class) relation. This is perfectly intelligible. Also, it is in line with a point that Marx was at pains to develop in the *Grundrisse*, namely that as soon as capital has carried through its "second circuit" then its "true nature" may emerge, and not before.[32] This is the "nature" of which the wage worker is now the immediate, and mystified, observer. In fact, in the *Grundrisse*, the development sketched in "Simple Reproduction" in *Capital* is foreshadowed in a passage that points out that the produced surplus value must be embodied, and in a *determinate proportion*, in the use values of precisely the factors of raw materials and instruments, and "as subsistence goods for labour during the act of production". If not, it is not possible that the process can start over again and "always begin again the diremption into the objective and subjective conditions of its self-preservation and self-reproduction". Consequently, the totality is once more seen to be the product of *wage labour*:

> [a]ll moments which confronted living labour capacity, and employed it as *alien, external* powers, and which consumed it under *certain conditions independent of itself*, are now posited as *its own product and result*.
>
> (Marx 1993, 451; 1953, 355)

However, before hailing the symmetry of this climax, one should note that Marx's own conclusion in the chapter in *Capital* uses rather dubious terminology:

> Apart then from all accumulation, the mere continuity of the process of production, in other words simple reproduction, sooner or later, and of necessity, converts every capital into accumulated capital, or capitalised surplus-value.
>
> (Marx 1965, 570)

This outright identification of "capitalized surplus value" with "accumulated capital" is not warranted by the argument. Indeed, it is potentially quite confusing, as is indicated, e.g., by the terminology used in chapter 17 in Volume II ("The Circulation of Surplus-value"), where capitalizing of the surplus value is taken to mean accumulation even of *material elements* in the process of production (Marx 1961, 324). It also comes to the surface in chapter 2 of the same volume, where it is said that

> [a]ccumulation, or production on an extended scale . . . becomes later . . . as was shown in Book I, by virtue of its development, a necessity for every individual capitalist. The constant augmentation of his capital becomes a condition of its preservation. But we need not revert more fully to what was previously expounded.
>
> (Marx 1961, 78–79)

In chapter 12 of the first volume, "The Concept of Relative Surplus Value", Marx talks about "a coercive law of competition [that] forces . . . competitors to adopt" new methods (Marx 1965, 319). However, this dictum is a result of the analysis of competition *inside* a sphere only. Therefore (among other reasons), it cannot be said to show that accumulation is a *necessity* in any serious, basic and material sense. An argument to that effect would have been quite unreasonable on the premises of Volume I, for accumulation cannot be shown to be a necessity for an individual capitalist if it is not first shown to be necessary for the totality of social capital. In a contrary case, the individual capitalist might have other options than to accumulate, options not excluded by the analysis.

The problem can be posed as follows: the phenomenon of capitalist competition has to be explained immanently, from basic tendencies in capital. It has, in fact, to be explained from forces inherent in the reproduction of capital and not the other way around. This way of thinking is, it appears, brought forward by Marx himself in the analysis of the intraspherical competition: he says, completely in line with the *Grundrisse* thesis of the methodological status of "capital in general", that the "coercive law of competition" is an expression of the (more basic) "law of the determination of value by labour time" (Marx 1965, 319). It is now necessary to look at some aspects of that law as it operates in the totality of social capital.

Notes

1 See the arguments in Rosdolsky 1968 and Wygodski 1970. It seems that the crucial date is January 1863 (Rosdolsky 1968, 26).

2 *Grundrisse der Kritik der politischen Ökonomie*, first published in Moscow in 1939; hereafter *Grundrisse*, and quoted, unless otherwise noted, according to the translation by Martin Nicolaus (Marx 1993) and the 1953 edition (Marx 1953). (The draft plan from 1857–1858 is reproduced in the foreword to Marx 1970.) *Capital* I–III will, as mentioned above, be quoted according to the English edition by Progress Publishers, and chapter numbering will also follow this edition.

3 The others were *Staat, Internationaler Handel, Weltmarkt*, i.e. state, foreign trade, world market, as Marx underlined during his work on the *Grundrisse* (see also Marx 1974).

4 Clearly, Marx was conscious of this last point. In chapter 10 of Volume III he says: "The really difficult question is this: how is this equalization of profits into a general rate of profit brought about, since it is obviously a result rather than a point of departure?" (Marx 1966, 174). If one reads his chapter 9, about the construction of that "general

rate", one cannot doubt that on the whole he treats the equalization as a point of departure only.

5 See Marx 1965, 765. See also Pappe 1951, albeit the author's methodological reflections on the theme are somewhat hampered by the fact that he wrote before the *Grundrisse* was commonly known in the West.

6 Some authors have felt that there is something forced about this way of concluding the volume. Maximillien Rubel, in his *Pléiade* edition of Marx's *Oeuvres*, wrote that the chapter on Wakefield (chapter 33) was arbitrarily added to the text because Marx was eager to hide the revolutionary agitation in chapter 32, "Historical Tendency of Capitalist Accumulation". Prussian censorship, Rubel argued, was renowned for executing its controls simply by throwing a glance at beginning and end of books (Rubel 1965, 541). Certainly, such primitive hermeneutics is open to ridicule not only for those familiar with Marx's planning of his work but also for any reader of chapter 33. In Elster (1985, 438) we find an uncritical reproduction of Rubel's viewpoint. On the other hand, Otto Morf (Morf 1970, especially 197), always eager to go to the foundation of things, is on the right track in the matter.

7 See, for instance, Marx 1966, 242. (To elucidate: suppose the effective interest rate of society is 5 per cent, and that a given landowner can cash $10,000 a year after the products of his soil have been sold (by the tenant). This money is then regarded as revenue consisting of interest of an advanced sum of $200,000. Generally speaking, this last sum constitutes the price of the plot of land in question. The "price of soil" is just compensation paid by the buyer for the liberty to exploit twenty years of future ground rent.)

8 In Rosenthal 1998 (chapter 6, 3) there is a good exposition of the price structures resulting from the existence of ground rent, and of the "character mask" of the landowner. However, Rosenthal is wrong when he thinks that, for Marx, after the introduction of "a capitalist order", "the specific social relations which define it *as* capitalist in no way depend upon the existence of landed property" (Rosenthal 1998, 75). (The necessity of expensive soil would, by the way, be satisfied even in the case of a bourgeois nationalization of land. While such a political operation would certainly do away with "absolute rent", which, according to Marx follows from private property in land, the prolonged existence of differential rent, yielding a bonus for the bourgeois state, could easily ensure a price structure of the soil similar to the one prevailing before the nationalization.)

9 On the other hand, it is precisely the said abstractness of the analysis of capital accumulation that makes it possible for Marx to use the criticism of Wakefield to describe the reversal from "the original law of appropriation" – a theme that he, as late as 1863, did not know how to place inside the frame of the first volume (Marx 1968d, 389).

10 I have altered Nicolaus' translation here, which has "landed property" where "ground rent" should be. Further, it must be pointed out that Nicolaus uses both "basis" and "foundation" for Marx's term *Grund*, a term that obviously is meant to refer back to Hegel's determination of reflection, *der Grund* (and rendered "Ground" in all extant translations of Hegel's texts into English). It should also be noted that when Marx characterizes the relation of the three class categories as a syllogism – *ein Schluss* (Marx 1953, 187) – Nicolaus' translation is "circle" (Marx 1993, 276), which is misleading. Also when it comes to Marx's treatment of the category of "measure", greater caution would have been appropriate from a translator.

11 See the exposition of the first plan: Marx 1993, 264; 1953, 175.

12 See the following words from Marx 1974: "Likewise, the transition from landed property into wage labour is not only dialectical, but also historical, since the last product of modern landed property is the general positing of wage labour, which then appears as the basis for the whole trash".

13 Among these are Hans-Jørgen Schanz (Schanz 1974) and James D. White, who writes that Volume II was meant to "act as a transition" between the two other volumes

(White 1996, 193). Furthermore, White seems to be ignorant of the debate on possible different draft plans by Marx. He takes it for granted that *Capital* I–III is the final version of the first book planned in 1857–1858 (White 1996, 158–159).

14 His classic "20 yards of linen" from the chapter on the commodity that opens *Capital* I stems from here!

15 Marx 1953, 975. This text is not to be found in Marx 1993.

16 See Roman Rosdolsky 1968, 61–71.

17 In addition, one should expect the existence of luxury producers. This could be vindicated by the fact that the capitalist, the only possible luxury consumer at this stage, is developed inside "capital in general" (as the "*Fürsichsein* of capital"). As soon as they are in place, we get the divisions of producers which later confront us in the reproduction schemes.

18 Here the translation is difficult. In everyday language, the English word "measure" does not convey a double sense that is present in the German *Maß* (as that word was used by Hegel and Marx), namely that of "measure" as well as that of being "moderate" or "bounded". Therefore, the German words *Maß* and *Maßlosigkeit* ("measure" and "measurelessness"/"boundlessness") will be used. When the word is employed in the form of the verb, the English is retained, but the reader should note that the German original was meant to keep the double sense.

19 It is important at this point to note Marx's terminology. Like Hegel, he uses the term *Schranke* ("barrier"), meaning something definitely other than *Grenze* ("limit"). A barrier, in this terminology, is a limit which has been abolished as such. A limit is a barrier which is not yet seen as a barrier and consequently is thought of as impossible to transcend. Marx is here exploring certain relations of production which create difficulties for the thinking subject. These difficulties, however, are not limits, but only barriers. They can be overcome. And they are overcome, as we shall see, through the category of *profits*, which shows itself as the relevant form of thought when it comes to grasping certain new and developed realities.

20 This aspect of the determination of value is taken up by Rosdolsky 1968, 116. It is an important theme in our treatment of Marx's theory of ground rents, in Chapters 3 and 4.

21 The rate of profit is given priority here, just as it is by Marx: "The way in which surplus-value is transformed into the form of profit by way of the rate of profit is, however, a further development of the inversion of subject and object that takes place already in the process of production" (Marx 1966, 45). It belongs to the deeper aspects of the matter, not to be followed up here, that this inversion also has the form of an inverse relation of factors in a fraction.

22 Just as Malthus – in giving up explaining how the exchange value of a thing can be transferred from the labour process it enters into to a finished product – simply tells us that "the capitalist *expects* the same return on all the parts of the capital he advances" (Malthus 1836, 268; see Marx 1968c, 46). This represents a conspicuous problem for bourgeois/Marxisant economics even today. See, e.g., Sraffa 1972 and his close follower Shaikh 2016, who both accept a principle (derived from Adam Smith) of determining the mass of forgone labour inserted in the product *only* through addition of the *value* of the *net* product (in Marx: "v + s" parts) of the series of commodities in its chain of production. This way of thinking shows that they simply cannot conceive what Marx calls the double character of the value-producing labour: *concrete labour* transfers old values to the product, while functioning as abstract it adds new value.

23 See especially Hegel, 1969, 442. In thinking "quality", the subject is forced to think "quantity" – that is, an entity which in itself is without measure, i.e. *maßlos*. When introducing the "measure", the subject brings forth a quality that is not totally freed from the measureless. The measure is itself without measure but in the sense that it is not an *essential* measure, since it is in itself coloured by the *indifference* of precisely the "measurelessness" that it is supposed to be measuring (since it must have precisely an essential oneness with it). Consequently, Hegel shows that the whole Logic of

Being – that is, logic thinking in its form of immediacy – is bound to end in a "complete indifference". At this stage, the only alternative is to drop the whole form of immediate thinking and pass over to the Logic of Essence, where one meets the world of thought not simply as immediately given but as a reflected "actuality" and "world of appearances". (It should be underlined that Hegel, as an idealist, cannot show that a transition to Essence is immanently necessary. He just points to the fact that no other alternative is open if one wants a progression. His way of doing this, however, points immediately to the logical structure of the passage between "transition" and reflective logic in *Capital*. Marx's and Hegel's thesis is that man, to think, must think *something*, a quality or a derivate of it. But nothing can be thought except in relation to another structure, and this can then be nothing other than "quantity". This means that basically thinking confronts a unity between the two, which is *measure*: a quality which measures a quantity, or a quantity which measures a quality. Now, Hegel develops diverse measures, but the highest and most negative, i.e. the one which can present the sublation of the whole qualitative logical sphere and its passage to Essence, is the indifference as entity to be found in form of *inverse ratio of its factors*. This is where an entity has a quantity or quality where a factor cannot be augmented without growing at the cost the other, and vice versa. In principle, this gives us a dead end – an indifference. The parallel with Marx's analysis of the world of "transitions", and the arrival of a world of *Erscheinungen*, is striking, for the oncoming entity (the rate of profit) constituted as "capital as measure" has its immediate ground in the rate of surplus value, where variable capital (wages) and surplus value (rent and profit) stand in inverse ratio inside the given working day and thus will soon force the capitalist to *accumulate* via machinery to soften up the possibility of surviving in competition. For Marx, an inverse ratio between a quantity and a quality alters the social measure and constructs what he calls an *Erscheinungswelt*. This is the sublation we are working on now.

24 For this conclusion, see Sandemose 2004, especially 44. In one of the last chapters of *Capital*, Marx says that "the average price of labour, i.e. the value of labour-power, is determined by the production price of the necessary means of subsistence", i.e. by the wage goods (Marx 1966, 868). This does not imply that wages are changed by the *prevailing* price structure. On the contrary, they are reflected by the price structure of the *foregoing* period of production. The wages are unchanged, but the mass of the gross social product making up the wage goods may change in the prevailing structure. That might mean that the value of labour power is changing, but not even that is a necessary consequence.

25 Commentators have tended to overlook the specific structure of the wage and the variable capital, which seems to represent one of the most important developments in Marx's thought between *A Contribution to the Critique of Political Economy* and *Capital*. The result is that many do not clearly see the reasons for Marx's decision to drop (together with the rest of the draft plan of 1857–1858) the thought of writing a particular book on "wage labour". This tendency reached a strange climax in Hardt and Negri 2000 (234). The authors, evidently knowing little about the research work on Marx's different draft plans, and without making any reference to the structure of the chapters on the wage in *Capital*, simply regard the absence of "the book on wage labour" as an unexplained *curiosum*.

26 Winfried Schwarz's polemic against Rosdolsky's theory of a change of draft plan by Marx is contradicted by the fact that modern landed property is treated at length in *Capital*, a fact on which Schwarz does not comment.

27 The thinking subject is emphatically present in the exposition of economic categories.

28 Here, it is appropriate to comment on the standpoint of Michael A. Lebowitz, which in principle is identical with Schwarz's. In Lebowitz 1993, he points to the fact that Marx, in *Capital* I and in "The Results of the Immediate Process of Production", writes about a more detailed study of matters concerning the wage (Marx 1969, 118: *die Lehre vom Arbeitslohn*). From a translation of this manuscript he quotes Marx writing that the

analysis of a certain type of wage variation "belongs not here but in the theory of wages". But a *desideratum* of a "theory of *wages*" is in principle something quite different from one of a theory of *wage-labour*. Further, Lebowitz points to a sentence of Marx's from the beginning of chapter 17 of *Capital* I (Marx 1965, 543), where he says that an exposition of the totality of wage *forms* "belongs to the special study of wage-labour, and not, therefore, to this work". He concludes: "In short, there can be no question at all as to a missing work on wage-labour" (Lebowitz 1993, 69). But the textual basis is far too scanty for this conclusion, all the more so as the German original's *die spezielle Lehre von der Lohnarbeit* alludes to a study prepared by Marx himself to a far lesser degree than the English translation. Further, it is clear enough that even if Marx in 1867 thought of writing such a work, there is no evidence that this is "the book on wage labour" that he planned in 1857–1858. For that to be the case, one should also, as I have argued here, provide evidence that 1) Marx at this time still planned a separate book on "landed property" and 2) the treatment of landed property given in *Capital* III has no relevance for the issue. No such attempt is to be found in Lebowitz 1993. On the contrary, when he quotes from Marx 1974 to try to establish the continuity in the Marxian stance on this issue, he refers only to what Marx writes about "the book on wage labour", omitting what he on the same occasion has to say about "landed property". Lebowitz should not be criticized for this, but a reader with a different point of departure might be convinced by this. (Paul Zarembka has pointed out to me that my arguments in these respects are made also by Kenneth Lapides (Lapides 1998, chapter 11). In fact, Lebowitz's arguments were directed against an earlier work by Lapides (Lapides 1992).)

29 Schanz, 44. Schanz's "Sketch" inspired me to write down a first version of some of the points presented in this chapter. See Sandemose 1971.

30 Marx 1966, 37. Marx might well have written "value of labour power" instead of "price of labour power" in this sentence. Indeed, it would have been only logical to do so. Anyway, in this discussion the reader should keep in mind Marx's remark concerning the priority of the *rate* of profits. What we are witnessing is a transition and reflection from the rate of surplus value and its conceptualization, i.e. from the *dominant inverse ratio* of society, which thus is the dynamic core here. Marx made it explicitly clear that Hegel's *Logic* had a great significance for his construction of the category of "profit" (Marx 1974a).

31 This interpretation is strengthened by Marx 1974.

32 Marx 1993, 514; Marx 1953, 413. (Nicolaus has "cycle" for *Kreislauf*, which is unfortunate.)

2 Historical and conceptual transition

Dual sublation of simple reproduction

The following reflections show how conditions mature for the new subjective form, the one belonging to the individual capitalist as well as the capitalist class. It is claimed that the transition to this form is effected by an immanently necessary passage from simple reproduction to accumulation present in Marx's texts. To clarify this, it has been necessary to make a thorough analysis of certain aspects of the Marxian "reproduction schemes" (details are to be found in appendixes to the chapter, at the end of the book). In the last section, conclusions relating to the structure of *Capital* are presented together with an evaluation of the relevance of that structure for Marx's overall view of history. One should keep in mind that the "intro-reflection" of the singular capitalist coalesces with the self-realization of the whole capitalist social class, i.e. the generation of the social economy as a totality.

A totality of the kind mentioned at the end of the last chapter is, by definition, not present in Volume I, nor in Volume II prior to the "reproduction schemes". If one scrutinizes those schemes, it will turn out that they do in fact contain an argument for the necessity of accumulation. Further, this argument coincides with an exposition of the conditions of the profit form. One might say, with reference to expressions used in Chapter 1, that the barrier made up by the aggregate consumption shows its relativity by turning into accumulation. But simultaneously, the reproduction schemes also furnish us with a solution to the problem mentioned above, concerning the need for "surplus money" to circulate a rising amount of commodities. In addition, these two themes are treated by Marx together at the end of the exposition of "Simple Reproduction" (Volume II, chapter 20), and they are even considered in a logical sequence. As we shall see, they immediately precede the analysis of accumulation in the schemes.[1]

To give a rough exposition of these points, it is necessary to present a general outline of the reproduction scheme in question.[2]

Marx's formula of equilibrium exchange in simple reproduction between Department I (the aggregate of producers of means of production) and Department II (the aggregate of producers of means of consumption) is, as many a reader will know,

$$I(v + s) = IIc.$$

The formula says that the sum of variable capital and surplus value in Department I must be equal to the value of the means of production in Department II. These are the aggregates that have to be "exchanged", or circulated, between I and II.

However, the value equivalence is only one side of the matter. The "exchange" formula also implies that material means of production with an aggregate value $= I(v+s)$ are technically adapted for use as constant capital in the industries producing means of consumption. Further (a condition much easier to fulfil), the demand for means of consumption from the workers and capitalists in Department I must equal the demand for new means of production on the part of Department II.

When it comes to exposition in monetary terms, Marx's main example is the following:

I   4000c   +   1000v   +   1000s

II   ......   2000c   +   500v   +   500s

The value composition and the rate of surplus value are uniform throughout the economy. For the sake of methodological simplicity, there is a preliminary condition that all constant capital is "fluent", i.e. "circulating" (as are, of course, the elements of variable capital and of surplus value), or, rather, that its turnover rate equals the production period under observation, namely one year. Besides, the scheme is realistic enough insofar as the existence of the two departments is deduced from the circuit of commodity capital, a circuit where individual and productive consumption are separated from each other, taking the form of two general branches of production. Furthermore, it is supposed that the economy has precisely the amount of gold money that is necessary to circulate the given commodities.

Let us now, in three subsections (1, 2 and 3) analyse two especially problematic points in Marx's exposition of this total social reproduction of capital.

2.1 Replacement of fixed capital[3]

In principle, a simple reproduction of the capitalist economy can go on indefinitely under the conditions set by this scheme, at least if it is only slightly modified (see the analysis of gold reproduction below). But it has its simplifications, and the most critical one is that fixed constant capital, which we can call the value expression of the *instruments* of labour, for short, is for the most part not consistently treated as the relatively inert magnitude which it in fact is.

However, in section XI of chapter 20, this simplification is given up. Here we meet a more realistic analysis, where the discontinuity of the renewal of fixed capital is taken up. Still, the ensuing problems are analysed only in connection with the aggregate IIc, because this is the only constant capital (consisting of both fixed and circulating capital, the last being the value expression of raw materials, etc.) entering the main "exchange" between the sectors as a magnitude of product value.[4] And it is in this exchange, for reasons already hinted at, that relations between the two main sectors, social consumption as well as production, i.e. the totality of human productive consmption, come to the fore.

The introduction of the analysis of the fixed capital inside IIc lets serious diffi- culties rapidly come to the surface. In the real world, fixed capital functions its whole lifetime with a capacity close to its average or optimal. When its use value (factually and/or "morally") is gone, it is renewed through the buying out of depreciating money funds. Since large fixed components of IIc consequently will not be exchanged annually with Department I, the amount exchanged by I must be reduced correspondingly.

Considered in its pure formality, this difficulty can be overcome. The analysis of reproduction is an investigation of a continuous, "fluent" phenomenon: the annual production we are handling represents a year in a longer row, and one can presuppose that the economy has already established a certain average ratio between the value amount of fixed capital materially worn out and the sums of money stored up for later renewal.

However, it is still unrealistic to presuppose that simple reproduction of a national economy can proceed under such conditions. The equilibrium now has turned into a purely theoretical one, since it has come to depend on a given mate- rial solidity and coincidences of production. From one year to another, there will naturally be divergences in the mass of material that has to be renewed. No kind of planning or storage policy can neutralize such facts. This means, Marx con- cludes, "crisis – crisis of production – in spite of reproduction on an unchanging scale" (Marx 1961, 467).

This result, which is given considerable weight by Marx,[5] shows that simple reproduction is impossible to uphold (although this is a point whose implications he might have elaborated more concretely).[6] Consequently, we have here an immanent explanation of accumulation – that is to say, an argument for its *neces- sity*, since accumulation now represents the only possibility left for any capitalist to escape disproportion in simple reproduction.[7] From now on, the thesis that maintenance and expansion of capital coincide is justified. The formal result of the investigation of simple reproduction in Volume I is being materially filled up by the result of the analysis of the parallel phenomenon in Volume II.[8] Holding this together with what we have said about the relation between reproduction schemes and average rate of profits, one finds a more concrete explanatory "model" for the genesis of said rate, a genesis that must be tied to the relation between a plurality of capitalist branches of production. We shall return to this point.

It is of prime importance to stress the link between, on the one hand, this *coer- cion to accumulate* and, on the other, the profit form. The crisis in the simple reproduction is precisely the *concrete* expression of the fact that there exists a discrepancy between the logic of value production and the logic of material repro- duction in the labour process. The conclusion is that "the form of profit is the only one wherein this antagonism can move".[9]

2.2 Gold digging[10]

If it was Marx's intention to prove the immanent necessity of accumulation by way of an exposition of the replacement problems of fixed capital, we would expect him to justify the thesis by showing that there are to be found (new) equivalents to a degree sufficient to take over the circulation of the resulting increased quantity of commodities. And such an argument is indeed present in Marx's schemes. Chapter 20, section XII, "Reproduction of the money material", contains an argument to the effect that there will be an accumulation of gold (hoarding) in the system of production, even when accumulation is otherwise absent, and no matter whether the whole mass of capital is circulating or not. In general, however, Marx's argument has been misunderstood. To a certain degree, this has to do with the fact that the texts left by him do not analyse all the aggregates in question.

What needs consideration, then, is the "*reproduction* of the money material", a material which for simplicity's sake is taken to consist exclusively in gold. When simple reproduction is presupposed, then the *aim* of reproduction is to renew the mass of gold that each year disappears from circulation because of wear and tear.

To do this, one has to analyse the production in the gold industry and the product value resulting from it. However, this industry also furnishes the system with gold as a means of production, so its market is more complicated than that of most other producers. (Further, as one can see, it is presupposed that the gold producer is placed in Department I.)

The analysis of the reproduction of gold should in no way be limited to an investigation of the exchange between the two departments. There can be no *a priori* reason for such a limitation. What is more, the investigation of fixed capital above has implications necessitating a much broader analysis, an analysis now to be followed up through the study of gold production.

Nevertheless, the exchange between the departments is the best point of departure, insofar as gold is involved in it. Also, this is the part of gold reproduction that Marx – to a degree – made the object of his analysis.

It is clear that of the aggregate product of the gold producer, only a certain part will function as means of production. The other part must be supposed to replace gold that gets lost through wear and tear in circulation.

According to the general exchange rule, both "v" and "s" of the gold producer are to be exchanged with Department II. However, since that means an exchange of both categories of gold, the equilibrium between the departments is endangered. The problem is that since a part of the gold does not consist of means of production, a corresponding sum of values will not take part in the necessary replacement of constant capital in II. Nonetheless, means of consumption to the presupposed amount will in fact be sold to I, since any commodity can be purchased for gold.

There thus emerges a problem not only concerning the full reproduction of IIc but also where a given part of the gold coins will end up. Since the social reproduction would get into difficulties if the workers in Department II had to reduce their wages, that part must be transferred from the aggregate IIc to IIs. So according to

Marx the result is simply that capitalists II store it up as a hoard. These coins do not take part in material production, so the simple reproduction is not disturbed in any way by this money movement.

The problem concerning the source of replacement money is still unsolved. Taking these stored money units to represent all or some of the new equivalents needed for the circulation of an additional mass of products resulting from an accumulation is unrealistic. For, in fact, there is already present a mass of commodities adapted for such a use, namely the means of production that could not be sold to II. If one presupposes a situation where they can in fact be realized, then this means that there is neither accumulation nor simple reproduction (or a reduction in production scales). We have an impasse. When gold is hoarded here, the point is that it not be used.[11]

In short, the hoarded coins cannot be the origin of replacement gold. They will not yet enter circulation, since they have no commodities to buy. Further, unlike the Kwakiutl, capitalists have no motive for throwing away precious metals.

The problem has some similarity to the one we meet in Marx's analysis of the transformation of money to capital (as it is presented in *Capital*, in contradistinction to the *Grundrisse*): we have a phenomenon that has to emerge from circulation yet cannot emerge from circulation. What is to be done?

Simply to posit that a replacement is initiated by some kind of state power is to beg the question. True enough, Marx presupposes that the presence of banknotes and paper money in the reproduction schemes would pose no theoretical problem, thereby hinting at the existence of a formal apparatus which might even have state character. But we have to presume that the state is an agency acting on the basis of a capitalist system that already possesses the means to operate as a self-processing unity (else, the bourgeois state apparatus could not have arisen). This is where we are up to after the economic transition from capital to landed property has been shown to be a fact.

Marx tells us next to nothing about the amount of wear and tear of the means of circulation. He just says that the hoarding in the aggregate IIs will take place "even after deducting the amount of gold being lost through depreciation of money in circulation" (Marx 1961, 472). We find no hint as to why that should be so. Furthermore, nowhere in the reproduction schemes does Marx explain to us the mechanism through which the replacement of outworn material of circulation takes place. The difficult point here is of course that no commodity owner will give away her ("worn out") coins without a guarantee of compensation from some state power. And given such a point, it is a mystery how the replacement is to be thought at all. Where do we go from here?

It is only fair to start with an analysis of the remaining aggregate in the product value of gold. The solution to the replacement problem may turn up when the investigation is otherwise brought to an end.

However, here, too, we are met with silence. Marx explicitly wrote he would investigate this aggregate – that is, the constant capital of gold production – but according to Engels no such analysis is to be found in the manuscript.[12] So we have to improvise.

The ratio between gold for production and gold for replacement symbolizes a critical fact for the gold producer. Typically, one would expect him to do as his fellows: use his reproduced constant capital in money form to buy new means of production from the other capitals inside the aggregate Ic. But these other capitals need to replace gold only to a value amount corresponding to the demand for means of production. They do not demand gold for circulation.

However, this certainly does not imply that the gold producer is left without means to renew his "c" in its entirety. For, as we have seen, the transactions in the schemes are mediated by money. The gold capitalist can simply throw the whole of his product into circulation and buy what he needs. But this of course means that a bundle of use values is missing from the reproduction of other capitals in Ic. Is there a crisis at hand?

In fact not, for contrary to the crisis arising from reproduction of fixed capital, this one can be overcome in theory without disturbing the simple reproduction. If we simply add to the aggregate Ic a value equal to its output of potential circulation gold, then there is once again a mass of means of production large enough to reproduce the whole of Ic in kind.

This implies a modification of the whole value magnitude of Department I or, rather, of all that capital less the one invested in gold production.[13]

Seen from the value angle, this leads to a disequilibrium, which is then compensated for by the hoarding in Department II. Seen from the material side, though, the exchange represents an equilibrium, since it is compensated for by the units that are produced in the gold industry without having any material function in production. From this it follows that the hoarded gold from now on can in fact be used as equivalents for excess products (and/or new labour power), initiating an accumulation. There is now present in Department I a commodity value that can be exchanged against the IIc that had its provenance in IIs. Of course, in buying it, capitalists I are using money that belonged to circulation prior to the last period of production.

The material reproduction of the aggregate is now possible in full. Yet each year, fresh gold, in a unit number equal to the value that we have added to the original size of Department I, pours out from the gold producer. As we have seen, in effect it cannot be properly used on the conditions that prevail in the discussion so far. However, it will not get lost: the modification of the proportions of the reproduction scheme gives us a clue to the dynamics of replacement of depreciated coin – and to still more.

That is, we must be allowed the conclusion that the compensation volume for wear and tear is generated inside the constant capital of the gold producer. As we have seen, Marx's general assumption implies that a large quota of the circulation money produced each year emerges from here. While it cannot be hoarded, it is reasonable that this metal is the source of a movement of replacement money, since naturally it is able to circulate in the whole two-department area (initially through the circulation acts that taken together constitute the aggregate exchange between I and II). And, in fact, if replacement money is assumed to be generated in this way only, it would vindicate Marx's contention that it is independent of hoarding.[14] Since "replacement of the money material" is the actual theme of the section XII, one might even say that the production for replacement creates a hoarding (in Department II) of gold as an unforeseen effect.

Here, it is crucial to keep in mind the genesis of the "excess" money in Ic. It is immediately *forced* upon other capitalists in the aggregate by an outstanding, single producer. And this is the *only* way excess money, or replacement money, can immanently enter the system of simple reproduction. Actually, even the money that is being accumulated in IIs enters "by force": it is supposed that capitalists II cannot resist the gold, even when a crisis of reproduction is the consequence.

2.3 The sublation in context

Of course, the above simply follows from the fact that we have to deal with individual, short-sighted capitalists. But this fact has *not* been emphasized in Marx's exposition in the schemes up to this point. Rather, he has treated the capitalist system as a quasi-rational entity, stressing the minimal conditions for a smooth interaction between value and use value. Why the change of angle?[15]

The point seems to be that the anatomy of gold production fits excellently with the situation that has arisen with the crisis of simple reproduction treated by Marx in the foregoing section (XI). The introduction of the gold producer is an icy anticipation of the surface of capitalist production, of hollow men flitting and crawling around, interested in profitable appearances only. In the study of a capitalist mode of production, one cannot abstract from the immediate profit motive. It had to come forward in this form, as an element *of competition*, together with the gold producer. But – as it is crucial to note – Marx could safely let him arrive, since the analysis of fixed capital had shown that the prevailing kind of reproduction was impossible anyway.

After pointing to how "storing up or hoarding" is necessarily included in simple reproduction, Marx points to a crucial result of the analysis:

> And as this is annually repeated, it explains the assumption from which we started in the analysis of capitalist production, namely, that at the beginning of the reproduction a supply of money corresponding to the exchange of commodities is in the hands of capitalist classes I and II.[16]

As one can see, it is not simply a question of showing that the possible barrier consisting of a lack of equivalents is "always already" sublated. It must also be shown how reproduction *ipso facto* and simultaneously is totalized, since the terminal point of the analysis coincides with its starting point, in the sense that it *explains* it. More concretely: Marx's result can be interpreted as the fundamental justification and concretion of the analysis of the simple reproduction in Volume I. When it can be supposed that there are sufficient means of circulation on a *capitalist* foundation, then it can also be shown that capitalists at the point of departure of the exposition, and on a *capitalist* basis, are to be considered as money owner(s).[17] Consequently, it is no longer necessary or reasonable to presuppose that the capitalist, "once upon a time, *became possessed of money, by some accumulation that took place independently of the unpaid labour of others*" (Marx 1965, 569, italics added).

In fact, this is a *crux* of the criticism of the leading classical economist David Ricardo (1770–1823) and his analytical method. Marx thought that when Ricardo dogmatically held competition among "many capitals" to be an adequate starting point, this was partly because his view of human nature led him to suppose that capital was generated from savings. With full justification, Marx combines this with the fact that Ricardo overlooks the generic relation between capital and modern landownership and therefore can imagine the existence of capital without an absoluteness of rent.[18]

Even a more general presupposition for (*inter alia*) the reproduction schemes, namely that they take their departure from a thesis to the effect that there exist only two classes (workers and capitalists), is now justified. The object of the analysis of reproduction is not only geographically closed (a national economy) but historically "closed", too. It can thus be shown that there is (at the end of Volume II) a whole skeleton for the totality which (according to Marx in 1857–1858) is produced by capital through its interaction with landed property and as a production of wage labour through landed property.[19]

This last result has to do with a demonstration of the power of self-reproduction inherent in the capitalist system. That reproduction, from this point on, is something very different from what we find in Volume I, where things are held together by the wage form. The *presupposition* of the analysis in Volume I is now shown to be something lying "ahead" of the wage worker whom we meet in that analysis. This "being ahead" has been unveiled as something that could proceed from a reproduction that was already given as capitalist. Likewise, it has been shown that the (formal) *result* of the same analysis, i. e. that the maintenance of capital coincides with an increase in its magnitude, can be defended only if one carries into the analysis the barrier found in the limited possibilities of consumption of the use values given. This barrier is most concretely investigated in the analysis of replacement of fixed capital. Simultaneously, the relativity of the barrier (i. e. that it *is* a barrier and not a limit) is immediately shown: accumulation follows as through coercion, and one sees a continuous relative increase in the possibilities of consumption.

Through this development of the simple reproduction, of "the pure repetition" of the process, the subjects consequently have changed place: it is now no longer the worker but the capitalist who initiates the process of reproduction, for *the reason why* the pure repetition takes place at all is shown to lie in the *accumulation* of capital, steered by the capitalist. At this moment, therefore, even the form of the new subject, namely the profit, must emerge. As we shall see, this happens in the guise of the socially *average rate of profit*.

All the movements we have considered here will also help to define the *specific nature* of that emerging category and its distinct reference to *material* production. Especially, when the surplus of circulating means (i.e. money) in capitalist commodity production follows from the context of that production itself, we are dealing with nothing less than the genesis of the *money market*. The inflation that leads to the existence of a finance sector is a result of material creation of *commodities*. Not only is "finance capital" no independent factor, it is a result of the need for reserves which is to be found in the productive sectors of the economy; besides, it consists of capital from productive firms which for technical reasons has to lie fallow if it cannot be lent out periodically; and, furthermore, as we see now, it is actually directly produced as marketable gold reserves by those sectors themselves.

In giving a 'monetary' problem from the reproduction scheme the privileged status of a major *barrier* to capital, Marx makes it clear *how* the role of the money market is *basic* for the *generation* of the totality of bourgeois society.

Through this construction of "capital in general" as a histological entity, where the logical solutions appear as products of waged labour, the bourgeois society delimits itself from the previous, feudal social formation, while at the same time a filter is created, through which it opens itself to its own transformation of elder forms of wealth inside its womb.

This evolvement of the totality of themes from Volume I as well as from Volume II is illustrated in Figure 2.1 as a scheme for the structuring of *Capital*.

Chapters in the different volumes are indicated by numbers along the lines. The evolvement of the volumes from earlier to later chapters is shown by the direction of the main arrows. The "direction" of Volume III goes athwart those of Volumes I and II. This is meant to underscore a relation we have seen is essential: since Volume III investigates the bourgeois production as it stands "in the world of phenomena", its prevailing mode of exposition breaks with that preceded it.

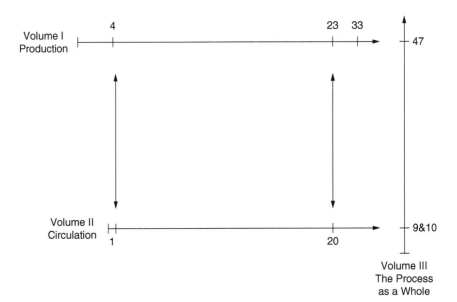

Figure 2.1 The structure of *Capital*

The fact that the two first volumes are investigations in terms of value-price magnitudes indicates, on the other hand, that they represent thematic parallels, also as regards method. In fact, there is, strictly speaking, no "transition" between them. Actually, the term *Übergang* was originally used by Marx at a time when his definition of "circulation" had not yet matured. The term reappeared in *Resultate*, possibly for a plan whose structure we do not know today.

The parallelism in question is at the same time a kind of reflection: it is of importance to stress that inside the capitalist production sphere proper, no *values* (nor prices!) are engaged. The capitalist economy does not know any "production of commodities by means of commodities" but merely a production through, on the one hand, concrete labour and, on the other, material means that are bought for capitalist consumption and consequently have lost their form of commodities. This processual form of pure use value is then *reflected* when it is put together with the circulation of the produced use values (turning into commodities after the production process) and their monetary expression: it is the pure form of production seen and reflected in its social context.

This has a methodological significance that can scarcely be underrated. If we meet production in its pure and simple form in capitalist society, it is a capitalist production process in the form it takes on when capital withdraws from the market and lets production of use values take over behind the fences of private property. This has its own significance: it explains the fact that Marx chose to insert an analysis of commodity fetishism into the investigation in his "commodity chapter". Now the methodological imperative of such an exposition becomes clear: we need to see through capitalist illusions concerning the nature of value. Since production manifests itself as production pure and simple, but still expresses itself in values and prices, the illusion will have it that values and prices are natural phenomena. The analysis of commodity fetishism sees through this and explains the spell which is laid on thought in its reflection of capitalist reality.

To return to our main theme: rather than the one passing into the other, the first two volumes of *Capital* supplement each other continually; it is only analytically that they are presented as separate. The parallelism is shown from Volume I, chapter 4 ("The Transformation of Money into Capital") onwards, since it is only from this point that a circulation of capital becomes possible. One should note that Marx labelled the first chapters of Volume I *vorchapters* to the exposition of capital itself.[20] In Figure 2.1, the vertical arrow between Volume I, chapter 4 and Volume II, chapter 1 illustrates this. The corresponding arrow between Volume I, chapter 23 and Volume II, chapter 20 is partly meant to expose the mutually supplementary character of the chapters on simple reproduction in the two volumes. It is meant to cover *as well* the relation between the money-possessing capitalist in Volume I and the reproduction of gold material in Volume II, *as* the demonstration that all capital must turn into capitalized surplus value (Volume I) and the analysis of the fixed capital (Volume II). It is also meant to underline the fact that the material in the third part of Volume II (the reproduction schemes) is of such a character that it is no longer simply a matter of parallellism but also of a *unity* of production and circulation, a unity that through *its own* oppositions produces "profit" and its subordinate forms (especially "ground rent"). The transition in question coincides with the step up to the level of prices of production. Thematically, it incorporates into itself the determinations that separate production and circulation (the barriers of equivalents and of consumption) and thereby also shows implicitly that the unity of production and circulation is of such an oppositional kind that the profit form and the "process as a whole" will introduce themselves. This transition we have indicated as starting in Volume II, chapter 20 and terminating in Volume III, chapter 9. But since the consumption barrier is so conspicuously present here, we will have to drag in chapter 10, too. For this text, entitled "The Levelling Out of the General Rate of Profits through Competition. Market Prices and Market Values. Surplus Profit", in fact considers the determination of value precisely from the point of view of the modification it undergoes relative to the consumption barrier. The chapter therefore forms a necessary link in an investigation of the reasons why the (average) profit gets the specific status of *Maß*.

Chapters 1–8 of Volume III must be thought of as an analytical introduction, with the aim of "dividing" – "analysing" – an average profit that is *already there*. In no way can they be considered its genesis. *Qua* analytical, they can be said to investigate individual capitals in their process of accumulation. As such, they can also be useful in the analysis of the extended reproduction in Volume II, chapter 21, for even if that analysis is made on the value-price level, it cannot be radically separated from Volume III, chapters 1–8, since value-price magnitudes (in the capital advanced) are presupposed even there. What is new in these chapters is that the form of profit enters the scene in virtue of the fact that surplus value is being related subjectively (as measurable) to the whole of (the individual) capital.

As I try to show in the scheme, there is a transition from Volume I (from the chapter on the theory of colonization) to around chapter 47 in Volume III, "Genesis of Capitalist Ground-Rent", since this chapter rounds off the theory of rent, so that the treatment of the factors that keep the workers in check are now at an end.[21] The term "transition" is justified, since it is proven in Volume II that the accumulation investigated in Volume I is of a *necessary* kind. It is then guaranteed that the coercion to accumulate that is present in the Volume I chapter on simple reproduction is a real one.

In other words, it is guaranteed that the accumulation that ultimately leads to a rising price of land is as real and total as the result of the coercion to accumulate deduced in the chapter on simple reproduction in Volume II. *Post festum* it is also shown that the system is characterized by a series of *necessary* transitions between the categories wage labour, landed property and capital – as described in the *Grundrisse* draft plan.

All the same, there is a difference in relation to the one central transition. In the *Grundrisse* draft plan, Marx had remarked that the "transition from wage labour to capital arises by itself, since the latter is here brought back into its active foundation"(Marx 1993, 276; 1953, 187). This must mean that he sees the transition as simply the purchase of labour power and its connection with the means of production. And it is this relation that lies behind the exposition in *Capital* I–II, where capitalist exploitation is considered from the standpoint of labour power and through a consciousness that corresponds to it.

To think of a "transition" as something that "arises by itself" is warranted by the tradition. In Hegel, *Übergang* or *Übergehen* is, as noted, the term used for *immediate* conceptual movements, where thinking one thought *is* thinking its counterpart. The three "categories" of the first draft plan do indeed have such a relation to each other. The concept of capital immediately presupposes the concept of modern landed property and wage labour, and respectively for each category all the way round.

The main problem with the 1857–1858 draft plan is that the reasons for this uninterrupted "transition" between the three categories of the "capitalist social formation" are not explained. In *Capital,* on the other hand, it is shown that such a movement is a product only of a fully developed relation between capital and labour (the categories of the "capitalist mode of production"). But it is also shown that it is a result of a "transition of wage labour to capital" which is subject to a deep and thorough analysis, not simply viewed as something that "arises by itself". The simplicity of the relation in *Capital* I is merely apparent. One of the central themes of the volume, a theme which was meant to be treated in detail in the section known as *Resultate des unmittelbaren Produktionsprozesses*, is the "real subsumption of the worker under capital", which secures capitalist stability by coercing the worker to assimilate himself to the *instrument* of labour (and not the other way round). It is in this fact that one can find the factor that up to this point has been conspicuously absent, namely the reason why there is in fact a differentiation in the production process as regards the relation between instrument and materials. By now it is clear that they appear as bearers of *different* social repressive forces vis-à-vis the worker.

The dynamic of the first volume widens to bring forward the *whole* capitalist social reproduction of material commodities and through this movement constructs the capitalist as a subject. In this way, it becomes a "transition" in the full meaning of the concept, since the *consciousness* of both classes in question has finally evolved. By this result, the whole movement of immediacy in the transitions between the class categories is explained: the transitional movement is there as a result of the class antagonism in capitalist reproduction. In Hegel, the slippery movement of *Übergehen* is finally held in check by the category of "Essence" – that is, by what he calls "Reflection". In Marx, the capitalist of Volume III has a similar function, and he too is constructed through a process of reflection: not through the production process itself but through a process which involves the circulation of the products, not just as material entities but as commodities.

The transition alluded to above, from the critique of Wakefield to the genesis of modern ground rent, is the transition of wage labour into modern landed property. Simultaneously, this latter is also the object of a transition (developed as the exposition of the third volume progresses) from the side of capital, for the same factors that made possible a capitalist subject are also necessary and sufficient for constructing the character mask of the landowner. At this point, the two stand up as conscious adversaries.[22]

Now, from what is mentioned above, as regards the function of the price of land, it follows that

> [t]he inner construction of modern society, or, capital in the totality of its relations, is . . . posited in the economic relations of modern landed property.[23]

And of course it is only as such a totality that capital dominates society, just as this dominance is the most essential distinguishing mark of that totality. Here, a new "parallellism" shines through: the one between logical and historical transition. The transition of capital to landed property is also a "transition" to the kind of relation of production (of ownership) that was dominant until capital took over. Thus it is also a scheme for the "transition" of capital to pre-capitalist relations in its own midst – be it with the purpose of destroying them or with an eye to maintaining them artificially.

Thus, having stressed the economic importance that Marx ascribed to the latent crisis in Volume II, chapter 20, section XI,[24] it is now time to point out its immediate importance for historical analysis. In this section, which in fact explains the *differentia specifica* of capitalist production in opposition to the potentially new historical epoch, namely the existence of *accumulation* of riches, Marx underlines the relation to communist society, explaining that the potencies of the said crisis

> can be remedied only by a continuous relative over-production. There must be on the one hand a certain quantity of fixed capital produced in excess of that which is directly required; on the other hand, and particularly, there must be a supply of raw materials, etc., in excess of the direct annual requirements (this applies especially to means of subsistence). This sort of over-production is tantamount to control by society over the material means of its own reproduction. But within capitalist society it is an element of anarchy.
>
> (Marx 1961, 469)

That is to say, in bourgeois society it has to express itself as a *crisis* of over-production as well as a continuous, relative over-production of a *spontaneous* kind. Conceptually, this is precisely the same thing as the kind of disproportion which is located in the different "diremptive" moments of capital.

So far we have only lightly touched upon this bourgeois foreshadowing of market expansions and upon the fact that it can lead to accumulation. Now we can hold on to it and see how Marx makes use of it to define the capitalist epoch in relation to its predecessors. In connection with the exposition of differential rent, he mentions that in agriculture as well as in all the other branches of capitalist production, there is

> [a] continuous relative over-production, in itself identical with accumulation (. . .). Under other modes of production this relative over-production is effected directly by the population increase, and in colonies by steady immigration.[25]

Accumulation, which Marx calls "the presence [*das Dasein*] of capital" (Marx 1993, 553; 1953, 450), is here in fact being compared with *population growth* in earlier societies. This demonstrates that it is precisely accumulation that differentiates bourgeois society as a specific *epoch* and consequently limits *all* the pre-capitalist societies to one single such epoch. This is underlined by Marx's tendency to make population growth, corresponding to accumulation in capitalist society, the real determinant of social change (or the lack of it) in pre-capitalist societies. For instance, he says:

> Since in all earlier forms of production the development of the forces of production is not the basis of appropriation, but a specific relation to the conditions of production (forms of property) appears as *presupposed barrier* to the forces of production, and is merely to be reproduced, it follows that the development of population, in which the development of all productive forces is summarized, must even more strongly encounter an *external barrier* and thus appear as something to be restricted. The conditions of society [were] consistent only with a specific amount of population.[26]

Thus one sees, e.g., emigration as a "structural" answer to threatening crises,[27] as well as other measures that are not compatible with a developed capitalist production, for the specific difference of pre-capitalist societies, the variations in populations and their specific significance, is sublated in bourgeois society; that sublation, however, is once again an *Aufheben*, and the sublated principle is *contained in* the specific difference of bourgeois society. Here, we have not had the time and space to demonstrate concretely how capital (according to Marx) through accumulation creates its own law of population and its own surplus population relative to its own existence. But it must be pointed out that when Marx says that it is only in capitalist society that a surplus population "appears as a result of labour itself"[28] this means that the historically created element itself takes over as the primary determinant in history, as opposed to the immediately dominating role of nature (and *a fortiori* of landed property) in pre-capitalist society.

It is only through the corresponding analysis of "The General Law of Capitalist Accumulation" in *Capital*, Volume I, that it is correct to say that capital is a *totality*. For capital cannot dominate remnants of earlier forms of society if it does not dominate, incorporate in itself, *the dynamic principle of these forms*. Through its power to construct an industrial reserve army, it "sublates" all society-changing factors other than its own. Thus it becomes a logical totality through its historical development; or, rather, it turns into a totality in which each element can also be logically exposed, i.e. subsumed under the encroaching capital. It is truly Substance: when it changes, it only changes itself.

Notes

1 Before we get the analysis of accumulation proper, Marx presents us with a last paragraph in chapter 20: "Destutt de Tracy's Theory of Reproduction". Clearly, its character is just historico-critical. It has no place in the immanent sequence of themes.

2 A reminder: the scheme is elaborated by Marx as a general analysis of the conditions of a *national* capitalist economy.

3 For a detailed exposition, see Appendix 1.

4 Of course, the I(v+s) are carried by means of production *in natura*. But as parts of a product value they just represent magnitudes to be turned into revenue as long as simple reproduction is presupposed.

5 Which, of course, is no wonder, given that he has already integrated the idea of "as much the constant positing as the sublation of *proportionate production*" into the concept of "capital in general".

6 In a letter to Paul Mattick, Henryk Grossmann points to the said "crisis" and possibly implies that he would like to make the same kind of use of it as here (Grossmann 1969, 112).

7 Formally, there is another way out, namely to reduce the volume of production and then to stabilize the simple reproduction on a lower level. But this possibility is not worth investigating, for the reproduction schemes always presuppose a given minimum in the value magnitude of capital, reflecting the technical level of production. The said "way out" would then mean a permanent shut down of capitalist production. A parallel argument is to be found in Marx's analysis of production time (Volume II, chapter 13), where a "shortening of the level of production" is rejected as a solution to problems raised by the many possible ruptures in a course of steadily crossing work periods and circulation periods inside individual capitals. (These are ruptures that show the necessity of additional capitals relative to the supposed starting point of the analysis, and which abstractly, i.e. on the level of individual capitals, concern the same problems focused on in the treatment of the transition from simple reproduction to accumulation in the model of total social reproduction. In reality, however, we have got to make do here with analyses whose development can be understood only in the background to the fact that the fixed capital undergoes a corresponding course. This last one (which, evidently, is most concretely analysed in section XI of chapter 20 in Volume II), however, must be exposed as independent of the first. In fact, it seems that in the reproduction schemes Marx finds it justified to presuppose a *harmonic* relation between working periods and circulation periods, precisely because he has already analysed them in the second section of Volume II.)

8 The first to point out a parallelism between the two volumes in this respect was, as far as I can see, Etienne Balibar (Balibar 1971, 279–285). (Balibar does not seem to be using the conclusions in the same way as here.) From a viewpoint of more "professional" economics, Hilferding (1968, 335–338), Fritsch (1968, 98), Campbell (1998, 141), Moseley (1998, 179) and Reuten (1998, 201) have pointed to the "crisis" in simple reproduction in Volume II. However, they are all generally more interested in the proportions inside the fixed capitals and do not concentrate on the aggregate Is, which is of decisive importance in Marx's exposition. Fritsch from the outset has closed the gates to an analysis of Is, since he (1968, 92, note) believes that it is unnecessary to follow the course of the parts making up the surplus value when one follows the movement of the parts making up the variable capital, since the first stands in a constant quantitative relation to the second. This implies that he overlooks important aspects of the function of use values and "the demand side" in the reproduction schemes.

9 Schanz, 1974, v. In Schanz, however, we do not find any concrete analysis of the reproduction schemes.

10 For a detailed exposition, see Appendix 2.

11 Campbell (1998, 137) says that "[t]he hoards Marx is concerned with in Volume Two are required for the continuity of the circulation of capital. Thus they are amassed intentionally or are voluntary hoards". Albeit she makes allowance for some "involuntary hoards", her propositions are far too strictly formulated, given the weight Marx himself puts on the storage under consideration.

12 Marx 1961, 472, note. The contents of Marx's manuscript of 1861–1863, as published in the new *MEGA*, seem to verify Engels' remark. Marx's most specific analysis of gold production (Marx 1980, 1701–1760) is here, by the way, kept on the level of revenues and prices of production.

13 In theory, the capital of the gold producer should have been augmented by about three per thousand, if the original proportion to the rest of the aggregate was upheld. We abstract from such adjustments here.

14 It is only fair to point out how Marx, in a paragraph in the same chapter (Marx 1961, 477), mentions the possibility of the gold capitalist holding back some of his surplus value as a hoard. Obviously, Marx here must be abstracting from the characteristics of his own scheme of simple reproduction.

15 In the chapter on simple reproduction, the importance and the volumes of the means of circulation have already been discussed in section V. Thus it seems that Marx consciously held back the theme of the material reproduction of money, to use it as a rounding off.

16 Marx 1961, 469. The use of a term like "storing" points to the possibility that Marx in fact never began the analysis of the reproduction of the constant capital of the gold producer. He says here that a "storing up or hoarding" grants money in excess also for the capitalists I. Such a term, according to my attempt at an analysis, is not quite adequate in relation to the situation of the gold producer's constant capital.

17 In Campbell 1998, 138–139 we read: "Marx does not explain the source of the social hoard in Volume Two of *Capital*, having already argued in Volume One that it is one of the results of the original accumulation". Obviously, this is wrong.

18 Marx 1993, 552; 1953, 450. Much is to be won if one makes such views the starting point of Keynesian "savings" theory, not to speak of Rawlsian dogmatic presuppositions about an ethical system having to be constructed to avoid the worst consequences of an inborn tendency in man to compete with other men.

19 It should be noted that in Marx 1974, in sketching the three-class dialectics to Engels in 1858, he writes that "the landed property is posited = 0" as long as the quantitative relation between capitalists and wage workers (here: especially the wage level) is under investigation inside the study of "capital in general". Also in this respect, there is continuity between the different plans and their results.

20 The term is used in Marx 1974a, where it concerns the construction of "the book on capital" in the *first* draft plan. However, as can be seen from a comparison between Marx 1970 and Marx 1965, the term is adaptable to *Capital*, Volume I.

21 Chapters 48–52, "Revenues and Their Sources" do not bring in anything new in substance but are focused on showing how the reader's acquired knowledge is to be used to penetrate the ideological surface, which has already been clarified.

22 Commenting on categories such as these, Helmut Reichelt (1970, 136) rightly saw that they represent "the constitution process of the bourgeois subject in its most abstract form".

23 Marx 1993, 276; 1953, 187. Such a formulation points to a well-known methodological reflection by Marx about the sequence of "the economic categories" in capitalist society in relation to their historical sequence. In the *Grundrisse* he says: "It would . . . be unfeasible and wrong to let the economic categories follow one another in the same sequence as that in which they were historically decisive. Their sequence is determined, rather, by their relation to one another in modern bourgeois society, which is precisely the opposite of that which seems to be their natural order or which corresponds to historical development" (Marx 1993, 107). These sentences have traditionally been seriously misunderstood (see, e. g., Meiners 1980, 272, where a good interpretation is presented). With "the categories" Marx here means capital, wage labour and landed property (and *a fortiori* their forms of revenue: profits and interest, wages and ground rent), a fact that can be deduced from the context, namely a polemic against the

"categorical" method of classical political economy. Robert Albritton comments on Marx's *dictum*, saying that in *Capital*, "the three first categories – 'commodity', 'money', 'capital' – do appear in history in that order" (Albritton 1999, 187). The implied error leads him to ignore Marx's words about a sequence being "precisely . . . opposite". Instead, he just says that the two sequences do "not follow" each other (Albritton 1999, 58). The practical consequences of a misunderstanding like this are made clear by the fact that Albritton ignores the closing function of the category of ground rent and transfers it to the interest on capital. He says: "In order to deal with the surplus profits associated with unavoidable qualitative differences between parcels of land [here, Albritton simply wants to abstract from absolute rent] or land-like resources, capital must generate the category rent. Finally, with interest-bearing capital, capital itself becomes a commodity. . . . A dialectic that started with the commodity comes full circle, ending with the commodification of capital itself" (Albritton 1999, 74–75). A similar position is presented in Sekine 1997, volume 2, 132. John R. Bell stands for views very close to Albritton's and Sekine's, writing that "[t]he concession of rent to landowners enable capital to develop a new self-image of interest-bearing wealth" (Bell 1995, 133). Such theses are, of course, flatly contradicted by the structure of the third volume of *Capital*, where interest is analysed before the transition to ground rent. In practice, the view of Albritton and Bell indicates severe problems for their methodological theses about a possible category of "pure capitalism" (for a criticism of Albritton, see Arthur 2002). In fact, in Marx's work, capital as a category comes "full circle" already in the circuit of commodity capital, representing a totality as against other forms of capital circuits (Marx 1961, chapter 3). It is used as the foundation for the reproduction schemes, which, in the form in which we have analysed them above, can be considered as the actualizations of precisely that circuit. Further, the two authors' attempt to reconstruct Marx's "dialectics" in *Capital* utterly fails, since such a conceptual movement by Marx is so evidently dependent on the position he ascribes to modern landed property. (It might be noted that Marx's remarks on "the categories" also led to problems for Klaus Hartmann. In his "philosophical investigation" on Marx, he produced an "excursion" on the subject, but his results were inappropriate (Hartmann 1970, 250, 254). The misinterpretation is also to be found in Postone 2003, 18.) As regards the viewpoints contained in Sekine's and Albritton's "pure capitalism", they are in part also nourished by the wish to construct a Marxian "pure dialetics", inspired by a faulty view of Hegel's thought. Their view is that the dialectic method should negate the category of ground, because this determination of reflection preserves a factor which is alien in relation to dialectic functions – as, e.g., is the case with Marx's positing of an absolutenesss of ground rent in relation to capital. But this is definitely impossible for Hegel, who stressed that dialectic method only exists because of the pressure from external unfreedom.

24 "This illustration of fixed capital, on the basis of an unchanged scale of reproduction, is striking" (1961, 469).
25 Marx 1966, 672. Marx is consciously making the supposition that all agriculture (*not* landed property!) is capitalist.
26 Marx 1972, 605.
27 "E.g. the colonies sent out in antiquity were overpopulation" (Marx 1972, 604).
28 Marx 1972, 605.

Prelude to Chapters 3 and 4

In the following two chapters, we confront questions related to the interaction of the three main classes in capitalist societies of today – some 150 years after the publication of the first volume of *Capital*. At the same time, we comment on some important tendencies in scholarly receptions of Marx's theory in later decades.

In overviewing the details of the reproduction schemes in Chapter 2, we saw that for a historical analysis, the economic relations of modern landed property are essential. What we are going to do in these chapters is depict the general structure of those relations in Western societies, from the times of the "primitive accumulation" up to today. Contemporary Western agricultural production and landed property in general have many forms, despite the fact that a homogeneous capitalist mode of production (based on real subsumption of industrial workers) dominates the core of these societies.

Among other things, these two chapters aim at recapitulating, in a more concise and empirically accessible manner than hitherto the structure of the Marxian doctrine of rent, and not least the different *forms* of rent. The leading thread is their methodological status inside Marx's theory of history. Sections 3.1 and 3.2 therefore focus specifically on the background for this status, and they accentuate Marx's theses of the interplay of the three main categories that we met earlier, i.e. modern landed property, wage labour and capital, inside the capitalist social formation. Sections 3.3 and 3.4 underscore the most important points of Marx's rent definitions through criticism of recent interpretations of his theories. Section 3.5 presents his theory of the genesis of industrial commodity prices as the necessary basis for the consistency of his view of all types of ground rent, while Section 4.1 shows the status of "absolute" rent in this regard. Section 4.2 analyses the question of the relation between absolute rent and monopoly rent in general, focusing on Marx's implicit assumptions of the status of effective demand. This theme leads on to a discussion, in Section 4.3, of the methodological foundations of concepts of monopoly rents. Section 4.4 criticizes a set of modern Marxisant theories of "urban rent" and explains them as illusions related to the operation of the money market. Section 4.5 sums up the author's view of the function of rent in capitalist society in recent centuries, while Section 4.6 rounds off the chapters with a view of the production crisis from 2007 on. Here, the "credit crunch" and the development of the housing market are taken as examples of the very form in which the class relations between capital, landed property and wage labour become apparent.

3 Karl Marx's theory of ground rent – historical elements in economic interplay

Part 1: the concept of rent in general

3.1 The historical significance of rent categories

To start this chapter, where the main weight is put on aspects of the Marxian rent concept which are relatively accessible without presupposing the typical network of capitalist prices, it is worth pointing out a well-known fact: according to Marx, there are to be found at least three types of ground rent in modern society. Landowners can in some cases enjoy a surplus profit based on the special and contingent quality of a product. This is the most usual form of "monopoly rent" in agriculture, forestry or mining (the main fields for ground rents). Also, we have "differential rents", based on the differences of quality of soil – given by nature *or* through human technical amendments.[1] In bourgeois society, these rents are in their classical forms paid to landowners by capitalists who lend the soil with the aim of appropriating the social average profit for themselves, paying the surplus profit resulting from the higher soil quality as rent to the owner. According to David Ricardo, who accepted only the existence of differential rent besides monopoly rent, the prices of the produce of the soil would vary according to the given differentials, with the centre of gravity the labour time necessary to create a given product mass on the *worst* soil on the market (the worst that can still be cultivated to fulfil the effective social demand). Marx agreed with this latter reasoning and in addition accepted a third sort, *"absolute"* ground rent, which, like the others, may appear in the prices of products of capitalist firms or other firms related to capitalist-dominated markets.

Absolute rent (if extant), like the other two sorts, constitutes an element which adds to Marx's"production price" of the product, i.e. the price that emerges as the apparent equilibrium price for an industrial branch. The majority of "landed" products will contain a differential rent in addition to the absolute.

The category of absolute rent is one of the most discussed in Marx's work. It is also, together with its interrelation with the other rent forms, a relatively complicated one. To present it in a form as accessible as possible, we lay primary weight on its function in Marx's theory of history in general. There are three central points to consider:

1   Absolute rent serves as a cornerstone and finishing touch for the validity of the labour *theory of value* in Marx's economic system in general.

2   The existence of absolute rent is the final proof of the all-pervasive priority of *property relations* in modern society. Thus, it underlines the significance of their opposition to *productive forces* in the Marxian theory.

3   The theory of "differential" rent, even in abstraction from absolute rent, presents us with a historical modification of the concept of value-producing labour in the Marxian corpus.

If point (2) is tenable, then it follows that we are speaking of private property, since value, or exchange value, is a form for the products of human labour only insofar as the producers are isolated from each other through their formally equal property rights, because these rights here are expressed in a certain volume of things "belonging" to an individual exclusively.

If point (1) is tenable, then Marx's settling of accounts with Ricardo's version of the labour theory of value is not limited to elaborating the double character of commodity-producing labour (its concreteness as well as its abstractness) but also to warranting the whole field of its validity in the economic sphere.

If (1) and (2) are both tenable, (3) gives us a historically adaptable evolutionary foundation for perfect determination of *aggregates of prices* in society's main branches – and in the totality of capitalist branches. It also contains the methodical principle for uniting the effects of aggregate demand and supply with a labour theory of value.

From 1817 on, when the first edition of Ricardo's *Principles of Political Economy and Taxation* appeared, influential readers (such as Thomas R. Malthus) protested against its thesis that an absolute rent could not exist. For Ricardo, the existence of a regular land rent (i.e. excepting monopoly rent) in addition to differential rent meant the knell of doom for any labour theory of value. For him, only differential rent could have a regular existence in agriculture and (*a fortiori*) in forestry and excavation industries.

Differential rent, according to Ricardo, follows from the (alleged) fact that the same human homogeneous labour in equal portions of extended time yields different amounts of produce directly proportional to differences in natural and/or man-made fertility on different plots of land. He was met by the objection that common empirical observation discloses that landowners can lease out their plots and receive rent even under unchanged effective demand for agricultural products and even if the homogeneous labour on that soil produces no more than on soil hitherto considered less productive than the least fertile in use.

Ricardo never since gave up his theory, so the price for a given item, regularly and on average – a bushel of corn, say – from the least productive process is sold at a price x which includes the lowest differential rent in the economy. This is the "market price" (Ricardo) of a bushel of corn. All corn producers sell a bushel at that price, and the owners of the most fertile soil get a differential rent which constitutes the greatest possible rate of the price. Any differential rent is a surplus over the average profit for any firm in society as a whole.

Let us say that a bushel of corn is produced through a total labour time (old and new taken together) of five hours on the least fertile soil engaged in production, which is the same as saying engaged in competition. This is what Marx would call the "*socially* necessary labour time" for that amount, i.e. for *any* producer. For, as we saw, Marx agrees with Ricardo that in agriculture it is this least fertile soil, or, better, the least productive firm (with market admittance), which incorporates the value-producing labour.

As for manufacturing industry, Ricardo's opinion is that it is no longer the least productive of the labour processes taking part in market competition which forms the base of the price but, as a rule, the average labour productivity in the branch. If a certain number of firms makes up a pig-iron-producing branch, then, if the effective demand is satisfied, it is the labour expended in the medium conditions of production which determines the value and the "natural price" ("market price"). Say that on average it takes five hours of simple, homogeneous labour to make and (physically) deliver five pounds of pig iron to the market: one might then believe that this amount must, on average, be exhangeable for one bushel of corn, regardless of the fertility of the soil in which it was produced. Let us say that the same goes for 1 metre^3 of timber, 5 litres of gaseous oxygen and one set of silver cutlery.

Now, according to Ricardo, there will in practice not be – or only very rarely – an actual equivalence on the market between the parts of the total circuit of such exemplars. The reason for this is differences in their conditions of production. Of these conditions, Ricardo gave outstanding priority to the differences in the proportions between fixed and circulating capital from firm to firm and from sphere to sphere.

If we consider the Marxian terminology, this is the relation between the value-amount of raw or auxiliary material, including of labour power, on the one hand, and, on the other, of durable buildings, tools and machinery. The difference between these kinds will vary greatly from branch to branch, leading to different claims on returns to the capitalist producers, something which in its turn leads to the deviation of actual prices of products from values, or, said in another way, from what would immediately correspond to labour time. However, Ricardo in practice has another definition of circulating capital, namely as covering only the payment of "labour" (since he has no clear concept of labour power as distinct from labour), partly (often) identified with the (payment of) wage *goods*. In practice, non-durable physical capital disappears from this analysis. In Ricardo's work, it is impossible to find the key factor determining such divergences of "prices" from "values" (to use the terminology which Marx found necessary for separating these phenomena). Actually, that shouldn't surprise us, since Ricardo held fast to a labour theory of value but was unwilling to separate out labour power in a clear fashion from labour material and instruments. Marx, in contrast, believes that a labour theory of value would have to let the main analytic separation go between *all* parts of physical capital, on the one hand, and labour *power* (i.e. the pure potential of targeted handling of that physical mass), on the other. Consequently, he separates capitals according to their composition between, on the one hand, the value of the whole mass of physical capital and, on the other, the value of the whole mass of labour power. This goes for each single capital as well as for the totality of national capitals. In this way, the value-producing power, the real source of value, is isolated ahead of all the material elements of labour.

It is through this relation c/v – the short expression for what Marx calls "the value composition of capital" – which stands in close relation to the corresponding composition of means of production and living labour ("the technical composition" of capital"), that Marx's concept of "the organic composition of capital" is formed. For technical and historical reasons, this composition is widely different from branch to branch, and an accurate concurrence between value and price magnitudes will be found only for the products of a capital which produces under precisely average relations between c and v.

Any such total of physical capital is called c, and the corresponding one is called v. The latter is Marx's symbol for "variable capital", i.e. the capital laid out in wages. Since that means the total value of the working capacity of the labourers, it is capital which buys the power which can augment total capital with a "profit", which has "surplus value" for its immediate form. Therefore, it is a "variable" capital, whereas the physical capital as such is strictly constant, if not diminishing in value.

In general, the understanding of the deviation of product prices from product values follows from these concepts. A capital with a "high" composition is one which produces relatively small amounts of value, since it has relatively few workers in relation to physical capital – and vice versa for capitals with "low" composition. Surplus value produced here is to a larger or lesser extent de facto transferred to capitals with high composition. Without such a transfer, which has the form of mutually competitive assimilations to the market, the co-existence of capitals would break down, i.e. free competition would end, while it is precisely this competition that effects the transfers.

All this gives a picture of what Marx calls "the transformation of values of commodities into prices of production". It gives the rule for the deviations of prices from values, with the proviso that each and every commodity is sold at its price of production, not at its value. The rule is limited by three reasonable constraints: a) the sum of prices does not exceed the sum of values, nor vice versa, and these totalities can ideally be measured as identical in a sum of homogeneous labour time spent in society in a period of production; b) the sum of new value (value added) is in the same way equal to the prices of the net product of society; and c) the sum of profits cannot exceed the sum of surplus value produced.[2]

Now, Marx's theory of land rent is built on this foundation, which he also developed through a criticism of Ricardo's general theory. It should stand to reason that if any element in Marx's logical edifice proves to be wrong, his theory of rent is undermined. But in order to verify that, and to show all the implications of the theory itself and of its eventual breakdown, it is necessary to depict the development of Marx's theory of the position of landed property in modern society.

3.2 From *Poverty of Philosophy* to the *Grundrisse*

Marx's first significant approach to the status of landed property is to be found in the *German Ideology* (1845), where an acute polemic against what he took to be petty-bourgeois inclinations, including those of Pierre-Joseph Proudhon, are to be found.[3] Present here is also a very general sketch of the place and role of landed property in what has become known as the "materialist interpretation of history".

However, the first germ of an investigation of the *method* necessary for analysis of landed property is to be found in *The Poverty of Philosophy*, from 1847 (Marx 1971), where the challenge represented by Proudhon was taken up in its specific *idealist* form.

In fact, Proudhon had come to incarnate precisely the naïve optimism of the Enlightenment (fundamental to Hegel's criticism of that movement), the belief that historical progress was a function of the capability to identify a "good" and a "bad" side in every social phenomenon – and then to just scrap the "bad" side. Furthermore, Proudhon's views implied that economic categories are essentialities that historically follow each other in a sequence which ultimately is dependent on their conceptual formation in human mentality. It is in harmony with Proudhon's dogma that human equality is to be verified through his own particular interpretation of the institution of division of labour. According to him, this division is an *acceptance* among individuals that their common plight should be evenly distributed.

Marx ridicules such thinking, where

> the singular man, this Robinson, suddenly has grasped the idea to make "his co-workers" a proposition of a known kind, and [that] these co-workers have accepted it without any kind of objection.
>
> (Marx 1971, 69)

David Hume once produced this kind of argument in his disclosure of the logic of contract theories. (If a man has the confidence to make a contract with an alien other, what is then the point in asserting that confidence by postulating that a contract is at the bottom of social affairs?) In Proudhon's case, it seems clear that such a theory implies that behind the "bad side" of the category of division of labour there stands a "good side" indicating a fundamental human equality. This mystical unity leads Man's mind to an anonymous "reason" which is the original fountainhead for the stream of economic "categories".

Marx, countering these views, underscored that Proudhon's method is nothing more than a theoretical destruction of the dialectical movement of a thing, as it comes to appear in his theory of circulation, where the genesis of money is misunderstood, while the commodities are taken literally to be "goods" that can do without money. This amounts to a gross misunderstanding of the contradictions among men and the ways to resolve them.

Ten years later, in the *Grundrisse* of 1857–1858, when we again meet criticism of Proudhon, it is transformed into a mature class analysis, where every singular "this Robinson" is acting as a *class* member, appearing inside a capitalist social formation with the class characters of landed property, capital and wage labour. It is here that we see Marx underline that the historical sequence of "categories" is other than their sequence of present structural importance and add that the latter follows from the opposite temporal historical relation.

The meaning of the stark thesis that determining factors in modern society have a way of functioning that is "precisely the opposite" (no less!) of what the bourgeoisie experienced in the feudal order is that the new society is putting the old order on its head. Here, we shall concentrate on the turning upside down of older rent relations in that new society.

The focusing on "sequences" passes over into the *Grundrisse* directly from *Poverty of Philosophy*, and there are many other methodologically crucial passages in the 1857–1858 work that have the same origin. Furthermore, while Marx in 1847 criticized Proudhon for not having understood Hegelian philosophy, he was himself definitely ambiguous in his relation to Hegel's thoughts on method – sometimes misunderstanding them outright. In the *Grundrisse*, however, his position is much more consistently Hegelian, and he uses Hegel's own method against the idealism of Proudhon.

Not only is Proudhon, according to Marx, wrong in postulating the sequence of categories as dependent upon conceptualization: he is also wrong in contending that their functioning is determined by their historical sequence in general. In the *Grundrisse*, Marx uses the Hegelian syllogism to underline this, insisting that "capital" is the factor that always appears as the "active middle" in bourgeois society, although its total movement may take both "wage labour" and "landed property" as its first or last point (Marx 1993, 276; 1953, 187). That is, the constellation expresses that an analysis of modern society is dominated by capital as the overarching power. The fact that landed property was originally the dominant factor vis-à-vis all kinds of labour relations and all kinds of capital tells us nothing decisive about modern society.

Nonetheless, interpretation of historical developments plays its part in establishing the totality of class categories in a given social formation. In *The Poverty of Philosophy*, Marx still had no clear conception of the fundamental condition of such a totality in modernity. Actually, he there took the modern proletariat to have an immediate background in a "feudal" proletariat (Marx 1971, 140–141), thereby ignoring those relations which he later ascribed to "the so-called original accumulation" of capital, and especially to its primary feature, namely the tendential expropriation of *any* type of non-owning stratum from the British manor economy, the "expropriation of the agricultural population from the land" (Marx 1976, 877–895; 1968a, 744–760).

The concept of an original ("primitive") accumulation was, however, well in place in Marx's mind by 1857.[4] The radical cutting of mankind's umbilical cord in Tudor times produced, according to this theory, a social formation whose main body is a function of the "action" (*Aktion*) of the three categories towards each other and among themselves. Such an *Aktion,* as we considered it in the first chapter, is a form of what Marx also calls an *Übergang*, a *transition* from one category into another.

To take "wage labour" (*die Lohnarbeit*), this implies that through the expropriation, a distinct part of the original accumulation, "*wage labour* in its totality is initially created by the action of capital on landed property, and then, as soon as the latter has been produced as a form, by the proprietor of the land himself"

(1993, 276; 1953, 187). This is "transition of landed property into wage labour".[5] But then Marx adds:

> *On the other hand, modern* landed property itself appears most powerfully in the process of clearing the estates and the transformation of the rural labourers into wage labourers. Thus a double transition to wage labour [*doppelter Übergang in die Lohnarbeit*].
>
> (Marx 1993, 279; 1953, 190, italics added)[6]

The two reflections contradict each other to a certain degree, a fact that scarcely has much significance in itself. However, (1) what is not mentioned is a possible third kind of transition, namely the immediate transition in which landed property transforms *itself* into a member of the "triad", fulfilling the "triangle" wage labour–capital–landed property, *itself* creating and expropriating free labourers, a fact which we meet in the Tudor enclosures, whose structure has not been replicated to this day anywhere else;[7] and (2) the possibility that such a "clearing" can be completed with the help of the forms of rent available for the "modern" landed property we are considering here.

Now, in introducing these reflections on the status of landed property, Marx treats the subject in a way in which his conscious affinity to Hegelian method appears to be undeniable:

> Capital, when it creates ground rent . . . goes back in the production of wage labour as its general creative basis [*in seines allgemeinen schöpferischen Grundes*]. Capital arises out of circulation and posits labour as wage labour; takes form in this way; and, developed as a whole, it posits landed property as a precondition as well as its opposite. It turns out, however, that it has thereby only produced wage labour as its general presupposition.
>
> (Marx 1993, 278–279; 1953, 189–190)[8]

In a similar way, Marx accentuates that there is a transition (*Übergang*) through wage labour "into capital", "a transition which follows by itself, since wage labour is here brought back into its active Ground [*in seinen aktiven Grund zurükgegangen ist*]" (1993, 276; 1953, 187).

It is here, and as the first and most important characteristic of modern *Grundeigentum*, that Marx points out that "landed property, as capitalized rent, is expensive . . . excluding the direct use of the soil by individuals" (1993, 279; 1953, 189), as we have already pointed out. As soon as the soil-price has turned into a function of capital accumulation, it takes on a form which in practice makes it impossible for wage workers to escape from the capital "Moloch" to the countryside. This is precisely the *reason* why Marx declares that "in the economic relations of modern landed property . . . the inner construction of modern society, or capital in the totality of its relations, is posited" (1993, 276, amended; 1953, 187).

The viewpoint is highly interesting. Not only is Marx, through his interpretation of the concept of the money market, making landed property a point of departure for the analysis of the capital relation: he is consciously joining sides with Ricardo's *general* view of capital. Twenty-odd pages earlier, Marx remarked how

> Ricardo, the economist of the modern age, with great historical insight, examined the relation of capital, wage labour and ground rent within the sphere of landed property, so as to establish their specific form.
>
> (Marx 1993, 252; 1953, 164)[9]

In the aftermath of this remark, which actually suggests some *concurrence* of modes of exposition between Ricardo and Marx, the author of the *Grundrisse* follows up with this observation:

> The history of landed property, which would demonstrate the gradual trans-formation of the feudal landlord into the landowner of the hereditary, semi-tributary and often unfree tenant for life into the modern farmer, and of the resident serfs, bondsmen and villeins who belonged to the property [*dem Grunde angehörigen*] into agricultural day-labourers, would indeed be the history of the formation of modern capital.
>
> (Marx 1993, 252; 1953, 164)

It is important to remind ourselves that in these same texts, the methodological proximity of Marx to Hegel is also conspicuous. That follows from a comment on what Marx might mean by employing the term "Ground" in the emphatic way present here. It is a central term in Leibniz's "laws of thought" and especially in Hegel, who treats it as the last of his "essentialities" (*Wesenheiten*, or *Reflexions-bestimmungen*) in his *Science of Logic*: Identity, Difference, Contrareity, Contra-diction and Ground. In Hegel's view, the dialectical contradiction is a necessary development of the thought of "Identity", but at the same time, its extreme form invites us to accept that a non-reflective, apparently *given, immediate* foundation has to lie at the bottom of our reflection (our understanding, intelligence). This basis, the Ground, turns out to be active itself and envelopes both matter and form. In this "material" guise, Ground is the *explanans* of contradictions – the refuge of the explanation of our social states of war.

Now, in the *Grundrisse*, when "the Ground" is introduced, the central theme in the exposition up to then has been *simple circulation*, concentrated in the chapter on money and the chapter on money as capital.[10] Here, the theme is the contradic-tory determinations of money and commodities, whose solution lies – as it was to do in *Capital* – in the discovery of the nature of labour power and thus *a fortiori* the relation between our three main categories. In their movement, the Ground of contradictions is to be found.

The term so eagerly employed by Marx, *schöpferischer Grund*, is somewhat idiosyncratic, but it adequately mirrors Leibniz's use of the "law of sufficient Ground", which he thinks reflects a ground which is always mixed with other causes or grounds, but which will always be in itself alone sufficient to create a given event. This is also one of the reasons for Hegel's predilection for it, along with his adoration of Spinoza's nature as productive, the *natura naturans*.

3.3 Recent discussions of the theme (1979–2017)

We shall now regard the sketch of the historical basis of the Marxian rent theory as accounted for, and turn to considering how the essentialities of Marxian theory, as depicted up to this point, are interpreted in contemporary debates.

One aim of this overview is to consider the discussion of Marx's rent theory from the angle of economists, historians and philosophy-minded theorists of science. However, it should be added, as a foreshadowing of the scope of the problems, that even the rather chaotic sentiments and viewpoints of postmodernist thought have found their way into analyses involving Marx's theories. The paradigmatic example might well be Jacques Derrida's attempt to interpret Marx's economic theory as based on *individual* consumption, while at the same time coupling the Marxian theory of knowledge with the Hegelian view of the genesis of the concept of the "Thing", interpreted not as a result of labour but precisely of individual consumption. This breathtaking misunderstanding (edited, appropriately enough, in the remarkable year of 1968) became the point of departure for problematic views on Marx's theory, such as those developed by Slavoj Žižek; recently, a consequence has been that the much misunderstood theme of Marx's absolute rent has even been wrenched into an abstract item in the ontology of *la condition humaine,* said to depict an "absolute scarcity" localized in "indebted man" (Lazzarato 2011). While perhaps welcome among marginal ideologists in economics, such conspicuous research results should, for other lines of thought, incite more sober investigations. The crucial question is whether it will.

Now, to introduce the theme proper: in a recent edition of the American journal *Science & Society*, an article by Joon Park, "Land Rent Theory Revisited" (Park 2014, 88–109) presents a series of influential views on Marx's theory of ground rent. This article is a convenient point of departure for overviewing the premises for contemporary discussions on ground rent, especially in Marx's work.

Park calls his article a "review" of Marxian views on the subject in the last five decades. As such, the article is welcome, albeit that one should make the critical remark that it is almost completely confined to Anglo-American debates, their weaknesses as well as their strengths.

Park writes:

> Marx's unique contribution, however, is the theory of absolute rent which is demanded even from tenants of the worst land and which thus becomes a part of the price of production. He argued that if landed property prevents the surplus value created in a sector from participating in the general equalization of the profit rate, it may demand a certain level of common rent in that sector for the use of the land. The amount of absolute rent is explained as the difference in value over the price of production of the product in a sector.
>
> (Park 2014, 92)

This passage is in need of some scrutiny. The first sentence defines absolute rent as part of a price of production of a commodity. The last one defines it as a surplus (limited by the total quantity of exchange value) over that price. In between these two contradictory definitional elements, there lies an ambiguous use of the word "sector". Marx generally leaves aside that term in his explorations of rent, since he generally treats all of agriculture as a single branch. Marx's theory definitely includes a monopoly of landownership and thus reduction in competition. But, for him, the social relation which excludes, e.g., capitalist agriculture from entering the intraspherical competition is precisely that which is expressed in the rent and cannot be separated from this in the way Park will have it. The "sector" yielding absolute rent is always a branch that involves private ownership *of soil* and the productive use of this soil, i.e. employment of the soil to generate use values for sale (i.e. commodities). Furthermore, since the "sector" consequently produces from a *given* resource (land, etc.), which therefore – as *"given"* – is limited in principle, Marx accepts (as we have seen) the thesis from British classical economy that the market-value magnitude is determined by the social necessary labour time on the *least fertile* piece of land in cultivation. (Opposition to this view will be commented on later.) Such a thesis is for Marx closely related to his general theory of history, as it has been depicted above; it is a remnant of older historical relations.

Furthermore, while this latter relation influences both the existence of absolute rent and the existence of differential rent, absolute rent can *appear* only on produce of the land insofar as the soil is cultivated by a capital which has a lower than average capital composition (between capital expenses and wage bill) in relation to the totality of productive branches in society as a whole, i.e. including both industrial and agricultural firms. This is because the condition of possibility for production on the soil, namely the consent of the landowner, constitutes a historically created yet *a priori* barrier to competition between capitals. While *free* competition leads to capital-intensive firms being furnished with some of the surplus value produced by labour-intensive ones, a low capital/labour average in agriculture (and mining, forestry, oil extraction, etc.) will not lead to such a transfer; instead, the corresponding sums will pass to the landowner as "absolute" rent.

However, to return to Park's exposition, he accepts Ben Fine's definition of absolute rent (Fine 1979), taking it to be an "accurate" description of Marx's theory to say that "the source of absolute rent is the difference between market value and price of production, after the equalization of the profit rate, across all sectors" (Park 2014, 97).

But, according to the above, this is a basic error, since the point for Marx is that the power of landownership *halts* such an equalizing movement, independently of any payment of differential rent, and reduces it to industrial capital outside agriculture and mining (etc.). Of course, it is possible to interpret Fine's words to mean that "equalization" is simply a calculation *a posteriori* of the level of rent. In that case, the result of the measuring, the aggregate amount of rent, would of course be the same. But one would miss the point as to what *generates* the amount. If "equalization" is meant to connote an active social movement of forces – as it clearly is by Fine – it is important to know that it pertains only to industrial manufacturing capital.

Again, the result in Fine is that all "sectors" without discrimination are placed on an equal footing, a manoeuvre that makes it impossible to see the actual specificities of agriculture in capitalist society.

As Park sums up his article, it turns out that he wants to highlight an article by George E. Economakis (2003), contending that it represents "one of the rare attempts to examine rent from the standpoint of *value theory*" (Park 2014, 105, italics added). He adopts Economakis' view that "the sectors with high organic composition have a higher rate of surplus value" and *a fortiori* "the possibility that *the value of a product* in a higher organic composition sector can be greater than that in a low organic composition sector" (Park 2014, 105, italics added). These points of view, correctly refuted by Jørgen Sandemose (the article in question (2006) is mentioned in Park's reference list), are, as has been underscored by Saverio Fratini (2009), "faulty [*sbagliato*]". Fratini (originally following objections presented by Sandemose) takes the point up in greater detail:

> the increment of labour productivity will influence the rate of suplus value only through the reduction of the value in labour added [*in lavoro incorporato*] in the commodities given to the worker as wage; but in this case, the higher productivity of labour would augment the rate of surplus value in all sectors.
>
> (Fratini 2009, 8, my translation)

Now, as implied in Sandemose 2006, there is a connection between Economakis' "isolating" of the movements in the rate of surplus value inside each and every branch from any other and, on the other hand, his concept of "excess surplus value" (indicating absolute rent) inside *specific* branches. In characterizing Economakis' summary of chapter 45 of *Capital* III, Sandemose remarked:

> There is no such thing as "excess surplus value" in the agricultural production process. The point of "monopoly of landownership" is not that it prevents "excess surplus value . . . from going into a general equalization of the rate of profit". This reasoning is tautological. The amount in question is an "excess" amount precisely *because* it is not taking part in the equalization. It shares this characteristic with all other parts of the product value from agriculture. It is the whole agricultural sphere that is exempt from inter-sectoral competition.
>
> (Sandemose 2006, 361)

In Economakis, and also in Park, there is a thesis to the effect that absolute rent is of the same nature as the monopoly rent of bourgeois market theory, leading to a "monopoly price". This would imply that there is no basic difference in price formation between agriculture and industry, since the same type of monopoly surplus would be possible in any kind of productive capitalist enterprise.

The two authors' misconceived theses on the nature of the rate of surplus value are de facto helpful in generating such a result. For they imply that Economakis' imagined subject matter, "excess surplus value", may be present everywhere, in any sector whatsoever. Consequently, no specific social force is susceptible to set obstacles to its free access anywhere in the system, and the theory of a monopoly of landownership would be meaningless. With such a point of departure, how to understand landed property and its historical role at all?

The contention that Marx should be understood along the lines presented by Economakis was launched by David Harvey in 1982, who took as his point of departure the following quote from Marx's chapter on absolute rent:

> if capital meets an alien force which it can but partially, or not at all, overcome, and which limits its investment in certain spheres, admitting it only under conditions which wholly or partly exclude that general equalization of surplus-value to an average profit, then it is evident that the excess of the value of commodities in such spheres of production over their price of production would give rise to a surplus-profit, which could be converted into rent and as such made independent with respect to profit. Such an alien force and barrier is presented by landed property, when confronting capital in its endeavor to invest in land; such a force is the landlord vis-à-vis the capitalist.
>
> (Marx 1968c, 770)

Harvey commented in the following way:

> Part of the excess surplus value produced in agriculture by virtue of its labour intensity (lower value composition) is "filched" (as Marx puts it) by the landlord, so that it does not enter into the equalization of the rate of profit. To be sure, the commodity sells at a monopoly price. But this represents a failure to redistribute surplus value from agriculture to sectors with higher than average value compositions, rather than an active redistribution of surplus value into agriculture, as would be the case under monopoly rent.
>
> (Harvey 1982, 351)

It is clear that this is a faulty interpretation. It is not "a part" of such an "excess" but the *whole* of it which goes to the landlord. If that were not the case, we would be confronted here by a differential rent, not an absolute one. It is quite another matter that this "excess" (Marx: *Überschuss*) may, by some of these producers, fail to cover the whole amount between their production price and their individual value. Harvey's misinterpretation underrates the power of landed property as an "alien force". This should be clear from the following remarks from Marx's chapter on absolute rent:

> In industry these various masses of surplus value are equalized into an average profit and distributed uniformly among the individual capitals as aliquot parts of the social capital. Landed property hinders such an equalization among capitals, invested in land, whenever production requires land for either agriculture or extraction of raw materials, and takes hold of a portion of the surplus-value, which would otherwise take part in equalizing to the general

rate of profit. The rent, then, forms a portion of the value, or, more specifically, of the surplus value, of commodities, and instead of falling into the lap of the capitalists, who have extracted it from their labourers, it falls to the share of the landlords, who extract it from the capitalists.

(Marx 1968c, 780)

Also, it ought to be clear that if landed property, as a *Schranke*, hinders *any* equalization into an average profit-rate on side of the "landed" capitalist, then it is acting upon *the whole* of the latter's surplus value, else it could not decide at what rate that surplus is to be transferred to the landowner.

It follows likewise that the excess in the value of agricultural products over their price of production can become a determining element of their general market-price solely as a consequence of the monopoly in landed property. It follows, finally, that in this case the increase in the price of the product is not the cause of rent, but rather that rent is the cause of the increase in the price of the product. If the price of the product from a unit area of the worst soil = P + r, then all differential rents will rise by corresponding multiples of r, since the assumption is that P + r becomes the regulating market-price.

(Marx 1968c, 771, italics added)

This means, and it is the effective guarantee, that the landowner class's monopoly has already made it impossible for any ground rent, all differential rents included, to influence a mass of surplus value that has already passed over into an equalization of rates of profits. The fact that agricultural capitalists sell their products at a production price is not a consequence of a competition with industrial capitalists. On the contrary, they have to accept a rate of profit already established by industrial capital in its settling of accounts with "wage labour". In other words: "The difference between the value and the price of production is (. . .) the surplus [*Überschuss*] of the surplus value of this capital over the one *assigned* to it [*ihm* zugewiesenen] through the general profit rate" (Marx 1968c, 771, italics added).

The modern ground rent, then, figuratively raises a "bastion" (Wygodski 1970, 102) around landed property, preventing investments on pure capitalistic rules. It will – under the general condition of a below-average composition of capital in agriculture – prevent cultivation of a given piece of land if the product of that soil cannot render a surplus over the price of production of general agricultural produce; this very fact may lead the capitalist farmer (*Pächter*) to raise the price of the product, creating a rent that goes to the landowner. This is *absolute* rent.

3.4 Historical guise of modern differential rent

In light of the above, it becomes all the more clear that it is of small importance that absolute rent, as a result of capitalist class-based action on modern landed property, may be kept low, purely quantitatively considered.[11] The point is that the underscoring of landed property as a creative independent power – its 'absoluteness', so to speak – is in line with both capital and wage labour. By precisely the same token, the historical provenance of modern differential rent is necessarily accentuated.[12] This historical background, which lets the whole of the phenomenon of land rent, even differential rent (despite its genesis in capitalist surplus profit), come forth as a modified form of patrimonial domination system based on landed property, is of central importance for Marx: after all, he is primarily a theoretician of history – a "historical materialist".

Historical developments are also decisive for the fact that the concept of socially necessary labour time has a significance in the agriculture–mining–forestry spheres different from that in manufacturing. The social exigencies for products from the soil, which are necessarily brought forward by capitalist industrial competition and accumulation, tend to enforce conditions that make the supply of "landed" products adequate to effective total demand. But this will, literally, only happen at a price: value production will be modified. By hook or by crook, landowners keep open an area sufficient for the demand. But the limited character of their resource leads not only to a restriction on society's total interspherical competition but also a to a restriction on the intraspherical competition "on the soil". The law of value in competition is upheld, with the modification that it is operative *directly* and *ostensibly* on the "worst soil" only.

The fact is that Marx's analysis of the main contradictions between capitalists and landlords has two decisive implications: an intraspherical modification inside the branch(es) of "landed" production and an interspherical modification barring the influence of society's average profit rate. And just as the latter is the centre of much anti-Marxian criticism, so is the former.

One category in Marx that has been the centre of much dispute, not least of misunderstandings, is"false social value" and its possible function in capitalist agriculture.

Let us look at a recent work by Christian Gehrke, which sums up the position and the issue excellently. Gehrke contends that Marx regarded agriculture as a sphere with the same kind of "value" determination as the industrial ones, thus "not by the 'labour time necessary under the worst conditions', as Ricardo had maintained". Gehrke quotes the following from Marx, *Capital* III – from a footnote in his chapter 10, on industrial competition:

> The controversy between Storch and Ricardo with regard to ground-rent (a controversy pertaining only to the subject; in fact, the two opponents pay no attention to one another), whether the market-value (or rather what they call market-price and price of production respectively) was regulated by the commodities produced under unfavorable conditions (Ricardo) (. . .) or by those produced under favorable conditions (Storch) (. . .) resolves itself in the final analysis in that both are right and both wrong, and that both of them have failed to consider the average case.

(Marx 1968c, 193)

And Gehrke comments:

> This would conform to the definition of value that Marx had given in vol. I of
> *Capital*, where he made it clear that the value of commodities must be calcu-
> lated on the basis of the labour-time which is necessary on average, or in
> other words, is "socially necessary".
>
> (Gehrke 2010, 21)

In an attempt to justify his argument by depicting the possible context of Marx's
terms and arguments, Gehrke writes:

> However, Marx regarded the determination of market value by the labour-
> time necessary under the worst conditions as a "distortion" which is intro-
> duced into the "law of value" by the capitalist mode of production: For Marx,
> the 'real' value of the agricultural produce is given by the *average* labour-time
> expended in its production, and the "real" price of production is a (weighted)
> average of the prices of production on the various lands. The market value of
> agricultural commodities which is established on the basis of competition in
> capitalistic conditions is therefore, for him, "a false social value".
>
> (Gehrke 2010, 22; see Marx 1968c, 193)

It is somewhat unclear what Gehrke aims at. However, it *is* clear that the problem
is that Marx's development of the category of false social value[13] *disproves*
Gehrke's very interpretation of the former's argument relating to the Ricardo–
Storch "dispute".

For the sake of brevity, Table 3.1 illustrates false social value through a modification of Marx's numerical examples, presented in a schema by W.S. Wygodski
(1970, 88):

While the "genuine" individual value of products is 27, the market value is 30,
being a "false social value", representing a surplus of 3 value units per (each and
every) produced entity.

It is true that Marx uses this as an analogue to the "artificial" price level caused
by differential rent in agriculture, but the example itself is meant to illustrate pure

Table 3.1 False social value

Groups of capitalists	Amount of products	Individual value of product	Market value of product	Individual value of total product	Market value of total product
I	1	60	30	60	30
II	12	20	30	360	360
III	3	30	30	60	90
IV	4	15	30	60	120
Totalling	20	Average value per product = 27		540	600

industrial relations. In such a case, this distortion vanishes through competition, while the illustration, presupposing equilibrium between effective demand and supply, is valid over time for agricultural markets. Here, the "artificial" surplus will persist, so that consumers in society at large will serve as victims for a para-sitic class of landowners (or, rather, for a class of landowners which to that extent is parasitic).

In the example above, we see how Marx emphasizes a most efficient group (IV) and a least efficient one (I) by letting two groups in between help to add up to what he takes to be the social totality of products. The "average" is consequently per definition represented here, and Group II determines the market value by generat-ing the great majority of products (see the identity (360) between value entities in columns 5 and 6). The "average" is duly considered and all in all leads us to a false social value, which equals the selling price.

It is such an "average" which is apprehended neither by Storch nor by Ricardo. Far from being an argument for an astounding thesis of value determination through the "average" firm inside the agricultural sector, Marx's example is the precise opposite: a confirmation (viz., the illustration transferred to differential rent) of the thesis that the least labour-efficient firm in operation determines the market value. This, additionally, is a confirmation of a relation that Marx takes to be a *historical* fact. His exposition of land rent in general (Marx 1968c, chapters 37–47) is rounded off by a chapter (790–821) on the "Genesis of Capitalist Ground Rent", where it is an essential point that in pre-capitalist conditions, market values dominate over any kind of production prices, and that consequently the domination of landed property over the upcoming capital relation is visible in the difference between definitions of socially necessary labour time in agriculture and manufacture.[14]

3.5 Implications of a historiographical argument against Marx

The advantage of giving priority to a socio-historical analysis as regards Marx's theory of rent can be illustrated well by the method commonly employed against his doctrine of the historical genesis of the capitalist rent forms.

As we have tried to show, the theoretical basis for interpreting absolute rent – or, for that matter, differential rent – as an entity without immanent connection to the law of value presupposed by Marx is weak. However, such arguments also appear in *historical* guise – e.g., in the work by Fine already mentioned, the author insists that it is only in the early stages of capitalist development that "absolute rent cannot exceed the difference between the value and the price of production in the agricultural sector", since "capitalists' investment was likely to be limited within the sector" (see also Park 2014, 97).

Similarly, Robin Murray is lauded for "noting that a historic feature of landed property and the immobility of capital in the early stage of the capitalist mode of production enables the systematic blocking of capital and the exchange of prod-ucts at their values" (Park 2014, 98; Murray 1977–1978).

Considering our reflections on the undeveloped state of pre-capitalist price formation, plus a further note on simple commodity production (to follow), we can see that Marx's conception is precisely the opposite: if there existed a systematic blocking of capital, it would only mean that the capitalist mode of production had *not* conquered society, and that no absolute rent of the kind could exist. The latter's only definition in Marx's corpus, as fulfilment of the labour theory of value, is that it follows from developed capitalism.

For, according to Marx's comments on Ricardo's theory of rent, "landed property can only affect and paralyse the action of capitals, their competition, to the extent that this competition modifies the determination of commodity values" (1968e, 330). That is, as we have seen, the transformation movement can be halted, but its ground cannot be destroyed.

Taking a developed capital competition and transfer system as an argument against absolute rent is contradictory to Marxian premises. Concretely, Marx says that

> transfer of new capital to the land and soil cannot . . . have . . . the effect of forcing landed property [to reduce the price to the industrial production-price level]; for the competition of capitals among themselves is precisely what makes the landlord able to demand from the individual capitalist that he satisfies himself with "an average profit" and to pay him the overplus of the value over the price that allows him that profit.
>
> (Marx 1968, 330)

In brief, the "historical" argument introduced by Harvey, Fine, Murray and others has no *raison d'être* whatsoever, and analysis lets it disappear dimly, like Eurydice, into shadowy ideological, or even populist, romantic kingdoms. No argument has been produced to the effect that a developed capitalist economy possesses any specific power against the investment barrier of landownership.

However, since we have raised this question as a case of historiography, it is appropriate to go further and make at least a general prospect of the situation of landed production in capitalist countries, especially as regards the play of forces between capital and landed property. The archetypical nations are the "northwest" areas in both America and in Europe, and it is justifiable to concentrate on them on this occasion.[15]

With the exception of the UK, landed agricultural property in developed capitalist countries is mainly in the hands of petty-bourgeois peasants, with holdings worked on a family basis corresponding to the size of the plot, or at least by a number of hands which on average is so small that the firms cannot be called properly capitalist and have not lost their "familial" character.

The case of the UK can easily be explained by the fact that an industrial revolution, and the expropriation of country people that was its necessary condition, could not have occured without antagonisms between landed class groups. Without this type of initial conditions, no "northwestern" capitalism would ever have been generated. On the other hand, such antagonisms were not requisite – at least not in the same grand scale – for the *spreading* of capitalism in Western Europe, given the extreme population-growth rate, the existence of an international market (once generated, mainly through British capitalism), advanced manufactural production and the pro-bourgeois political effects of the Napoleonic Wars. Here, the dominance of a small-holdings property structure could continue into the new era, and was in part a revolutionary result of the political struggle against feudalism.[16] Among the immigrants to North America, this structure was copied and accelerated though state action, that very state being, as far as the US is concerned, an organized petty bourgeoisie.

All in all, as regards the historical development from Tudor times to now, in the lands inside a mighty parallelogram from Alaska's Point Hope to Norway's Hammerfest and further on to Italy's Lecce and California's San Diego, including for good measure the old British Pacific dominions, we must admit that a genuinely capitalist social formation dominates, while it is only on the British archipelago that its genesis corresponds with some accuracy to the relations that formed the background for Marx's 1867 warning to German workers: "De te fabula narratur" (1976, 90; 1968a, 12). The "classical triad", as Ellen Meiksins Wood persistently named the three-class configuration (e.g. 2002, *passim*) seems at first sight to be a somewhat limited configuration.

However, this should not be taken to invalidate the extension or significance of a conspicuous thesis from Marx's side in his treatment of the three main categories, namely that capital is simply dependent on "ground rent" as representing an "Other" to itself. Accumulation, he stresses, leads "capital" to expand in such a way that against the background of landed property it "has to posit a value or form of wealth specifically distinct from capital. This is *ground rent*" (Marx 1993, 276; 1953, 187). This should follow as a general feature from Marx's reflection on the status of the landed population in capitalism.

Marx indirectly treats this subject in some detail, especially in the first book of *Theories of Surplus Value*. He concentrates on the social position of what we today would call the average small independent and self-working landowner, the petty-bourgeois peasant, and it seems that his method and conclusions can be taken to be valid – with some modifications for other ownership forms (in the "northwest") lying between the ordinary peasant and the absentee landlord.

Marx is here analysing the farmer as a person integrating more than one class character, abstractly belonging to each of the functions of the classical "triad". As a landowner he is limited by his own role as a capitalist, inside which, so to speak, he employs himself as a wage worker. As a capitalist he may slow down his investment and thus indirectly his own physical plight, while a rise in efficiency may limit his rent income as a landowner, and so on.

Far from being a case of ideological "concept imperialism" relating to independent farmers or peasants inside capitalist society, this model serves as an illustration of the ambiguous position of many a producer in that society and is, according to Marx, realistic for that very reason. It reflects the situation of a farmer in a developed capitalist society, where an advanced credit system confronts him to his detriment as well as for his welfare and – first of all – as a partial result of the *Aktion* of landed property, even in its small-holding form in the agricultural sphere.

In fact, Marx (in 1862) writes on capitalism that

> the *division* [*die Trennung*] appears as the normal relation in this society; where it actually is not present, it is presupposed [*supponiert*], and . . . in so far correctly: For (in contradistinction to old-Roman or Norwegian condi- tions, or to American, in the US Northwest) the union [*die Vereinigung*] appears as contingent, the division as normal, and therefore the division is held fast even when the person unites the different functions. Here it appears very strikingly that the capitalist is only the function of capital, the worker the function of labour power.
>
> (Marx 1968d, 384)

Needless to say, most of Marx's exceptions mentioned above have disappeared today, so the following should, albeit to a different extent, be valid for the whole of the "northwest", even for landless *petites-bourgeoises*:

> As proprietor of the means of production he is capitalist, as worker he is his own wage worker. That is, as capitalist he pays his salary and draws a profit from his capital, i.e., he exploits himself as wage worker, and in the surplus value he pays himself the tribute which labour owes capital. Possibly he pays himself also a third part as land proprietor (ground rent) . . .
>
> (Marx 1968d, 383)[17, 18]

The political power and prestigious position of the peasant or farming landowner in the "northwest" should, according to Marx, be functionally explained through the necessity of keeping wage-workers out in the cold. The capitalistic develop- ment in industry is at least as effective and advanced in many areas where the *classical* triad is absent as it is in British ones. The mechanism of worker exclu- sion is also just as efficient, for the falling rate of profit and of interest is clearly there, albeit modifications are present for Mediterranean countries (Italy, Spain, even France).

Marxian historiography concerning this kind of landownership still has much to explore, but at least the theory of rent seems adequate for a thorough under- standing. It deserves mentioning that it is odd to think that contemporary capital as a matter of course is in a stronger position versus landed property than in earlier days. Concretely, the "bastion" position of landownership, which eventu- ally can be expressed in the existence of absolute rent, may be the best option in constructing an explanation. It should be noted as especially relevant for the most developed of the developed nations that a weaker position for capital does not mean that the capitalist system is being weakened. On the contrary, *capitalism*, or the capitalist *social formation*, is, and remains, a triad, with capital as the "active middle". It *consists* precisely in the dialectic of the said "categories". The better the triad functions as such, the stronger is *capitalism*. The *active* middle, the middle *in actu*, is the capitalist production, to the extent that working people are integrated in it, producing surplus value. It is, consequently, the capitalist *mode of production*.

3.6 Fulcrum of rent theory: the transformation from values to prices

We have underscored how the force of Marx's theory of rent is dependent on the validity of certain pillars related to his concept of the organic composition of capital. It is now time to check the consistency of those theoretical pillars and *a fortiori* how critics of the Marxian theory are apt to interpret it. To continue with recent interpretations, we will look at Miguel D. Ramirez's important "Marx's Theory of Ground Rent" of 2009 (ignored by Park).

Ramirez notifies the reader of the viewpoint that Marx's theory of rent might be "fatally flawed" (as it is put by Howard and King, 1985) simply because of a faulty procedure in composing the "Transformation of Labour Values to Prices of Production" (Marx 1968c, 164). This procedure, according to Ramirez, is "obviously incorrect". He gives no argument but is aiming at the Ricardian criticism rendered by Bortkiewicz in 1906–1907. Still, he thinks he can abstract from the alleged incorrectness by relying on a variation of that criticism, developed by Francis Seton (1957), presenting a "solution" which Ramirez holds to be acceptable to Marxian thinking.

It is necessary to underscore that this "transformation" problem, if extant, does indeed have a very close, and crucial, connection with the question of the possibility of rent. This has been pointed out in Sandemose 2006 (363); however, as that article also showed, this criticism of Marx depends on a blatant misunderstanding of the latter's theory of measure of value and of the *numéraire*. Seton repeats this error just as blatantly, since his "solution", as he puts it, aims to "permit money prices to be expressed in terms of the *value* of gold" (Seton 1957, 156).[19] This possibility was refuted by Marx, since it would amount to the sublation of the concept of money (Marx 1968b 105; 1968e 198; Sandemose 1973, 1976, 2004, 2010). Since all parties in the debate in question accept(ed) that "money prices" (an irrational expression, by the way) are based on value magnitudes, Seton's thesis must be said to imply an attempt to define the quality "value" precisely through the quality "value". However, in the real world, it is the partitioning of the *material* (*use* value) of gold on the measuring rod (*numéraire*) which expresses prices. Also, without a "solution" based on such an evident premise, there cannot exist any justifiable theory of ground rent in the Marxian system, since rent is there a development of capitalist surplus profit, which, in turn, has to be a surplus over a uniquely determined level, the average rate of profit, which gives the frame of quantitative price relations.

The point is precisely that the level in question can be neither defined nor determined if one posits the *numéraire*-commodity as a quantity of *value*, or even at =1. For here, the quantity of a production equation (relating to the *numéraire* material) is presented as nothing more than an *unqualified* relation, which simply means a pure number. This, again, means that the number is taken not only to quantify relations between industrial branches but even to ensure the existence of some *quality* that has the capacity to represent the likeness between the productive material represented by the equations. A number pure and simple cannot account for such a phenomenon.

In this case, even Fratini has difficulties, since in his article, seeing the necessity of determining the basic level of production prices (the "fulcrum"), he uses equations from Piero Sraffa (1972) to "integrate perfectly" the absolute rent in the general system of *Production of Commodities by Means of Commodities* (Fratini 2009, 25). But since that system presupposes that one can find the level of prices through the "standard commodity" as = 1 (plus, alas, operating with a will-o'-the-wisp type of independent variable, like Seton does), the attempt is to no avail.[20]

Notes

1 This concerns the difference between what Marx calls "Differential rent I" and "Differential rent II". These two are not treated separately in these chapters.
2 Sandemose 1973, 1976, 2004, 2010, *passim*.
3 See especially Marx and Engels 1968, section A, 18-27, and the section "Der Verein", 373–401.
4 See, explicitly, Marx 1993, 459; 1953, 363. It is important to note for a full understanding of the views that follow below that there are small imperfections in the *Grundrisse* text relative to the one in *Capital*, not to speak of the fact that the latter text contains an attempt at a full historical-*empirical* overview of the whole of "the so-called original accumulation of capital", while nothing like that is present in the 1858 text. In addition, the empirical overview in *Capital* has its problems. See Sandemose 2012.
5 Translations amended.
6 Marx's preposition "in" indicates that the preposition "to" is misplaced in the translation. The transition is an organic movement between realities corresponding to the categories, not a mechanical interaction between them.
7 It begs the question when David Harvey without discussion uses the British Tudor experience to argue as follows: "Primitive accumulation off the land produces wage labourers. A definite form of landed property fulfils this historical role and continues to fulfil it in so far as the widening and deepening of capitalism on the world stage requires it." Apart from the fact that Harvey then immediately starts to contradict himself, the confusion between "original accumulation" and "expropriation" is all too characteristic (Harvey 1982, 359).
8 The English version is amended by using the preposition "in". Furthermore, Nicolaus, as mentioned already, has "landed property" instead of Marx's *Grundrente*.
9 Once more, note Marx's preference for the term "ground rent", where one could have expected "landed property".
10 *In toto*, this covers Marx 1953, 35–162. In Marx 1993, that should correspond to 115–250, but the chapter division has been blurred by the editor.
11 *Contra* Harvey 1982, especially 353.
12 See, in addition to my following remarks in the text, Marx's note on the relation between the amount of absolute rent and the structure of rent "differentials" in the same agriculture: 1968c, 763.
13 Marx 1968e, table on 260.
14 As concerns the background for such a definition, the reader should take the pleasure of surveying the acute comment made by the Ricardian Thomas Corbet (Corbet 1821, 53–54) on the theme, quoted by Marx in 1968c, 193, note.

15 In other continents or subcontinents, the appearance of a dominant capitalist industrial sector is restricted to firms where the subsumption of workers is only "formal", and where capitalist competition can at most be said to exist inside spheres, not between them. This is a result of the widespread cartelization through "business groups", and it means that we do not find "Marxian" prices of production, nor soundly developed forms of land rent (Sandemose 2010 and 2012a).

16 Sandemose 2012; 2015, 25–29.

17 It goes without saying that the producer then defines his means of production as if they were "constant capital".

18 It should be noted here that Marx's point of view has been turned upside down in Elster 1985, where manipulations with quotations, etc. are used to make it look as if Marx refuted the "trebling" and "doubling" of the producers in question, taking it to be "imperialistic" (there are other, sometimes even more drastic, manipulations of Marx's viewpoints in the work in question – see Elster 1985, especially 490–492 and, for the concept of justice, 106 and 219, as considered in Sandemose 1988).

19 For a criticism of the Seton "solution", and also of its forerunners in Dobb 1953 (1937) and Meek 1956, see Sandemose 1973, 67. Here, it is fruitful also to consider Meek's investigation of the post-WWII debate in *Economic Journal* on the "transformation problem"; there, an original point of view was put forward by H.D. Dickinson (1956). A similar approach, taking the unknown in simultaneous equations as not the being individual equations as such but their reciprocal quantitative relation (though still getting wrong the concept of the *numéraire*) is presented in Emmanuel 1969, appendix V. See also Sandemose 1973, 75, note.

20 See Sandemose 2013, 566–567 for criticism of Lapatsioras, Milios and Laibman in these respects. In notes to which he gave the title "Anti-Marshall", Piero Sraffa seems to focus on the "one", taken as number, as essential for expressing the reciprocal equality of commodities:

> Of course this should not be understood to mean that there are [sic] no difference in quality in utilities: on the contrary, such differences are very great, and far too much neglected by economists. We only mean that the only means available for economic theory, not only for measuring, but actually for understanding (apprehending, perceiving) them, is the money test – which is *one*; and its being measured by a positive or negative number is purely a question of arbitrary convention, and cannot be made the basis of a qualitative distinction. The utilities of salt and of music are fully [sic] as different in quality among themselves as they are from the disutilities (utilities of non) producing salt and music.
>
> (Sraffa Papers at Wren Library, Cambridge: D 1/13.5.
> I am indebted to John Eatwell for permission to quote this.)

4 Karl Marx's theory of ground rent – historical elements in economic interplay

Part 2: rent structure and the capitalist price system

Prelude

In this part of our investigation into rent, the main themes are absolute rent and its criticism by traditional economists. The development of criticism of Marx in general, and the emergence of outright untenable positions on "urban rent", is kept in sight. It is shown how these positions, which definitely cannot reflect class relations in capitalist society, may entertain some false degree of plausibility for nations where capitalist production is based on formal subsumption of labour. In this way, we approach themes to be highlighted in Chapter 5.

4.1 From the fulcrum to absolute rent

In this section, and in the next, we shall attempt to demonstrate how landed property, through its connection to the concept of labour value, and through its ability both to enable and to restrict modifications of the law of labour value, demonstrates the unity of the capitalist economic system. It consequently also unveils the unity of the "triad" of the central categories, pointing to the unified totality of population, civil society and state.

Since this is a result we are trying to vindicate through the analysis of the possibility of a stable unit of account for the *economic* system, it will be in order to restart with criticism of Ramirez's opposition to Marx, for in Ramirez we find an attempt to soften up the concept of absolute rent, quite in line with the relativity and ambiguity expressed in his view of the system's *numéraire*. In fact, he contends that Marx's view is that absolute rent will, "*per se*", "not disappear in the course of capitalist development, but it will assume a different economic form, *viz.*, the form of monopoly rent". This latter concept he still tries to define in compliance with Marx (Ramirez 2009, 73).

Ramirez does not point to any textual evidence in the Marxian corpus for this metamorphosis of absolute rent, and it should be noted that it is in conflict with Marx's well-known remark that the *punctum saliens* is to prove the *possibility* of absolute rent in capitalist society, not its actual existence (Marx 1974b, 374). When the logical argument is delivered, the *frame* is given for any analysis of the actual existence or non-existence of absolute rent *in concreto*. This will be a matter of investigation mediated through the theory of economic class antagonism between capitalists and landowners (be they "absentee", peasants or whatever), added to the possibility of below-average organic composition of capital in "landed" branches. As is clear from many other sources, Marx's position is that absolute rent would *disappear* as an empirical phenomenon if the producers of agricultural basics (like corn) as a totality acquired a higher composition than the average in society. But it is also clear that it would *reappear* in the case of the "landed" composition *sinking* from that higher point to a point below the social average. The reason is that absolute rent is dependent not only on the immediate empirical fact of below-average composition but also on the deeper relation of private property to the soil.

To this extent, absolute rent follows from a class monopoly (of landowners). It definitely cannot be said to derive from any other form of monopoly, as treated in monopoly theories related to more or less arbitrary price-setting on the part of bourgeois producers or as Ramirez's "monopoly rent". The reason is as follows.

The incongruence between the two forms of monopoly follows from class relations developed in *free* competition between *industrial* spheres and between privately owned firms in general. Landowners are – in this respect precisely like the working class – dependent on the capitalist, i.e. on the latter's class monopoly on *manufactured* means of production, for earning and materially realizing their livelihood – however extravagant – from the produce of the soil. The landowner is *also* dependent on an agricultural production led by a competitive force (in the "triad", a capitalist farmer or his equivalent), an effective processuality based on abstract labour and on a steady reduction of labour time per product to what is socially necessary, to acquire wealth from the produce of the soil. If that cannot be realized, the capitalist will abstain from investment in agriculture, just as the land-owner has the power to abstain from leasing out his soil unless a rent is paid. Given the exigencies of competition-adequate (both inside and between spheres) production, that rent must be a function of the free-competition level of the industrial average rate of profit, and the same exigencies delimit the level of the rent to the actual socially necessary labour time of the product, i.e. to its value. The "average maximum" of this type of rent per product is thus the difference between the corresponding industrial production price and the monetary expression of the whole of the socially necessary labour time per product on the least fertile soil in use – on the slough, so to speak.

This can be expressed also in premises like the following, from Fratini:

> Monopoly rent thus has characteristics which are decisively different from absolute rent. In fact, even if absolute rent may gush [*scaturisca*] from the resistance which landowners are capable to generate against the extension of production on the soil, this resistance is not unconditioned. The capitalists pay the rent in order that the obstacle be removed, so that the owners hold back [*si astengano*] from employing their power to refuse the use of the soil, which is their right. It will then be the task of the habitual mechanism of capitalist competition to fix that there will be employed precisely the quantity of

land necessary to satisfy, under normal conditions, the effective demand; while the pieces of land which have been left uncultivated are drawn away from the market.

(Fratini 2009, 19–20)

Instead, monopoly rent, as Fratini underscores, does not lead to this result, since "the obstacle to satisfying the demand remains even if the rent is paid" (Fratini 2009, 20).

These reflections should be compared to the very precise definitions implied in Marx's criticism of Ricardo's theory of rent. In his passages on Ricardo in *Theories of Surplus Value*, Marx takes up Ricardo's well known example of agricultural monopoly price on a tiny island. Here, Marx agrees, monopoly prices pure and simple can be thought to be the rule rather than the exception. He continues with the following, important overview (a sentence of which has already been reproduced above):

> Abstracted from such an exception – of which there can be no talk in European countries; even in England a large part of the fertile soil is *artificially* kept out of agriculture, actually out of the market, to *rise* the value of the other part – landownership can only affect and paralyse the action of capitals, their competition, to the extent that the competition of capitals modifies the determination of the *value of commodities*. The transformation [*Verwandlung*] of values to prices of production is only a consequence and result of the development of capitalist production. The original state [*Das Ursprüngliche*] is (for the average) that the commodities are sold to their values. In agriculture, the deviation from this [is] stopped by landed property.
>
> (Marx 1968e, 330)

Three points are of general importance here. Firstly, it seems that Marx, contrary to some interpretations, had good reasons for taking seriously a thesis of the existence of a "simple commodity production", with commodities traded to their *values*, historically prior to the capitalist mode of production. Here, one should note that he consciously speaks of the *selling* of commodities, even in a not fully developed capitalist stage; that must mean that he has in mind a society with a well-functioning *circulation* of commodities (albeit nothing of the extent or status of commodity economy inside that society is presupposed), not one that is limited to immediate exchange.

Secondly, it seems clear that such a simple commodity production may not only be prior in time both to the bourgeois *production-mode* and to its specific national form of appearance but indeed is a forerunner of the establishment both of the capitalist *social formation* and of its political organization. The national frame of the object that Marx sets out to analyse is presupposed in the first chapter of *Capital*, not least in his implication that when both *intensity* and *productivity* of labour are kept constant for analytical purposes, one is talking about *national* averages.[1] Similarly, "foreign trade" is called trade between nations, where national differences in average labour quality are of the greatest importance for the analysis. Other examples are *legio*. The market for products from agriculture (and mines, forestry, etc.) is integrated in the dynamics of the three main classes of the capitalist social formation.

Thirdly, and not least for this last reason, the presupposition that absolute rent can be transformed into a monopoly rent pure and simple is unjustified. On the other hand, it is clear that a monopoly rent can exist, and that it is – and must be – independent of absolute rent.

According to Ramirez, however, the case is in fact different, as we saw. Here is formulation in more detail:

> if the organic composition of capital [in agriculture] were raised to the level of manufacturing industry, landowners would continue to receive rent for all their land, including the worst land. The only difference under these changed socioeconomic conditions is that absolute rent would now assume the social form of a monopoly rent . . .
>
> (Ramirez 2009, 84)

But how is this to be thought? Ramirez insists that it "follows" because the prevailing absolute rent is something that is "filched by the landlord". The latter may be true enough, but how can it be said to lead to the former? Obviously, we here have to remind ourselves of the quantitative limit of the value dimension. Why is it that landlords can "filch" only the margin up to the magnitude of *value*?

An important point is that, as far as conscious acts of will are concerned, it is the capitalist (the farmer) who is *the seller*. He sets the price. What is set by the landlord is the amount of *rent to be paid*, which seems to be a function of the rate of interest (a capitalizing) but is just the function of the law of value. If a capitalist, or, rather, a commodity producer, is to sell a commodity at a price above its value, corresponding to a socially necessary length of labour time, then he is competed out of the market. (The regulating price is the creation of the worst land in use, i.e. from the amount of labour necessary there.) The argument turning the tables in this connection, however, is the point underscored above – all too often underrated – that landownership is economically dependent on the capitalist division of labour and the level of industrial efficiency. A point integrated in this argument is that a rising organic composition in the total agricultural capital will as a rule signify a rise in the volume of goods from this "sector" in its totality, even with an expanding population. A fall in prices of agricultural goods can well follow, hindering absolute rent on the worst soil.

The *locus classicus* relating to Marx's view on the relation between "traditional" monopoly and rent from the landowner's monopoly is to be found in *Capital* III, chapter 46:

> When we talk of monopoly price, we mean in general [*überhaupt*] a price which is limited only by the lust of buying and capability of payment on part

of the buyer, independently of the product-price determined through the general production price or through the value of the product.

(Marx 1968c, 783)

Such a price, Marx points out, can, e.g., be set on a special wine from an area of extremely good conditions and is sold at a surplus profit which may transform itself to "rent": "Here", Marx continues, "the monopoly price consequently generates the rent" (1968c, 783), while

> on the contrary, rent would generate the monopoly price if corn was sold not only above its production price, but [*sondern*] also above its value, owing to the barrier [*Schranke*] set by landed property to the investment of capital in uncultivated land without payment of rent.
>
> (Marx 1968c, 783–784)

This conclusion corresponds precisely to the one presented by Fratini. The "monopoly price" is here defined as an "overplus" which is temporary and subject to domination of the law of value in general on the market. It should be noted that the expression that rent *generates* (*schafft,* from *schöpfen*) the monopoly price has nothing to do with the illusion, partly fostered by Adam Smith, that an amount of rent takes part in the constitution of the value of (agricultural) products. Marx's point is, rather, that the definition of "ground rent" includes not only an amount of money passing from one man to another but implies the very *regularity of the form* of the redistribution of riches, as was once (in the Soviet industrialization debate) excellently argued by Evgeny Preobrazhensky (1965, 148). This *constant form makes up* a relation of production, and this relation may "generate" a quite specific, temporary monopoly price, while the monopoly price in Marx's first example is not produced by petrified social relations, as such, but by whimsical extravagant consumers.

4.2 Absolute rent and effective demand

This last comment reminds us that it is natural to view the whole theme of the contemporary debate on Marxian ground rent theory in light of the original Bortkiewicz criticism. To some extent, that is simply a question of proximity to the source: one should expect Bortkiewicz, who in the great majority of cases showed a fine sense for finesse in the history of economic dogmas, to have a keen awareness of the consequences of his own criticism.

In his critique of Marx's theory of modern landed property, Bortkiewicz described absolute rent in the following way:

> When Marx says that absolute ground rent corresponds to the excess of the value of the agricultural produce over its price of production, reference is to the value and price of the entire agricultural produce and not to individual units of agricultural products, and accordingly also to the aggregate amount

of rent and not to the quantum of rent which is contained, for instance, in the price of a quarter of corn.

(Bortkiewicz 1910–1911, 409)

This is a timely reminder, and it underscores Marx's dictum, reported above, that

> if the price of the product from a unit area of the worst soil = P + r, then *all differential rents will rise* by corresponding multiples of r, since the assumption is that P + r becomes the regulating market-price.
>
> (Marx 1968c, 771, italics added)

In this same connection, Bortkiewicz also underlined:

> Absolute ground rent is indeed nothing but the excess of the value of the agricultural products over their price of production. It needs to be noted, however, that the latter must be calculated on the basis of the industrial rate of profit – not the rate of profit which would emerge under the assumption of the non-existence of landed property and the participation of agriculture in the transformation of values into prices of production implied by it. (. . .) It would therefore by no means be in accordance with Marx's point of view, if one were to define absolute ground rent as the difference between the actual price of the products and the price they would have assumed if the competition between capitals in search of the most profitable investment opportunities were not hindered by landed property.
>
> (Bortkiewicz 1910–1911, 409)[2]

Now, in his article mentioned above, Gehrke, fully justified, supports Bortkiewicz's view in this regard, with the acute remark that the latter's

> interpretation seems indeed to be the only logically possible one: If agriculture were supposed to be involved in the transformation by which a uniform rate of profit on the capital advanced in the various branches is formed, the possibility of absolute rent on the marginal land could not have been admitted by Marx.
>
> (Gehrke 2010, 29–30)

But, unfortunately, Gehrke also agrees with the following remark from Bortkiewicz, focusing on the role of the rate of surplus value:

> it is a somewhat crude and contrived idea that *first* a particular rate of surplus value is established on the basis of the production conditions in both agriculture and industry, and that *thereafter* a definite rate of profit is formed within industry alone, which is then transmitted to agriculture by conferring to it the ability to regulate agricultural profit.
>
> (Bortkiewicz 1910–1911, 409)

Here we once more redirect the discussion into Ricardian waters, for we should remember that Bortkiewicz's "solution" of the "transformation" issue will lead to a pressing need for an exogenous, independent variable to stabilize a set of equations. Such a variable was de facto present for Ricardo in his thesis of the central role of the commodities making up the use-value bulk of subsistence for workers, produced on the rent-less land margin.

However, for Marx such thinking is inadequate, given his radical break with Ricardo's theory of the *numéraire*. Furthermore, as Fratini has shown, the denominator in the Marxian rate of surplus value is determined by the same factors for workers across both industry and agriculture. Equally important, competition among rural and urban producers tends to equalize methods of production, and consequently value content, for commodities making up the use-value background of both numerator and denominator.

Thus, when it comes to mending what Gehrke admits should be called "Ricardo's blunder", namely the exclusion of the value of means of production from the profit rate, few things could be more natural than to keep the rate of surplus value constant when comparing the organic compositions of capital and thereby the individual rates of profits in industries – all the more so, since the conceptualizing of "constant capital" – in its opposition to the variable part – is won precisely through a correction of Ricardo's way of expressing the crucial diremption inside productive capital.

In a work from 1919, Bortkiewicz puts his point very distinctly, asking: "why should landed property, if it has the power to oppose the laws of capitalistic price formation, be bounded by the limit of value?" (Bortkiewicz 1919, 254).

But this way of thinking, followed up by innumerable other critics of Marx, depends on an impermissible abstraction from the presupposition of the analysis, and from what we called its "fulcrum", namely the existence of production prices as transformed exemplars of values in the industrial sector. These prices, the guiding mechanisms for the average profit rate steering relative agricultural prices, are by definition quantities transformed to reflect the necessary technical differences between sectors. In principle these differences, or at least their general characters, are unchangeable (unamendable) and must necessarily be accepted by any producer.

This fact by itself implies that capitalist market prices of products are interwoven with demand and supply, in the form in which these factors appear on the market. A sort of technical "equilibrium" is therefore always presupposed in the capitalist social formation, and the same goes for agricultural products. The totality of their prices and of their physical mass is always given and kept at certain levels in competition. Existing prices reflect such moving "equilibria". According to Marx, they are limited by, and steered through, laws of labour value. In principle there are no shortcuts to extra-profits. In fact, Bortkiewicz's objection simply represents a blunder. Aggressively spoken, it could be seen as an expression of subconscious reluctance to accept that his interpretation of Marx's theory of the *numéraire* is obsolete. But the fact is simply that Bortkiewicz, like Marx and every other, is seeking to uphold a consistency inside his own theory.

What he overlooks, in other words, is that Marx's concept of the value-producing socially necessary labour time is not confined to the immediate result of the competition inside a sphere but is also an appearance which follows from inter-spherical competition. This latter is by no means confined to generating production prices: among other things, it shapes changes in the demand for certain products at the expense of others. Competition consists, to that extent, in provoking shifts in buying or selling patterns, shifts whose most important and basic feature lies in the capitalists' market for means of production apt to generate a rise in the rate of surplus value. Through such mechanisms, any capitalist steadily experiences local over-production of non-realizable commodities, containing labour that is wasted and cannot take part in the overall description of the labour that can be added to the socially necessary amount. The example regarding "false social value" is useful here: it may appear at one point in time but is then ruled out through industrial competition, and the products bearing it no longer port in the pool of value products.

Seen from this angle, one will have to modify the Bortkiewicz–Gehrke definition of absolute rent, which, as we saw, assumes that "absolute rent is indeed nothing but the excess of the value of the agricultural products over their price of production" (Bortkiewicz 1910, 409).

While Bortkiewicz's thesis is strictly speaking correct on the conceptual level, it is open to misunderstandings as regards empirical results. For Marx, the existence of absolute rent is made possible by the capacity of agricultural (etc.) prices to reach a maximum identical with their *values*. Therefore, the commodity value *magnitude* is a "fulcrum" of absolute rent. Still, such a rent exists even if the commodity is sold at a price furnishing the owner with a surplus profit below the value:

> But since the value of commodities produced by agricultural capital which according to the presupposition stands above their production price, this rent (. . .) makes up [*bildet*] the surplus of the value over the price of production or a part of it. If the rent is equal to the whole difference between value and price of production, or is equal only to a larger or smaller part of this difference, would depend solely on the size of the area being drawn into cultivation.
>
> (Marx 1968c, 770)

Marx continues by pointing out that in the latter case there will always be "a part of this surplus which enters into the general equalization and proportionate distribution of all surplus value among the different individual capitals". The rest constitutes the actual absolute rent – its empirically measurable quantity – and is "pulled out of this equalization [*dieser Ausgleichung entzogen*]" (Marx 1968c, 771).

For Marx, this fact in no way changes the concept of absolute rent. It is *precisely* in this same passage that Marx describes modern landed property as "the barrier [*die Barriere*] which does not allow any new capital investment on as yet uninhabited or unleased [*unverpachtetem*] soil, without a customs charge [*Zoll*]".

Or also:

> Because of the barrier [*Schranke*], which is set by landed property, the market price must rise to a point where the soil can pay a surplus over the price of production.
>
> (Marx 1968c, 770)

Consequently, "capital, in its investment in soil [*Grund und Boden*], encounters an alien power and barrier [*Schranke*] in the form of landed property, i.e. the landowner faces the capitalist in this form" (Marx 1968c, 770).

The problem with Bortkiewicz's question about upper limits in agriculture lies in his not accepting that it is quite possible to have the power to oppose a difficulty without having the power to surmount it. In opposing the capitalist (price) system, landownership is bound to stay within the range of possibilities defined by that system. The fundamental determination of value inside the landed sphere can be modified but not surmounted: necessary labour time determines the pivot point of landed products but only through dislocating it from extant average conditions to extant worst conditions; similarly, the value-producing labour time in those worst conditions makes an absolute rent possible in the next turn but also defines the insurmountable upper limit for the profit provided by an absolute rent rising on the conditions on the best of the (as yet) uncultivated land. That limit is the value of the produce of those latter conditions, once more limited by the proviso of below-average capital composition.

The examples from the general movement inside capitalist competition show us the reason: there is no contradiction in saying that a product cannot be sold as soon as its price is set at a point higher than its production price, or eventually at a point higher than its value, *and* saying that it is rendered useless by the limited size of effective demand.

There is nothing in this argument that makes concessions to marginalist-subjectivist thinking. What is said is simply that the concepts of supply and demand, as well as these phenomena themselves, are functions of human work and labour and are determined through a total of the labour-time relations pervading a society. This is neither the time nor the place to go into this in further detail.

Nonetheless, it should once again be pointed out that the *national* frame of the Marxian economic model is unquestionable. This frame in principle was presupposed by the Physiocrats as well as by Adam Smith. Its organization implies a general balance of forces between investments in agriculture, excavation and manufacturing. It is a reasonable conjecture that the further development of this entity to a political nation-*state* is bound up intimately with the emergence of an average intensity and productivity related to a labour that produces use values *as values*.

Such a homogeneous productivity-*cum*-intensity is the foundation of a *culture*, and differences related to its appearance in different regions and zones are the basis for what are called different "cultures".

4.3 Monopolies and method

Bortkiewicz and related theorists are quite conscious of the difference between absolute rent and monopoly rent in general. But in their own theory, any such separation is apt to disappear, since they are unable to grasp the reason for its existence. Since they do not put absolute rent in its reasonable position, they will in practice treat it as a monopoly rent in Marx's meaning of that word.

Seen in relation to Marx's theory, the nearest consequence of the position of Bortkiewicz, Gehrke, Ramirez and others would be to let the question of absolute rent be a matter of personal, individual initiative separated from social lawlikenesses. And, conversely, what is in fact a feature of social lawlikeness is turned into a display of more or less arbitrary economic behaviour. We shall now – in this section and in the next – take up some consequences of such voluntarism in economic theory and method.

In general, readers' consciousness of specificities in Marx's theory of rent is weakened by a limit to the understanding of the very operation of capital itself as a monopoly. A cure for such reasoning could well consist of a reminder of the status of the very concept of capital in Marx. We start *in media res*, focusing first on theories in Gehrke and Negishi.

Gehrke says the following:

> Marx's concept of absolute rent has sometimes been identified with a "monopoly rent" in the sense of Smith and Ricardo, because Marx repeatedly uses the word "monopoly" in connection with absolute rent.
>
> (Gehrke 2010, 32)

Gehrke goes on, contending that "there is a serious problem with Marx's notion of absolute rent if it is interpreted as referring to competitive conditions, which can be seen very clearly" in a definition from the 1861–1863 manuscript, here rendered from the edited *Theorien über den Mehrwert*:

> just as it is the *monopoly* of capital alone that enables the capitalist to squeeze surplus labour out of the worker, so the monopoly of landownership enables the landed proprietor to squeeze that part of surplus labour from the capitalist, which would form a constant *excess profit*.
>
> (Marx 1968e, 88)

Adhering to standpoints expressed by Takashi Negishi, Gehrke contends that "monopoly" by Marx here should be taken

> not in the modern sense that capitalists or landowners act jointly so as to maximize common gains, but in the classical sense that the supply of capital or land is limited (at least in the short run) so that it is scarce or in the Marxist sense that capital (land) is owned exclusively by capitalists (landowners). The monopoly of capital, therefore, does not exclude competition

among capitalists. Otherwise, there would be no equality of the rate of profit. Similarly, the monopoly of landownership does not exclude the possibility that each landowner acts independently. Though Marx made some confusing statements (. . .) it is clear that he did not have joint action of all the land-owners in mind.

(Negishi 1985, 97)

Both Negishi and Gehrke, as is immediately visible, identify the vital characteristics of two monopolies and then simply identify them *tout court*. For all practical purposes, capital and landed property are here considered as the same relation, not as the two opposing forces they are in Marx's work.

On the other hand, both authors realize that Marx's theory implies that monopoly in what they call "the modern sense" is simply a case relating to the "lust of buying and capability of payment on part of the buyer, independently of the product-price determined through the general production price or through the value of the product" (Marx 1968c, 783), for such characteristics cannot change simply because a plurality of subjects band together on a spontaneous basis.

Still, it is seriously misconceived to say that there is a "Marxist sense that capital (land) is owned exclusively by capitalists (landowners)". Such a wording is tautological on these premises, since for Marx the ownership of capital by definition is ownership of *alien wealth and power* in relation to workers and in relation to landed property – capital which capital can, as a Frenchman might put it, *transiter* as into its own "creative basis". Both capital and landed property are here economic processes which are monopolistic in themselves and develop their specific monopoly to higher levels: capital through its process of accumulation and landed property through excluding workers to an ever higher degree (in tendency), locking them up with a "golden link"[3] in a paved greenfield marked "no admittance except on business".

Before we move deeper into this, let us add Negishi's comment on his remarks above. He concludes with the following thesis:

But if landowners on the marginal land are supposed to act independently, each one of them will have an incentive to invite additional investment on his land (because this would increase his rent), until absolute rent has completely disappeared on the marginal land.

(Negishi 1985, 20; see Gehrke 2010, 31)

That is not all. The competition inside and between industrial sectors is an act of monopoly in the sense that it is the very way and structure of capitalist behaviour. To say that capitalists in this manner act independently is just to utter the absolutely true statement that their very act is a monopolizing act. For Marx, the "monopoly" of capital means only that capital is dependent upon a class (of wage workers) definable as not-owners of means of production.

The monopoly of landownership should not be placed in line with such a definition. In modern times, it indicates simply that the globe, undeniably a measurable and scarce resource, is in the possession of certain ostensibly definable individuals.

Historically, the act of owning the land is not connected to any especial economic activity at all – except to archaic landownership in Neolithic times. As a member of bourgeois society, the landowner is not a *bourgeois* but a *citoyen* and consequently an independently acting person by definition. But as a victim of the prevailing materialism of history, he is of course steered and limited in his independent actions, since his very independence is a material-historical product.

As we saw above, Negishi contends that "though Marx made some confusing statements (. . .) it is clear that he did not have joint action of all the landowners in mind" (Negishi 1985, 97). This expresses the same confusion, in the sense that it is undetermined and both true and false. When Marx speaks of the *Aktion* from one of the three class categories, he obviously has in mind a concerted action in the sense that all individuals, as class members, take part in the act, at least through a passivity vis-à-vis the "iron laws of capitalism" and at most in full loyalty to them. A "cartel" action is quite out of the question. A member – e.g. a land-owning peasant – may act against his immediate class interest, e.g. by selling a product at a lowered price, but this act of course exposes his monopoly of landownership (as well as his existence as a partly capitalist bourgeois).

In discussions on absolute rent, the status of its possible historical appearance plays a steadily self-repeating role; and the prospect of its "disappearance" is often a theme too. In Robin Murray's well-known work, "Value and Theory of Rent", a unique conclusion is to be found:

> Marx certainly foresaw the possibility of agriculture's organic composition rising . . . and thus liquidating absolute rent. But he did not deal with the resulting objection that marginal land would not be given gratis. The conundrum is easily answered once we understand the material basis for rent of any kind. The existence of differential and absolute rent is dependent on capital's inability to reproduce the conditions of production. Rising organic composition reflects, as Amin acknowledges, capital's subordination of the soil. Output increasingly varies with the inputs of capital rather than the inputs of land. The material basis for rent of all kinds is thus dissolved. The marginal plot will tend to disappear [sic] along with absolute rent, and the conundrum.
>
> (Murray 1977, 112)

Ismail Hossein-zadeh, in a brilliantly clear exposition of the relation of classical and Marxian theories of rent, presents a crushing objection to this:

> the problem is that the rise in the agricultural composition of capital to social average, or even above it, is not tantamount to capital's ability to reproduce the conditions of agricultural production. It is unrealistic to assume that in the presence of monopoly landownership there can be independent reproduction conditions of agricultural production by capital.
>
> (Hossein-zadeh 1992)

One of the fine points in Hossein-zadeh's article is a realistic view of the claims that have to be present for one to dismiss the empirical presence of an absolute rent. For example, as regards Murray's contention, Hossein-zadeh believes that it

> cannot be valid unless capital's penetration in agriculture goes hand in hand with the dissolution of an independent landowning class (i.e., the capitalists themselves come to own the land as more capital is invested in agriculture).

Such a way of thinking helps to uphold a more realistic view of the conceptual tenability of this type of rent than is all too usual. It also has to do with the question of the form of causal explanations in social science. Take some sentences by Vladimir Lenin as a point of departure:

> It is not true to say that according to Marx absolute rent results from the low composition of agricultural capital. Absolute rent arises from the private ownership of land. . . . The non-capitalist monopoly created by the private ownership of land prevents the leveling of profits in those branches of production which are sheltered by the monopoly.
>
> (Lenin 1962, 301–302)

Here, as if we were chased by an irony, the category of Ground and its relation to the formal cause enters the picture. The *actual* existence of absolute rent depends on a lower *average* composition in agriculture. The claim of an average reflects the point we have seen mentioned *inter alia* by Bortkiewicz: the price level in question is calculated with "reference . . . to the value and price of *the entire* agricultural produce". However, without the private character of landownership, there would be no such rent at all. Consequently, the active ground lies in the form of property, the economic "category" itself.

This is another timely reminder, and it furthers the reflection mentioned above, that even if payment of absolute rent disappeared by force of technological progress in agriculture (compared to industry), it is by no means clear that such a result would be permanent. Technological development (progressive change in the organic composition of capital) has its up and downs whenever capitalism exists, and uneven development has been just as common as even.

These reflections push aside any credibility of theories of absolute rent being dependent on a "cartel" – a way of thought that is scarcely more realistic than the idea that, in a given situation, a band of rentless landowner *mafiosi* might conspire to press the average composition in industry upwards, with the aim of enriching themselves.

However, there is a difficulty even with Hossein-zadeh's conclusion. In fact, if it is valid, absolute rent cannot disappear from empirical capitalism at all, for if "capitalists themselves come to own the land as more capital is invested in agriculture", this will certainly result in cartel building – this time pervading the whole of what we might call the "real existing capitalist social formation". That is, private landownership will just continue, with capitalists taking the role of their historical opponents – as landowners. At best, the economy will continue as before. Landownership can never be capitalist, except in a figurative way, namely through a nationalization of land effected by the bourgeois state, sluicing differential rent into the state treasury. Under other circumstances, Hossein-zadeh's capitalists will be landowners part of the day, and landowners will be capitalists for another part. In fact, one would envisage the kind of cartelized economies that are common in the so-called Third World, based on an Asian mode of production, without interspherical competition.[4] If such a solution could be a reality, it would definitely be a "worst case".

4.4 A landslide of land rents

Turning now to some direct political consequences of the voluntarism mentioned above, the example of Allen J. Scott may serve as illustration (see also Park 2014, 96–97). Scott de facto excludes absolute rent from modern society with the argument that a "cartel" of landowners is inconceivable, and that "the real economic *and political* power of landlords . . . is probably fairly negligible" (Scott 1976, 131).[5] However, Scott's method for measuring powers is not accounted for, and rent cannot be said to rely on political power in the West today. Of course, one nonetheless might take state price regulations of agricultural products (which may lead to prices above as well as below a level corresponding to any rent) to be functions of the *possibility* of rent inside the agricultural economic structure of different nations. We will look at that possibility more in detail.

However, the most important objection against Scott is that the reason for the absence of any cartel is simply that it is unnecessary. A "cartel" could not generate more windfalls than the ones already present for self-owning peasants connected with the capitalist credit system, in possession of means of production and on the brink of acquiring land rents. If the implication of the power of landownership per se is simply not comprehended, one is unaware of the fact that it is a class society that is being analysed in the first place. The rent is a consequence of a certain structure of property constellations, based on the workers' sole property (which is a product of the "primitive accumulation") and on capitalist property as it comes to the fore in the system of an average rate of profit. A theory of "cartels" at this level of analysis would mean a return to a sociology of stratification and then methodological individualism in the next turn.

The lack of understanding of the basic class elements of rent leads to even more fanciful constructions. Several self-declared supporters of Marxism have for decades copied the tendency among more outright bourgeois economists to concentrate on politico-psychological mentalities and their alleged significance for investment, savings, etc. This flight into the field of what Marx called "vulgar economy" has taken the form of so-called theoretical explorations into "ground rent in an urban context" (to use an expression in Park's summary). Let us take a look into the true background.

One of Marx's most important insights into the class conflict in the wage labour–capital–landed property triangle was, as we have seen, the functional theory of how the development of capital accumulation must lead to a rising price of soil. The reason for this can be deduced from the phenomenon of the "price" of land as capitalized ground rent: if a field delivers products which are sold for x $ a year, and the rate of interest is 5 per cent, then the price for the field itself is set at 20 x $ *mutatis mutandis* (the invested capital reincarnated in twenty years, in this case). But since the accumulation of capital leads to a sinking profit rate and therefore *ceteris paribus* to a reduced rate of interest, the soil price will rise steadily, ensuring, as we have repeatedly underlined, that workers, having access solely to wage means, cannot escape from the capitalist mode of production.

Marx's point of view seems to be that, having made this circle, landed *property* (not simply "ground rent") is shown as a force that can be viewed as trumping what we have to presume are derived or secondary economic categories in landed economic activity: the *price of land*, the *price of products* and the existence of *any ground rent*. Property is *the* basis for the activity of any landowner and in practice unites all possible landowners, just as all capitalists perforce unite themselves reciprocally through the mechanism of the price of production, and all workers are forced to unite in the common fate of bearing a labour power in commodity form.

These basics in Marx's theory of capitalistic class dynamics are often overlooked by Marxisant authors. This is so in spite of the fact that Marx makes concrete mention of them in his treatment of rent in *Capital* III. And, there, he also makes the existence of any soil price, even "at building-places in big cities" (1968c, 781), dependent, in one way or another, on agricultural rent (mining and other excavation activities included). His view is clearly that even if the price of soil is an artificial concept, it is not more irrational than an irrational number and, therefore, it is allowed to exist. Its existence is, however, also dependent on its derivation from a real and qualitative kind of quantity, namely the labour value (and its derived prices) of *material, agricultural or excavated commodities*.

Also, Marx takes it as given that a *"monopoly price"* dominates the market for leasing or buying housing facilities, dependent on the price of the soil where they are situated. But this price is actually also adequately described by bourgeois theorists of traditional schools, with the important reservation that they have no sense of its ultimate dependence on agricultural rent.

Clearly, there is a marked tendency among Marxisant thinkers today to break away from Marx's implicit assumptions. Park's article is, once more, a useful example. He takes it as a healthy, positive fact that authors like David Harvey, Lata Chatterjee, Richard Walker and Matthew Edel have been making attempts to construct a new theory of rent adapted to urban structures. Instead of conceptualizing housing prices, related to workers' incomes and levels of wage, as phenomena derived from *production* (agriculture and excavation), these are now imagined to be functions of social relations taken as interpersonal pure and simple, without material mediation. Lessees are taken to be "rent" payers for the cost of "*a space*" (Park 2014, 96), not the material content of space. Park faultlessly quotes from a paper by Edel to the effect that absolute rent is simply scarcity rent and is

[a]pplied for "a level affecting all of a large sector (agriculture, urban areas in general)", while monopoly rent is applied for "specific, detailed land uses" by "racial minorities, immigrants and other subgroups.

(Park 2014, 96)

In the discussions among economists who in one way or another share this thinking, the awareness, even if subconscious, of problems arising from the loss of material content has had to enforce itself to some degree. The post-modernist affinity to thinkers like Derrida or Lazzarato in truth makes itself felt. For instance, Michael Ball thinks that "buildings" is a typical product in the area which Edel would call "urban areas in general" and sets out to presuppose "the commodity produced in agriculture being 'corn' and on urban land, 'buildings'" (Ball 1977, 400). Park partly adheres to this, accepting that "the space in buildings and the rent from the space are still based on the use of land, as a building is a type of fixed capital for improving the productivity of land use" (Park 2014, 101).

Here, the class character of these writings, or, rather, their insistence on a way of thinking that allows society's class contradictions to be ignored, is apparent, for it is not the productivity of "land use" (whatever that may be) which is in the picture but the productivity of *land*. If a "building" per se amends productivity *of the soil*, then the same would be the case with any industrial building placed on a greenfield, serving to produce new building materials, machines, tools or whatever. This incredible scenario would give us an identification of the class interests of capitalists and landowners, and it would crush any Marxist picture of a working class, since such a class, as we know, is necessarily generated through the contradictions between capital and landed property.

Investment in *agriculture* proper – abstracted from forms of property – is investment in the productivity of *the soil,* in its fertility and self-renewal through the "death" of sowing seed, an apparent mystery which in earlier times was the theme of a John the Evangelist or a John Barleycorn or of Orphic hidden rituals, while now it is actively mystified by economic theory. Investment in "land use", to a fault, can denote any investment whatsoever, because every human productive endeavour must be based on *terra firma* in some way.

Thus, we are here presented with a logical consequence of the viewpoint of Fine and others, to the effect that capitalist competition in some original form pervades all branches with an equalization principle *prior to* the coming into effect of the monopoly of landownership. And, furthermore, the logical result follows that any economic activity or product can at will be taken to represent absolute rent. Also, most of this problematic thinking can be combined with the thesis that absolute rent can be found in "in *a* branch", so to speak, at random.

Arguments by Alain Lipietz are all too clear as regards this issue. For him, as Park correctly reports, "the product of land is the built environment itself" (Park 2014, 98). That is, while rent in the classical meaning depends on the labour value of a product generated by means of pieces of techno-natural land that yield different fertilities (in addition to a power of monopoly), it is here ritually and mysteriously transformed into a manufacturing-industrial phenomenon while simultaneously crossing over from an analysis built on labour values to one built on marginalist versions of "scarcity" for the economy as a whole. Not only Marxian theories but Sraffian ones as well will suffer.

It is something of a wonder that such views are accepted today, while more serious, relevant and distinctly formulated methodical arguments in these respects against Marx or his classical forerunners at first sight seem to be completely lacking in the literature. It is not unreasonable to suppose that the way of thinking in question has been generated inside some kind of "authorized" Marxisant reasoning on the matter from theoreticians with prestigious clout; I tentatively point to Ernest Mandel's *Der Spätkapitalismus* (1972) as a possible first source. Mandel treats agriculture inside twentieth-century capitalism with some unjustified suppositions, which may be seen to anticipate what Park presents as "the Renaissance" for Marxian developments in rent theory (Park 2014, 93).

For instance, in *Late Capitalism*, Mandel holds it to be an important fact that "the yearly expenditure to constant capital in US agriculture in 1948 was higher than the 'soil-capital-costs' [*Bodenkapitalkosten*] based on regional soil prices" (Mandel 1972, 346) and adds that an "element of the fixed capital" in agriculture is "spent in the buying of the soil" (1972, 347).

It is indeed problematic to consider the price of fertile soil a part of constant (fixed or circulating) capital. In fact, the price of soil is a ("capitalized") form of the ground rent itself and, far from making up and/or inflating any part of constant capital, derives from the social existence of an excess over market value (absolute rent and/or high levels of differential rents) of the *products* of that capital in use (see also Sandemose 2010, 259–263.)[6]

To inflate constant capital with the price of the soil itself is an error that might be understandable from the point of view of well-developed peasant farming, where the landowner's role is to be found precisely in the person of the farmer himself, and where, as we have seen, not only two but even three class characters may belong to him, since he may also be taken as employing himself as a wage-labourer. We should analyse his interests and position in society *after* having analysed in pure form the role of profit, rent and "wages" in the economy of which he forms an element.

In fact, David Harvey has delivered some theoretical reflections paving the way for a true Marxist analysis into this field. His view is that the development of the division of labour inside capital circulation leads us to a point from where land-ownership is integrated in bourgeois economy:

> When trade in land is reduced to a special branch of the circulation of interest-bearing capital, then ... landownership has achieved its true capitalistic form ... Once such a condition becomes general, then *all* landholders get caught up in a general system of circulation of interest-bearing capital and ignore its imperatives at their peril.
>
> (Harvey 1982, 347, italics added)[7]

4.5 The heart of the matter: ground rent in a totalizing view

The view quoted from Harvey should be compared to a crucial remark in the *Grundrisse*, namely Marx's intermediate reflection leading him from the concept of "capital in general" to the dialectics inside the "triad". Here the central passage follows, this time in full:

> In the money market, capital is posited in its totality; there it *determines prices, gives work, regulates production*, in a word, is the *source of production*; but capital, not only as something which produces itself (positing prices, materially in industry etc., developing forces of production), but at the same time as a creator [*Schöpfer*] of values, has to posit a value or form of wealth specifically distinct from capital. This is *ground rent*. This is the only value created [*die einzige Wertschöpfung*] by capital which is distinct from itself, from its own production.
>
> (1993, 275–276; 1953, 186–187)

In the same way that the *Grundrisse* contains long-range foresights to such an extent that it has been suggested (Rosdolsky 1968, 499–504) Marx predicted the development of digital technology, so it includes an impressive premonition of the capacities of the money market inside the "triad" economy. At the same time, he never launched theories of a necessary sublation of peasant-like holding systems in the same social formation.

And, in fact, it seems that the development of the money market is a crucial factor in explaining both the force of resistance of the older property relations and the development of a fetishized thinking that opens the way for unrealistic theories of rent.

Clearly, we are back in the problematic we left at the end of Section 3.5: despite more than a hundred years of "social cleansing" in the countryside of the northwest, with non-Tudor exclusions of poorer people and less well-to-do peasants, allowing for highly mechanized work in the most agricultural areas, it is improbable that the farmer or peasant holding has been weakened; on the contrary, it seems reinforced, or at the very least has retained its relative strength. And, as depicted earlier, a motley rural population has been unified "into the modern farmer", a term that now should cover even the traditional peasant associated with agricultural day-labourers (*Ackerbautaglöhner*) (see, again, Marx 1993, 252; 1953, 164).

If so, and *if* the Marxian view of a dependence of the capitalist social formation on the wellbeing of the "triad" is correct, *then* the development of landed property has to be explained by still one another factor, namely the function of an absolute rent, eventually combined with differential rents. It is, under this hypothesis, the contention of this book that in the absence of a "Tudor" expropriation, the present standing of landed property in the northwest (again, Britain excluded) has to have had another special "transition of landed property into wage labour" as its basis. Simultaneously, this explains the specific form of the whole of the capitalist social formation in the Western world.

But on the other hand: aside from the fact that such a development could not possibly be realized in full without the capitalist money market – developed by the "triad" itself – how realistic is this thought of a transfer from British relations – and of their reappearance inside the "parallelogram"? We have seen how Marx speaks about "a double transition to wage labour" from the part of landed property. Obviously, a critical question is whether "a double transition to wage labour" can be realized on the condition that

> modern landed property *itself* appears most powerfully in the process of clearing the estates and the transformation of the rural labourers into wage labourers.
>
> (Marx 1993, 279; 1953, 190, italics added, and
> see Chapter 3, Section 2, this volume)

As argued above, such a powerful creativity is not to be found in any nation-state outside Britain. Only there was the purge so thoroughgoing that no elements from intermediate strata could remain to cool down the contradictions between landed property and capital. In England, the old feudal *Gefolgschaften* – retainers – were thrown out, annihilating any mediaeval "master and bondsman"-relation in between the new oppositional main classes.

Indeed, this evolved to such a degree that it is problematic to say – as Marx does – that it was *modern* landed property that acted. Rather, it was the developed feudal landownership that prevailed and which eliminated itself in one and the same *Aktion* – seemingly confirming a main thesis in Marx's own "materialistic conception of history" – that sublation of old relations created "modern" landownership.

But then what? How could a modern landownership come into existence outside British shores? Implicit in Marx's formulation lies the presumption, as we saw, that capital, as an "active middle", can trigger it in this manner:

> wage labour in its *totality* is initially created by the action of capital on landed property, and then, as soon as the latter has been produced as a form, by the proprietor of the land himself.
>
> (Marx 1993, 279; 1953, 190)

The British "experience" is thus like a four-step ladder:

1   *Feudal* landownership throws out agricultural population and retainers from the land, thereby opening itself to modernity;
2   Capital, acting on that landed property, transforms the expropriated populace into wage labourers;
3   Landed property becomes modern landownership and allows for the use of wage labour hired by farmers;
4   The result is a rent system where the modern landed proprietors take part in the general creation of the modern proletariat.

One should underscore that Marx says modern landownership creates wage labour in its *totality*, which must mean something more than an opening up for wage labour in agriculture, mining and forestry. Since Marx holds the capitalistic rise in soil prices to be a priority feature of "modern" landed property, it seems clear that he puts primary weight on this function, which is vitally dependent on a money market. That, in its turn, should imply giving priority to capitalized ground rent and consequently to the whole tendency of capitalization (not least of labour power as a commodity), i.e. to features of the modern credit system and the rise of fictitious capital.[8] The only way that the British system can be reproduced inside the "northwest" is, then, by the function of absolute rent. Of course, the rising soil price is a consequence also of all differential rents. But if we are to speak of an *Aktion* from the landed proprietor "himself", i.e. from the category of landed property, a force barrier-separated from capital, one is relegated to absolute rent.

Absolute rent is the only rent form which can be ascribed to the existence of landed property itself, albeit that this is the case solely inside the capitalist social formation. Differential rent originates as capitalist surplus profit, belonging to the capitalist farmer role and transferred to the landed-proprietor role. But absolute rent belongs to the proprietor from the start, since he is free to abstain from it as well as to collect it – briefly, free to decide whether some low-quality soil should be used in the capitalist national economy.

If the proprietor chooses to allow production on a new piece of land "at the margin", he is individually entitled to an absolute rent for his piece of land, while at the same time, as an anonymous class member and representative of the category of landed property, he is raising the price of the whole mass of agricultural produce, as pointed out by Marx and Bortkiewicz.

It is also possible to find a "purely" terminological backing in Marx for taking him to have predicted that the force of absolute rent would enable any landowner to manifest himself as a class member. For it is precisely in the definition of absolute rent, as presented in *Capital*, that Marx once more, and for the first and only time since the *Grundrisse*, returns to his term from the introduction of the triad: *der schöpferische Grund*. As we have seen, there is a sort of movement in prices which can alone be said to be caused by rent, thus making the latter absolute, i.e. making it the pure expression of landed property as a subject:

> then landed property is the creative basis [*der schöpferische Grund*] of this rise in prices. Landed property has itself produced rent [*Das Grundeigentum selbst hat Rente erzeugt*].
>
> (Marx 1968c, 763)

Also, Marx goes on to underscore that the same causal nexus (*Grund*) then lies behind the emergence (*[ist]* . . . *Ursache der Schöpfung*) of the higher differential rent that follows on the hitherto worst land and subsequently all over agriculture (Marx 1968c, 763).

According to this view, landed property, and with it the possibility or actuality of such a rent, is the way that the capitalist system, in the absence of Tudorism, in a more slow and lenient way than the abrupt "clearing of estates", produces a proletariat – partly through a potential for rises in prices of necessities, partly as a continuous rise in land prices. Nonetheless, it was only with the assistance of earlier mass migrations (especially from Europe to America) and state-sponsored harassment of peasants that the result was possible. A further, important aspect is internecine competition among peasants. This petty-bourgeois, landowning class segment, having accepted a market-based system, also paid the price: the strengthening of its class had to take place through decimations of its numbers.

But, in fact, there is a robust possibility that it is not the "absoluteness" of landed property alone, i.e. the absoluteness of its rent alone, that ensures the results which Marx could sum up from Steuart, which we recognize in these words:

> clears, as Steuart says, the land of its excess mouths, tears the children of the earth from the breast on which they were raised, and thus transforms labour on the soil itself, which appears by its nation as the direct wellspring of subsistence, into a mediated source of subsistence, a source purely dependent on social relations.
>
> (Marx 1993, 276; 1953, 187)

The situation is, rather, that the bourgeois state, rightly convinced of the strength of the landed monopoly in its society, ensures the well-being of "cleared" soil-based economic spheres through subsidies to uphold their production in spite of potential market competition that in many cases might oust them from their home ground. Even so, this would not have taken place without the might and "absoluteness" of landed property; absolute ground rent is the sempiternal fulcrum of bourgeois society, at least in this meaning. What theory building related to ground rent should avoid is the construction of new, fanciful forms of "rent" inspired by forms of state action. To avoid political voluntarism, one must hold fast to the view that rent is a more basic source of wealth, from which a political superstructure loaded with forms of distribution may follow, without changing the Ground that created it.

The following is the full rendering of the important formula in Marx's draft plan, mentioned earlier:

> The inner construction of modern society, or, capital in the totality of its relations, is therefore posited in the economic relations of modern landed property, which appears as a process: ground rent [sic] – capital – wage labour (the form of the syllogism [*des Schlusses*] can also be put in another way: as wage labour – capital – ground rent; but capital must always appear as the active middle [*tätige Mitte*].
>
> (Marx 1993, 276, amended; 1953, 187)[9]

This thesis is the background of the main stream of the argument in the present chapter: turning Proudhon's perception of dialectics and the sequence of categories on its head is an operation that must lead to a detailed analysis – in Marx's case, comprising 200 pages in the third volume of *Capital* – of the economy of modern agriculture. In view of the relatively static nature of agriculture's property relations in the century and a half that have passed since Marx rounded off that analysis, it is imperative to make clear to what extent landed property in general, and in all capitalist nations, can be subsumed under the *Grundrisse* schema.

As argued earlier, it is plausible to do so. But, as also argued, it is dependent on the acceptance of dichotomous or even tripartite subjects in the economy, and of the internal necessity of the corresponding concepts. Important here is the earlier quote from Marx to the effect that "it appears very strikingly that the capitalist is only the function of capital, the worker the function of labour power", to which we surely might add, "the landowner only the function of landed property" or, actually, "the function of *ground rent*".[10]

For Marx, the capitalist system – *to the extent* that it actually functions as an organic system – reduces its participants to character masks:

> I do not by any means depict the capitalist and the landowner in rosy colors. But individuals are dealt with here only in so far as they are the personifications of economic categories, the bearers [*Träger*] of particular class relations and interests.
>
> (Marx 1976, 92; 1968a, 16)

In fact, as soon as the capitalist social formation has reached the point where it is dominated immediately by a capitalist money market (Marx 1993, 276; 1953, 187), the triad characters originally seen in the British capitalist breakthrough and its afterlife spread themselves to each and every direct or indirect producer of material goods in the "northwest". The existence of dichotomous-tripartite masks in fact just underlines the pure *Träger* function of any member of the main classes.

In this way, the capitalist social formation is realized precisely in the money market, whose existence so often provokes analysts to fall for theoretical abstractions removed from the *schöpferischer* core of the capitalist mode of production, i.e. from the "active middle" of the social formation. This leads to much confusion, where the specific fetish-character of money and money market gets the upper hand in the process of vulgarizing economic science. The extreme example is that the ten-year-long crisis of the capitalist world is still called "financial", despite its obvious core in productive capital and reduced production volumes from 2007 on.[11]

On the background of such a view of capital's historical development, it has been fair to stress the danger of going astray through unrealistic conceptions of what a land rent can be said to be. For behind the lack of realism in those analyses there obviously lie illusions and mystifications that can be common to us all. In practice, the dangers they involve are immediately connected with the fact that even the secondary, purely distributive form (land rent, for instance) of a social relation (such as landed property) approaches us only in a mediated form. Let us now look at the main "form of appearance" of landed property in the sight of the working class.

4.6 Social formation, housing debt and credit structure

The necessity of underlining the differences between fundamental income relations (the three main categories and their distributional aspects) and relations in
the money market proper are all the more important against the background of the
actual interweaving of the money market and its credit system with what has traditionally been called the "housing question". For, in fact, it is via this market that
any worker is in the most direct way oppressed by landed property. While the
wage worker is typically not reflecting on buying farming land, he is absolutely
dependent on a dwelling place. With his family, the condition for his reproduction
as a member of the working species, he has to live in a certain place, be it his
privately owned house or apartment or on hired premises. The price he pays, one
way or another, is a sum of money in part laid out for possession of the piece of
land where the dwelling is situated. Of course, the portion of extant and current
ground rent is by no means the only component of the rent he pays:[12] building
costs, etc. are also in the picture. Furthermore, pure monopoly rent, generated by
the intercourse of supply and demand, has its real native land here. But the fact in
question is important enough to count as the primary reciprocal "action" between
workers and landowners in modern society. Furthermore, the existence of private
landownership (or, one could even say, of landownership as a separate economic
relation) is the primary condition for the fact that one has to pay a housing rent at
all. The same goes, *mutatis mutandis*, for the capitalist's payment to rent or purchase factory "greenfields".

Housing expenses are among the highest single components of the budget of
the common worker (if he has actually bought a dwelling place, the payment of
interest and instalments is surely no less dominating). They will be the dominant
in every consideration he might make concerning leaving his way of life for an
agrarian alternative.

It is no wonder, then, that the worst general economic crisis of our days (since
the one starting in 1929, calmed only by the war ten years later) now *appears* as a
direct disturbance not in productive capital as such but in the capitalist social formation in general. According to the overwhelming common view, deceitful as
ever, it was generated in the sphere of the money market and, furthermore, sprung
from the closest possible economic relation between the working class and landed
housing sites.

The major events of the first of the superficial showdowns of the crisis, namely
the credit crunch culminating in 2008–2009, had an international or even global
character. Fictitious capital expanded to enormous dimensions through foreign
buying of US bonds. But the crunch clearly had its provenance in the expansion
in US-generated credit from at least 1995. Expanding credit followed from the
policy of "scraping the barrel" from the side of big (and small) credit institutions
in their construction of credit "derivates": the poorest potential borrowers of all,
workers or proletarian elements living just above the pauperist layer of the
industrial reserve army, were tempted to secure their life by establishing risky
mortgages.

Friedrich Engels once said of the social conditions connected to the industrialization of the German rural areas:

> Like the ground rent of the landlord in Ireland, the interest of the mortgage usurer in Germany cannot be paid from the yield of the soil, but only [sic] from the wages of the industrial peasant.

> (Engels 1973a, 654)

In such a way, the expropriation of the landed people and their transformation into a modern proletariat was (and is) accomplished. In the form of mortgages, capitalist credit is capable of turning traditional labourers into wage workers and of perpetuating their new condition. There are many lower-class US citizens today that are no better off than Irish or German peasants more than a century ago, abruptly having to pay the price for mortgages contracted at a time of speculation and soaring soil prices – not to speak of the legions of homeless in that country.

On the other hand, if we look at the US farming class proper – mostly independent landowners producing in a manner that can sensibly be called capitalist (or bourgeois) – they have important features in common with Western European farmers, combining two, or even three, class characters in single persons. Nonetheless, even if their mode of production is capitalist, their mode of original ownership of the soil is, as pointed out earlier, non-capitalist. Like their European colleagues, they take part in a structure of ownership-*cum*-production whose primary result is the extant price of the soil, including its tendency to rise. They are somewhat better sheltered than wage workers from the immediate misery of crisis.

Furthermore, as long as one confines the analysis to the aspect which is most critical for capital seen as a totality, namely what Marx calls "overproduction of capital", the mode of production is the necessary starting point. Over-accumulated money from the core of capitalist production also makes up a big share of the means of credit. However, as capital develops historically, it is only natural that the sources of credit available from the wages function systematically swell up the total means of finance of the capitalist class, especially when the latter's monies tend to be exported as capital.

Today, the structure in countries in the Northern American and Western European cultural sphere is fairly equal as regards mortgage debts.[13] In 2005, the ratio of total household debts to GDP in the US, in all nations in the northwest of Europe and in Canada, Australia and New Zealand, taken together, averaged well over 80 per cent, and the average mortgage debt reached about 70 per cent of the total debt (OECD 2006, III, 137). Warnock and Warnock (2008, 244, table 2) estimate the maximum relation between outstanding mortgage debt and GDP for ten representative countries in these areas in the period 2001–2005 to be about 69 per cent.[14] These are not simply proportions that underline the function of keeping workers in place: they also point to the fact that the actual completion of the grand relation of Marx's three main "categories", i.e. the actual and perennial completion of the capitalist social formation, is a crisis-producing factor in itself. Let us look at some additional examples.

In the last two decades, total household debts in the areas mentioned have "risen to record levels", according to OECD reports, "particularly [for] mortgages" (OECD 2006, III, 136). In a corresponding table covering later years, they show that "countries that experienced faster and deeper innovations in mortgage markets (United States, United Kingdom, Canada, Australia, and the Nordic countries) tend to have higher shares of household loans from nonbank financial institutions and a higher stock of mortgage debt as a ratio to GDP". OECD material from 2016 shows how these tendencies have by no means been weakened through the "financial crisis" (André 2016, 17–19). On the other hand, such material always shows a substantial general variation between the "northwest" and, e.g., Eastern European countries or periphery euro areas (André 2016, 7, 10).

In addition to this development, due to the aggressive loaning tactics of new types of institution since the start of the millennium, "[t]he share of mortgage debt has been rising over time, accounting for approximately two thirds of total household debt in most countries by 2005" (OECD 2006, III, 136). Furthermore, the "composition of the pool of homeowners" has changed steadily, "in part because of new mortgage products facilitating housing acquisition by borrowers with limited funds" (OECD 2006, III, 143). This, again, suggests that workers' wages in most of Western capitalism (Germany is a significant exception) have been making up an increasing part of the credit market *pari passu* with a growing reciprocal "action" between landownership and "wage labour".

This, in fact, is a tendency about three decades old. In the general picture, the part of the low-income groups' share of indebted households "has increased the most since the end of the 1980's, reflecting the effect of the liberalization of credit markets on the group of households which were previously most subject to credit rationing" (OECD 2006, III, 147).

In more "theoretical" terms, what is happening is that the capitalist class is harvesting windfall benefits in the form of means of credit from wage labour, generated by the reciprocal "action" of classes. The credit is essential to keep the economy going, while the threatening crisis is softened.

History will judge whether the breakdown from 2007 on should be considered as the first one to express, in an actually immediate way, the contradictory interests of all the three main classes of bourgeois society. The crash of 1929 was not an immediate fruit of constellations of landownership, and the agricultural crisis in the US anticipated it by five years. Panics in 1837 and 1857 were connected with land but through speculation in publicly owned soil. The so-called crash of 1873 was tied to railroad building but scarcely to speculation in land. The crisis starting in 2007, on the other hand, involved all the central class interests simultaneously. Because of the centrifugal effects of the credit system – of the *Geldmarkt* – that is still the case.

As Engels underlined in "On the Housing Question", "[it] is [the] transaction between capitalist and worker which creates the entire surplus value which later is distributed to the different sub-species of capitalists, and to their servants: ground rent, commercial profit, interest, taxes, etc." (Engels 1973, 223). Since the wage in any period is paid only after the end of production, we may add that the transaction "creates" the incomes of all the three main classes, plus their derivative forms.

A precondition for such a distribution is that incomes are measurable and can be determined independently of the magnitude of the capital advanced. In bourgeois economics, this represents a problem, since its spokesmen without exception take the price of the products to be determined in (a more or less fictitious) exchange between money and commodity. It leads them to lay undue weight upon possible changes in the price of the money commodity, an endeavour that in its turn leads to meaningless equation systems with no final determination.[15] If this structure actually reflected realities, credit-creating confidence would be hard to explain!

As we noted above, Marx, on the contrary, sees the price system as generated together with circulation, which has as its precondition that all commodities compare themselves in *physical* quantities of the money commodity. What is valid for his analysis of the commodity must also be valid for commodities as products of capital.[16]

The upshot is that since the "transformation problem" depends *exclusively* on the misapprehension of the money commodity indicated above, it has no real existence as such.[17] Consequently, it is fair to suppose that the distribution of the net product between the three main classes is measurable through and through, even with a given magnitude of capital.

However, the epicentre of the vortex of illusions, and its generating core, lies in the methodological confusion of the understanding of the origin of rent, namely what here has been called the "fulcrum" of the whole price dynamics: the transformation of values of commodities to prices of production. If the Marxian, i.e. (as this author would say) the actually functioning, *numéraire* in our daily and concrete economy is not understood, the whole system is open to arbitrariness. It is this position, and the loss of a pivot point, that led Sraffa to contend that the rate of profit might be generated through the "money rate of interest" (Sraffa 1972, section 44), thus, in the decisive moment, with an Orphic turn of the head, sacrificing the world of material production to some shadowy realm of finance and speculation.

It should be quite clear that if a theory of the capitalist system is not capable of demonstrating the unity of measurement of prices, rates of profit and capital magnitude, it is *a fortiori* of no use in reasoning out a political line for the overthrow of the capitalist system as such. It may, however, be a tempting tool in creating superficial slogans against exploitation, serving no one but lower-age groups of ruling strata and their longing for a sempiternal life in material well-being and spiritual illusion. In that manner, Yanis Varoufakis some time ago declared that one should give up every attempt at in-depth analysis of the economic core:

> The essence of the economists' inherent error is that they erred into thinking it is possible to tell a credible story about how values and prices are formed in complex (multi-sector) economies that grow through time.[18]

Confronted with such traditional Greek Apollonianism, might we not be tempted to reclaim dialectical analysis and yield to Plato's claim for scientific method, at *Republic* 533d:

> It is literally true that when the eye of the soul is sunk in the barbaric slough of the Orphic myth, dialectic gently draws it forth and leads it up.

Notes

1 See the example of the development of early English manufacture (Marx 1968e, 53) and the labour intensity in its "*nationale* Unterschiede" (*ibid.*).
2 On Bortkiewicz's role, see also Sandemose 2006.
3 "Rising price of labour as a consequence of capital accumulation in fact only means that the scope and weight of the golden link that the wage worker has already forged for himself, allow of a relaxation of its tension" (Marx 1968a, 646).
4 A main theme in Sandemose 2010 (see also Chapter 5, this volume).
5 Scott offers no alternative to the expression "landlords", and we have to suppose that we can argue against him while taking any landowner as example.
6 A further weak point to be mentioned here is that Mandel makes use of the fact that many functions of traditional farm work are industrialized in ordinary factories where they are combined with a higher technical composition than is common in farm environments (Mandel 1972, 347). There should be no need to point out that these are relations that belong to investigations of the composition in the industrial sector and not in agriculture. Unfortunately, Mandel's reasoning spreads confusion not only about the relation between agriculture and industry but also agriculture and land speculation, since he knits the circuit of the phantasmagoric "soil-price-element" in constant capital with "the specific laws of land speculation in late capitalism" (Mandel 1972, 347). As such, it seems as if the way was opened for the uncritical view so persistent today, that the genesis of ground rent should be treated as implying immediate relations to the sphere of circulation, not to mention financial superstructures.
7 On the other hand, Harvey on the next page seems to presuppose that such a social development implies that "peasant proprietorship has been eliminated". This leaves the reader at a loss as to what his general meaning is (mark well that Harvey's formulations do not involve a thesis to the effect that landownership has become capitalistic, only that its form has been adapted to capitalist relations).
8 "The creation of fictitious capital is called capitalization" (Marx 1968c, 485). One should also remember that Marx is often taken to be the "inventor" of the term "fictitious capital".
9 Nicolaus renders the term *Schluss* as "circle", which seems unfortunate.
10 See again his terminology at 1993, 276; 1953, 187.
11 See Sandleben 2011; "The State of Manufacturing in the United States" 2011; MCG Blogs de Economía 2011.
12 For the composite parts of the tenant's rent, see Engels 1973, 230.
13 The possibility, or the impossibility, of establishing a regular mortgage market may be among the factors that help explain the constant relative backwardness of nations. Housing markets are diminutive outside North America, Europe and the Pacific region. As pointed out by Warnock and Warnock, "no emerging market appears to have widespread availability of long-term fixed rate mortgages. In contrast, many developed countries have mortgages with terms of 25 years or greater, and roughly half have predominantly fixed rate products" (2008, 243, especially table 2).
14 Averages weighted by GDP (author's calculation).
15 See, again, Sandemose 1973, 1976, 2004.

16 See Sandemose 1976, 156–175, where there is a lengthy analysis of the possibility that the Bortkiewiczian critique should be valid as regards capital circulation but not for other forms of commodity circulation.
17 The "problem" in question cannot *basically* be taken to indicate a problem of equilibrium, because without a theory of prices one cannot measure the factors in the eventual equilibrium, nor know their common denominator and form of expression (see Sandemose 1976, 55).
18 As quoted by David Laibman (2012, 428).

5   Modes of production on the world market

Prelude

In this book up to now we have been through the definition of the capitalist social formation. This is effectuated in such a way that the three basic classes of this formation are presented as "character masks" of social actors and activities. For historico-geografical reasons the landowning class is the one which presents the most complicated picture, but it is also the one where the use of that mask concept is immediately the most fruitful. The reason for this is that a single concept that encloses the greatest circuit of variations shows all the more distinctly how individuals, no matter their differences, are not responsible for the social relations in which they engage, so long as society in general has an alienated form. Their class interests take on anonymous forms, and they act according to iron laws and rules – which does not diminish *their* specific felt or experienced freedom of action.

However, as we have seen, the geographical expanse of the capitalist social formation is by no means "global". Outside of its "parallellogram" it confronts territories organized in other ways. These forms certainly deserve to be considered.

One severe obstacle to reasonable anlysis of the present global economy is the idea that landownership in areas peripherical to capitalist ones are taken to be "feudal". In fact, the emergence of a real-subsuming system of capital in the West brought with it the *dissolution* and sublation of all kinds of feudal production. As Marx underlined, feudalism was, precisely in this way, a historic precondition for capitalism.

As for feudalism itself, it had its preconditions in the Asian social formation and then in ancient slave society (Marx 1972, 9: "Vorrede" to *Zur Kritik der politischen Oekonomie,* 1859). Since the latter was a strictly Western phenomenon, from the time of the industrial revolution the "global economy" consisted of only *two social formations* – the Asiatic and the capitalist one. Nonetheless, the capitalist *mode of production* to some extent emerged as an important field inside "Asiatic" communities – African and South American areas included.[1] Actually, a capitalism could even flourish inside them, since large strata of the population were turned into wage labourers, producing commodities industrially and through the cash nexus, and apparently watering down the traditional dominance of phenomena like the Hindu caste system and the Chinese *hukou* organization of the populace. However, the latter forms have remained all too strong to permit anything more than a capitalism relying on workers' formal subsumption under capital.

Actually, civilizations like the Chinese or the Indian have even less to do with feudalism than with real-subsumptive capitalism. The grotesque habit of calling the Asiatic system a feudal one derives, probably, from the Stalinist-Kominformian feeling of inferiority, according to which any acceptance of Marx's thesis on the Asian mode of production was shunned, because it would allegedly stamp Russia and Eastern Europe as immature for a development of socialism. Correspondingly, a prolonged debate arose as to whether wage labour in "Asian" societies can be called "free" in Marx's meaning of the word, i.e. as "birdfree" in the form it took in the Western "Tudor" expropriation. The answer should be simple. It certainly cannot have such a character, as long as Asian (et al.) workers are not expropriated from *jati-hukou* terrorism. Readers of *Capital* all too often forget that in the English case, yeomen and freeholders were expropriated not only from the good but also from Evil.[2]

In this chapter, we venture to analyse the world market as it appears as a resultant of exchange and circulation of *material* commodities produced in different countries. The reason for this is that it is only through the mechanisms of this market that the world economy can be depicted as one *active* totality; it is only here that "globalism" acquires a meaning. Without a material market at bottom, financial operations are bubbles and nothing else.

The countries in question will have different dominating modes of production originally producing for their domestic supply (and/or markets). Today, most such modes have a capitalist affinity, albeit it is only in the Western developed nations (older dominions included) that the working class is the victim of real subsumption under capital. Strict work discipline adapted to specifically capitalistic machinery is here in principle an untouchable cornerstone of the system. Culturally, it was further developed through the "general will" of the Enlightenment age, as acutely described and analysed in Hegel's *Phänomenologie des Geistes*.

Elsewhere, wage labour is present in a form corresponding to formal subsumption of labour under capital. Here, social discipline is not developed "intrinsically", as it is in the West, where class oppression mainly progresses through peaceful means. Mass discipline in the productive sector can, if at all, be kept alive not through typical Western capitalist fetishism and alienation but, rather, by non-economical means like coercive gymnastics and personal cults.

In an ambience dominated by formal subsumption, capitalist oppression is, then, closely accompanied by what in the West should be called pre-bourgeois violence. Or, rather: in these socio-geographical areas, once rightly subsumed under the label "half-colonies", where the internally ruling, possessive strata fought for their relative freedom against imperialist capitalism, the liberty they have now won takes the form of direct, violent oppression against their own labouring strata, while the growth of formal capitalism has scarcely managed to soften the forms of oppression.

Perhaps even more important: in the latter kind of societies, landed property has not reached the level where it represents genuine private property.[3] This means that land has no general commodity status and, consequently, the system lacks a fixed expression of capitalized ground rent and the true social foundation for ficti-tious capital.

Thus, the differences between such "modes" are accentuated through the recip-rocal combination of the class characters of wage workers, capitalists and land-owners inside them. Such differences inside extant forms of capitalist production modes are in their turn decisive for the forms of social formations in each case.

The pure physiognomy of a material thing produced inside a nation opens up the possibility of saying more about that country's physical potential for produc-tion than any financial manipulation related to the banking system of the nation in question. And the wealth of nations consists of useful things constructed by qual-ified labour melded together with natural processes – qualities made of qualities. The value relation between different commodities, in a home market or on the world market, is something quite different. It has no more material content than has the *Wechselkurs* (Marx 1976, 176; 1968a, 97).

Even in the case of trade between full-fledged capitalist nations, where, as we have seen, their class structure is guaranteed through their money market, the mate-rial trade in commodities forms the "cell form" of the economic development in question. However, the *value forms* which appear in international exchanges are quite different from those that emerge in national markets. An advanced value form, such as the *price*, for example, has other forms of appearance internationally, because the structure of competition is completely different – be it between capital-ist nations, between non-capitalist nations or between exemplars of both types.

The world market is, then, here understood strictly in its basic feature, as a market for material products, in the universal form of *commodities*, in principle produced capitalistically – whatever the form of subsumption of labour. The con-cept is used to cover – at the very minimum – what is called an *exchange* of two or more products from two different countries, with no limit fixed for a maximum of transactions.

The term "exchange", which has to be used with some indeterminacy to begin with, is explained in greater detail as we proceed. In that connection, we will sum up the most important social species of commodities on the world market, i.e. study them through the mode of their production. As the reader will have antici-pated, the term points back to some of the most basic concepts in the Marxian theory of history.

We primarily analyse the capitalist mode of production through the concept of *intensity of labour*, which plays a main role even in Marx's theory of the "modifi-cations" of the law of value on the world market. Also, this author finds what is often labelled Marx's "theory of international values" to be correct in its founda-tions, and I will use it as an operational point of departure – especially apparent in the first sections. As I proceed, I hope the usefulness of employing it for the Marxian materialist ecomomy will be clear to the reader.

A target for criticism here is the modern mainstream theory of "factors of production" insofar as it is found feasible for an analysis of the movements on the world market. This is briefly taken up in Section 8. In Section 7, I consider

David Ricardo's theory of "comparative advantages" as a counter-example to that theory, while I also point out that inconsistencies in the Ricardian theory must have been productive for the rise of a factor theory, i.e., for the "vulgar" theory of international class relations which in the twentieth century became the bourgeois answer to Marx.

I use some terrain to show that the *real* historical and social background of the economic functioning of the so-called "factors" – capital, land and labour – must be a measuring rod for whether such a "factor theory" is viable or not. To do this, I seek support in Marx's theory of those factors considered as forms of organized class forces, which we have considered in detail earlier in the book.

However, it turns out the Marxian theory is also useful for analysing the aborted or undeveloped state of those modes of production which, beneath the *advanced* capitalistic one, supply the world market with material products. This should become clear especially towards the end of the text.

As the text continues, I try to show how the said inconsistency in Ricardo's model is based on self-contradictions in his value theory, especially in his thoughts about money and prices. I also try to demonstrate that Marx's criticism of Ricardo's value theory has the potential to overcome precisely these weaknesses; the fact that these last are now mostly ignored in public debate represents perhaps the most deadly threat to competent socialist theory-building today. This makes it appropriate to comment on some typical Marxisant attempts to understand Marx's position (Section 5).

5.1 Introduction

In the discussion on "radical" political economy in the last third of the twentieth century, Karl Marx's theory of foreign trade and/or world market was to some extent overshadowed by the debate focusing on theories whose interpretation of a "labour theory of value" implied that workers' wages in some fashion had to be taken as an independent variable. In fact, this was a tendency grounded not only in misunderstandings of Marx's theory of value and money but even in David Ricardo's presupposition that the value and material content of *the real wage* was the source of profits and land rents and, consequently, for analysis of the distribution of riches to the three main classes of society – classes whose existence was hidden by later mainstream theory in the conceptualization of what were called the "factors" of production. The most acclaimed of these works, as regards the field of foreign trade, was Arghiri Emmanuel's book *L'échange inegal*, from 1969, which the author called "a study of the imperialism of trade" (Emmanuel 1972). In fact, scores of Marxisant authors wrongly presupposed that Marx had a theory of unequal exchange on the world market, of whom Emmanuel was a worthy representative. Likewise, many of them believed in Emmanuel's main methodological point, namely that each and every nation, regardless of other circumstances (geographical, historical, sociological) owed its degree of economic strength to the height of the prevalent wage level. In this theory, the wage (real or nominal) was certainly an independent variable.

Emmanuel, adopting the traditional division of world economy into "rich" and "poor" countries, accepted that an "unequal exchange" can only be one of several mechanisms which stand for transfers of values from members of one group of countries to those of another, and that its direct effect was responsible for just a part of the difference in standard of living between the two; but he still held "unequal exchange" of material commodities to be the elementary mechanism of transfer, which enables the developed countries to regularly start up the uneven development characterized by igniting all other mechanisms of exploitation, fully explaining the forms of distribution of wealth (Emmanuel 1972, 65).

There was a rational point to this view, for as long as the analysis of world trade concentrates on imperialism as a basic *bourgeois* phenomenon (Emmanuel's Marxisant stance), it has to start with a theory of exchanges of *commodities*, i.e. exchanges of the form determination which Marx calls the cell form, or elementary form, inside bourgeois society.

Any transfer of value proper, outside the one accomplished by concrete labour in the production process, has its background in an exchange (in the wide sense of the word) of commodities. It would seem to be a fair presupposition, then, that transfers of value in the form of loans, advances, interest, etc. should be investigated from a point of departure in such a basic form. Actually, Emmanuel had some important methodological points to make in that respect.

Even though Emmanuel's presuppositions are otherwise definitely at odds with those of Marx, the point accentuated above in itself quite in line with the way of thought behind Marx's approach. This is the case even if the latter is not directed at explaining "uneven development" in general. When Marx takes the world market into analytical consideration for the first time, it is connected to his investigation of immediate commodity production (and the structure of international wage levels) in the first volume of *Capital* – probably because he wants to study the theme in a conscious abstraction from streams of credit, which are thematized only in the third volume of the work.

Otherwise, progressive bourgeois theoreticians (of whom Emmanuel is an example) obviously take a point of departure quite alien to that of Marx. The latter's actual stance is frequently misunderstood. To begin with, consider the following remarks from chapter 20 of the first volume of *Capital* (chapter 22 in the English edition), "National Differences in Wages". Marx here insists that the law of labour values is subject to certain modifications in world trade:

> In every country there is a certain average intensity of labour, below which the labour for the production of a commodity requires more than the time socially necessary, and therefore does not count as labour of normal quality. In a given country, only a degree of intensity which is above the national average alters the measurement of value by the pure duration [*durch die bloße Dauer*] of labour time. It is otherwise on the world market, whose integrating parts are the individual countries. The average intensity of labour changes from country to country; here it is greater, there less. These national averages

form a scale [*bilden also einen Stufenleiter*] whose unit of measurement is the average unit of universal labour. The more intense national labour, therefore, as compared with the less intense, produces in the same time more value, which expresses itself in more money.

(Marx 1976, 702, see 1968a, 584)[4]

Although the main focus here is on wages, the content is valid for all movements on the commodity world market. We shall now explain why they stand for a criticism of most applied money theory of our day and certainly of Marxisant theories of world market and foreign trade.

5.2 The concept of money and the functioning of gold

Let us keep in mind this contention of a clear discrepancy between Marx and modern Marxisants while we analyse the passage in question, first with the theme of "money"and "universal labour" as our point of departure. When Marx uses the latter term, he is not (as one might have believed) introducing a new concept ad hoc. The origin of the term "universal labour" is to be found in section C, "World money", of chapter 3, "Money or the Circulation of Commodities", in Marx's work *Zur Kritik der politischen Ökonomie,* from 1859 (Marx, 1972, 125–128). "World money" is the money commodity in its form of being available to people from all nations on the world market. Consequently, we are not talking here of coined gold (which would have brought us back to a confusion of the Babel type) or of perceiving gold as belonging to a specific national currency. In this very problematic, the secret of the concept of "world money" is unveiled: It can only be the money commodity without coin imprint – that is, bullion, gold bars. (As far as this goes, Marx is in line with David Ricardo's brilliant scrutiny of the function of the commodity bullion pure and simple.)

Marx writes that as soon as money ascends "the domestic sphere of circulation", i.e. enters an international sphere, it

> falls back into its original form of precious metal in the shape of bullion. In world trade, commodities develop their value universally. Their independent value-form thus confronts them here too as world money. It is in the world market that money first functions to its full extent as the commodity whose natural form is also the directly social form of realization of human labour in the abstract. Its mode of existence becomes adequate to its concept.
> (Marx 1976, 240–241; 1968a, 156)

In the text that follows, Marx underlines in diverse ways how world money functions as "universal wealth". It becomes clear that no other world money is possible save bullion. The bar *form* is necessary because it characterizes the precious metal as a (formed) *product*, and therefore as a product of human labour, and can be amassed as such a form in relatively large quantities. As bars, gold can function in clearly delimited unities of weight and volume and thus as *numéraire*, standard of prices, for commodities. Therefore, gold in bar form is the form of appearance of abstract labour (i.e. Marx's concept of labour considered as producer of exchange *value*) in a universal context. The value of any commodity is a specific amount – measured extensively and intensively – of living labour. The exchange ratio between two commodities can be shown in a precise manner, and not only as a representation but also as real and material.

The existence of such a universal wealth, and, all the more, in the "form" of a "content", i.e. as an actual comparable unity, is what determines the generation of the category of universal labour. Since experience shows that world money does exist, there has to exist a value-producing labour that counts as universal labour. It is this labour which makes up the measuring unit for different national averages of quantities of value (abstract labour time) in a given common unit of weight. As is the case in national economies, where abstract labour appears most adequately in gold produced by a national average intensity-*cum*-productivity, so universal labour is most adequately expressed by the existence of a gold-producing labour which compares national averages on a scale.

It becomes clear that it is untenable to think of national currencies, like the US dollar, or US bonds, or "T-bills" (Treasury bills), as world money, in the way it is often done. Such forms are only a specific type of currency materialized in paper. World money, on the contrary, is imagined abstract labour, i.e. clearly defined with the help of a product of labour. On the other hand, it is of course a fact that different guaranteed papers can at any time serve as auxiliaries for the realizing of specific functions adhering to world money, such as speedy transfers of bullion, be it in material or symbolic form.

To understand Marx's concept of world money as well as of money in in general, one has to realize that money must be defined as imagined gold. On the face of it, it is easy to see that there is nothing odd about such a description, since gold cannot be money by its nature. Clearly, money is a social form of determination – a form being related to something material.

But although it is nonsense to identify gold with money in an analysis, simple understanding has often tried to accomplish precisely that. According to Marx, it is even a necessary feature in capitalist production that such an identification take place, and tends to become a *Volksvorurteil*, or popular prejudice. Thus it is not surprising that many take the position that to have a theory that money is gold one must imply that gold be present in every economic transaction.

One historical background for such a socially valid mystification lies in the fact that gold once was used physically as means of circulation. Also, gold's actual role as such a means originated in its function as a hoard (tesauration) and its existence as plain *commodity* (not just as plain product pure and simple, i.e. as *use* value).

Gold's immediate physical presence in circulation was almost entirely abolished before Marx published *Capital*. There existed a so-called gold standard, i.e. a claim that states could make on one another for gold as a replacement for bank notes (paper money). Later, the remnants of the gold standard were abolished (partly through the Bretton Woods agreement of 1944, partly through President

Nixon's declaration of a de facto US state bankruptcy in 1971, in which its last form, the liability of the US government to exchange gold for dollars vis-à-vis other states, vanished).

It has been a common belief that the money system in some way or other lost its connection to gold in 1971. Surely, that is to attribute infinitely exaggerated power to a handful of Washington officials. On the contrary, the money–gold unity is rather more decisive today than it has ever been.[5] The mass of commodities which has to circulate on domestic or international markets, has long since grown to such an extent that it is unrealistic to suppose that the money needed to circulate them should be guaranteed directly in gold; consequently, gold bars function in monetary matters exclusively as national or international reserves. On the other hand, it is no less necessary than before. Furthermore, the status of commodities as imagined gold has *not ever* been dependent on the physical presence of that gold. To imagine any commodity as an amount of gold is only dependent on 1) the power of imagination itself and 2) that gold is present in the world as something to be perceived materially, verified and imagined as such. *Au fond*, it is in this last respect that the development of a specific, homogeneous matter in bar form is so important: it is a defined product and, as such, the recognized point of departure for a representational abstraction.

5.3 The concept of "exchange"

If we want to study an object like a possible "unequal exchange", we are certainly required to check the content of an exchange *tout court* and in general, be it equal or unequal. A precondition for the viability of such a theoretical construction must be that one can determine in what proportion two commodities are exchanged on the world market and that some regular non-equivalence of value magnitudes is apparent in it.

However, what we observe in such cases is that different commodities are *sold* to customers in foreign countries. Also, since sale presupposes purchase and vice versa, we observe customers *buying* a commodity. That is, we do not observe two commodities being exchanged against one another in the fundamental "barter" meaning of the word.

That a commodity has been sold signifies that it has been alienated for money and that somebody has alienated money for it. But it is wrong to say that it has been exchanged against money or vice versa. It has not been exchanged for money as a commodity but "sold", alienated, for imagined quantities of gold. As Marx points out in his work from 1859,

> nothing can be more erroneous than the presentation {*Vorstellung*} that money and commodity inside the process of circulation step into the relationship of immediate exchange [*des unmittelbaren Tauschhandels treten*] and that their relative value is mediated through their exchange [*Austausch*] as simple commodities.
>
> (Marx 1972, 72)

This remark is equivalent to his comment in *Capital* I to the effect that

> [t]he difficulty lies not in comprehending that money is commodity, but on the contrary how, why and through what commodity becomes money.
> (Marx 1968, 107)[6]

Put briefly: that a thing is money signifies that it is non-exchangeable inside simple circulation. Thus, money is a material-social phenomenon incorporated in a specific processed physical matter, it is a measure of value and a standard (*numéraire*) of prices; from this basis, in its relation to other commodities, it is *capable only* of "circulation".

As implied above, to be in the position to circulate commodities in its ambience, money itself has to be incarnated in some commodity. For money cannot enter the world of commodities without itself having their common substance. Thus, the world market is not a sphere (just as little as a national one) where products are "exchanged" inside the simple circulation: it is where they circulate, so to speak, around a golden calf. That a commodity circulates, means, in Marxian language, that it is allotted, *without exchange*, to a certain quantity of gold.

Money, then, is integrated in such a quantity of gold – in a certain weight of precious metal. That the commodity A has a "price" is a sign of this fact; it means that A is evaluated to be a certain physical quantity of this specific other commodity. That the commodity A circulates means that it can be bought or sold like any other; consequently, circulation means that any commodity can compare itself with any other. That two different commodities have the same *value* means that an identical quantity of socially necessary labour time has been consumed productively in their generation. But that two commodities have the same *price* means that they can be counted and calculated as identical with one and the same physical quantity of gold (the standard, *numéraire*). Already at this point it can be anticipated that two commodities on the world market may have the same price but still express two quite different values.

Now, as regards this simple commodity circulation (Marx's *einfache Warenzirkulation*) in its international form, the whole case is based on the fact that universal labour implies a measuring (and comparison) of given national differences on a scale. The presence of a scale means that there is no dynamic or unifying principle to be found in the competition on the world market. Inside a developed capitalist nation such a principle makes itself felt through the tendency of prices to adjust uniformly according to exigencies of an average rate of profits, whose level is determined by competition 1) inside branches as well as 2) between branches. These two points imply that 1) there is established a certain socially necessary labour time for a *certain physical* mass of products and 2) there is established a certain average rate of profits which in principle can be afforded by firms in *any* branch inside capitalist production, *irrespective* of the different compositions between mass of living labour and mass of capital goods in those spheres. Ideally, all capitalist products can then be sold at what Marx calls their "production price".

5.4 First comments on the concept of intensity of labour[7]

A first, approximate definition (but an insufficient one, as we shall see) of a world market might well be that it is the meeting place of commodities that are all produced according to the rules mentioned earlier but in nationally diversified circumstances (different intensity and productivity levels).

The very acceptance of such a possibility, logically acceptable as it is, shows us at least that on the world market there cannot exist anything like the equalization of profit rates we have been considering. The equalization must take place in a national frame (of which still more later), and the world market is by definition a common contrast to national frames or nations.

On the world market, defined as an institution for buying or selling at least two products from two different nations, we have before us only what we might call static competition between productive firms from these different nations. This means, to use an expression from Guenther Sandleben's outstanding overview, that there does not exist any "average intensity" on the world market:

> In contradistinction to the relations inside a country, there consequently does not exist on the world market any globally valid "socially necessary labour time", an entity which has precisely "an average intensity" among its preconditions.
>
> (Sandleben 2011, 9)

Also, Sandleben points out that it is not only the national intensities which remain side by side on a scale on the world market. For if we, setting out from the lack of middle intensity (*mittlere Intensität*), can conclude that there does not exist "a global social necessary labour" (Sandleben 2011, 10), then the scale-principle has to be valid, on the world market, for the other factors entering the definition of "socially necessary labour time" inside a nation. According to Marx's original definition in the first chapter of *Capital*, these are certain "socially-normal conditions of production" which underpin a definite degree of productivity of labour inside the nation, such as scientific and technological levels and (we must assume) social infrastructure. On the world market, these factors are either missing or significantly modified, and already for such reasons a dynamic form of competition is out of the question.

Thus, in the wake of his remark on how a more intensive national labour will express itself in more money (gold), Marx contends that in the absence of dynamic competition, where intensity differences can present themselves as such, the more productive national labour appears as more intensive (Marx 1976, 702; 1968a, 584).[8]

Such a result is reasonable. Even resultants of competition inside branches (or "spheres") in a national sample of the capitalist social formation will include cases where one or more capital(s) acquire(s) a supreme productivity that allows commodities to be sold far above their individual values. In such cases, the augmented productivity counts as if there was produced a larger amount of values, i.e. (as we shall substantiate in the last sections of this chapter) as a rise in intensity. But as a rule, such phenomena will in such cases be overcome by competition. That is not so easily done on the world market, since here it is national capitals – or other national wealth forms – with completely different infrastructures in the background which oppose each other.

It is clear, then, that Marx's theory cannot be used to argue that an equalization to an average rate of profits takes place on the world market. On the contrary, single nations initially stand, as capitalist *or non-capitalist* economies, unmediated against each other, and at most it is only slowly and in the long run that, *on this market,* possibilities open up for equalization of productivities. And, we might add, when that happens, it is not through a mechanism of competition via production prices as is the case inside a nation with *developed* capitalism.

Therefore, it is not the case that single capitals (Marx: *Einzelkapitale*) have a priority in exchange (via buying and selling) on the world market. On that market, in its selling and buying, a singular capital represents a national total capital; that is its primary characteristic as far as that market is concerned. This is clearly revealed in the fact that all single capitals of a given nation fall back on the use of its original national currency.[9] This currency has a "value" (as the expression goes) which is connected with, and corresponds to, the average labour productivity and labour intensity of its nation. The nominal exchange rate between currencies expresses how much gold a given amount of labour hours inside a nation can produce in comparison with other nations.

In this way, as it is expressed by Marx, "the more intensive national labour . . . as compared with the less intense, produces in the same time more value, which expresses itself in more money" (Marx 1976, 702; 1968a, 584). That Marx ties the measure unit of "universal labour" directly to this constellation must mean that "money" is used as a synonym for gold material. Consequently, it seems that Sandleben commits an error when he says that these movements presuppose that "the value of money remains constant" (Sandleben 2011, 10). For irrespective of the question of whether it takes more or less time to produce a certain weight of gold material, the value, which always is exchange value, of any other commodity will still have the same relation to the quantity of labour used in the production of gold. The reciprocal relations of commodities, i.e. their relative prices, will be the same.

At this point, there is no evidence for a possible "unequal exchange" on the world market. What is evident is that the above-mentioned, different national averages of what Marx calls the organic composition of capital (OCC, for short) do not appear as visible entities on the world market. The OCC is, for any productive capital, a functional unity of 1) the technical composition, of mass of workers in relation to mass of means of production as well as of (2) the (corresponding) value composition between wages (as variable capital) and objectified capital.

Since the OCC for historical and technical reasons differs considerably between different branches, the surplus of each branch inside the *national* economy has to undergo changes in the processes of competition, which goes even for the nominal prices (changed values) of any piece of objectified capital. These modifications Marx treats without difficulty (albeit with unclear language) in chapter 9 of the third volume of *Capital*, casting shame on all those who, even today, lament the aforementioned alleged "transformation problem" of the relations between values and prices in his system.[10]

OCCs do not come directly to the fore in international trade, in contradistinction to what goes on on the national level. Inside a given country, the rate of the surplus on capital, taking the form of the *average rate of profits,* can be observed directly even in a capital with an average composition. When a commodity produced inside a *developed capitalist nation* is laid out for sale on the world market, its price is set not according to its relative OCC but according to the relative productivity and intensity of labour in all branches on a national level.[11] That this is so follows immediately from the fact that it is priced in the nation's own currrency, which reflects those average domestic conditions.

Now, this may in general not make much difference for the producer, since the relative average of the OCC is always reflected in productivity and intensity. Countries with a high OCC are precisely countries with a high productivity and intensity.

Inside a national economy, through the competitive movements mentioned earlier, capitals or spheres with a high composition can "compensate" for their relatively low share of variable capital. But the precondition for this is a complicated historical process, incarnating the very construction of a capitalist social formation, with an average rate of profits, an advanced system of soil prices, etc., which cannot inmediately be traced on the world market: thus, in foreign trade it is not primarily the composition of capital but immediately labour productivity and intensity itself that counts. In addition to being rewarded for a high productivity and intensity, an advanced capital can get hold of monopoly rents and thus raise its individual prices. But it cannot expect a windfall profit directly as a result of pecularities in its OCC. Here, there lies an immediate temptation for advanced capitals to continue on to pure imperialist policies, seeking support from their own state apparatus to maintain on the world market the position which they possess without extra-economic force on the domestic market.

It would be hard to understimate the theoretical value of Marx's theory on "the international application of the law of value". It deserves to act as the fulcrum of a renovated and revived theory of the imperialist aspects of capitalism, or at least of a general analysis of the interaction of all economic systems expressed through nations which approach each other on the world market.[12]

The imperialist export of capital, which we recognize as an essential element from the international crisis of 1873, goes necessarily back to an international trade with use values dressed as exchange values. These commodities, aimed at individual or productive consumption, whether in rich or poor countries, are what capitalist imperialism basically needs to function – as the prevailing core behind the nebulous shadows of "financialization".

5.5 Illustrations: motley reasoning among Marxisant authors

We shall now try to expose the heart of the matter *via negativa*, by dragging contrasting views into the picture; these will be views which are influential in the debate.

In an acclaimed textbook by Ian Roxborough one reads:

> In *Capital*, Marx presupposes the equal exchange of equivalents, that is, a commodity embodying X hours of socially necessary labour-time will exchange with another commodity, embodying the same amount of socially necessary labour-time.
>
> (Roxborough 1979, 60)

Let us first concretize these theses, which are valid only under the simplified conditions Marx makes in the two first volumes of *Capital*. We should remember that such an exchange of equivalents will take place only in the case of two commodities produced by capitals which both work under socially average conditions. In addition, we should remember that we are talking about circulation, so that the "exchange" is no barter-like relation but a transfer mediated through money.

Roxborough continues with the following passages, apparently presupposing that he himself makes use of common knowledge about a Marx-based theory:

> There are a number of different theories of unequal exchange. What they have in common is a proposition that labour is rewarded unequally in different parts of the world and hence identical commodities may embody different amounts of socially necessary labour-time. When one commodity is exchanged for another, behind the transaction is an exchange of a greater quantum of socially-necessary labour-time for a lesser. The exchange is unequal and works to the disadvantage of of the underdeveloped countries. The same amount of labour-time may be embodied in each commodity, but the remuneration of that labour is different. If the value of labour-time is the cost of its reproduction, that is, a certain basket goods at any determinate historical epoch, then more value goes into the commodity produced in the metropolis (real wages are higher) than into the identical [sic!] commodity produced in the periphery. So that a commodity which embodies X days labour is exchanged against an identical commodity produced in the Third World which embodies more than X days labour [. . .] This is the essence of the unequal exchange.
>
> (Roxborough 1979, 60–61)

Here, we are presented with an unjustified use of a series of categories, such as "underdeveloped countries", "third world", "metropolis" and "periphery". These expressions are not explained anywhere else in Roxborough's book, nor is it explained how the author can accept a thesis to the effect that an "unequal exchange" may be to the detriment of "underdeveloped countries" without first evaluating if such an exchange might be what leads to the very definition of "underdevelopment" in a country.

Still, let us concentrate on other contentions in this problematic text.

Firstly, in the attempt to make a point of departure in the "reward" of labour in explaining an unequal exchange, Roxborough combines his thesis with a concept of "the value of labour-time". But labour time cannot, no matter which theory we are investigating, have a value. Concretely, it is, contrariwise, through labour time that value is *created*.

Furthermore, a contention presupposing that the reward of "labour" (if consistency is aimed at, it ought to be the rward of labour power) has nothing to do with the fact that "identical commodities"can embody different amounts of socially necessary labour time. On the contrary, it is important that a product does not take the form of an exchange value if it is not to be exchanged against another and non-identical product. When Roxborough wants to argue from a situation where identical commodities are exchanged against each other, the misunderstanding is of a form that scarcely makes any reasonable criticism viable.[13] Still, there is certainly room here to point out that the value created in the course of a given length of labour time does not stand in any rational relation to the value of the wage goods, as Roxborough seems to think. We are obviously talking about incongruent magnitudes.

In fact, Roxborough's focus on such a theory might well be meant as a tribute to Emmanuel, whose influential thesis, as we have mentioned, was built precisely on the difference of wages in poor and rich countries.

As a parallel example of uncritical repetition of presuppositions, all too often present in Marxisant models, let us look briefly at Minqi Li (2005). Here, inequalities of exchanges on the world market are taken as given, i.e. the "unequal exchange" is simply presupposed as an institution. The author further says that the "value added" consists in what each state can gain in the exchange (where the unequality consists in one state gaining more "value added" than the other). This kind of "value added", Minqi says, the state will split in wages and profits. Poor states will be coerced to pay lower wages than richer states, and so he can point to a correlation between high wages and rich states and vice versa (Li 2005, 430). But, alas, every presupposed causal connection is here taken completely out of the blue. As if he was willingly trying to expose himself as a vulgar economist to the highest possible degree, Li adds that the wage, this presupposed but unexplained independent variable, is not determined by socially necessary labour time at all:

> The wage rate, or the price of labour power, is, like the price of every commodity, determined by "supply" and "demand" . . .
>
> (Li 2005, 431–432)

Li presents himself as a Marxist, and, as such (on the pages of a self-declared "Marxist" journal), he should be informed of the fact that for Marx, the value of labour power, determined through the socially necessary labour time spent on the production of the wage goods, is certainly not determined by abstract "social forces" (in which Li takes explicit refuge). We have shown (in the case of Emmanuel) that there is no rational connection at all between wage rate and labour time; so how should Li's explanation be any more rational?

As for Roxborough's misunderstanding of the claims of theories of exchange on the world market, it is underscored by the following contentions:

> Once it is accepted that equal amounts of equally productive and equally skilled labour, with identical technology, are rewarded unequally, (that is, that real wage rates differ from one country to the next), then it is no longer possible to assume that the of value – socially necessary labour time – has any unique value. Marx's assumption was that, at any given historical period, the notion of a single value for average wages was a meaningful one. This was to be the measure of value. Once it is accepted that real wage rates differ greatly on the international scale, this assumption is untenable.
>
> (Roxborough 1979, 61–62)

This gives the impression of being fierce imagination, beyond control. Marx's theory has nothing to do with conceptions like these, as we shall presently see.

As already remarked, time, irrespective of what one wants to call it – "measure of value" or whatever – cannot incarnate value. Besides, the expression "value for average wages" is totally without meaning in a Marxian context.

In fact, Roxborough's reasoning, precisely like Emmanuel's, Li's and others', silently takes as given what should first be shown, namely that the economic inequality between nations is grounded in wage differences. Consequently, he manages to construct an "unequal exchange" which operates with all (or potentially all) other factors as equal. But it is meaningless to take the work performances in a poor country and a rich one as "equal amounts of equally productive and equally skilled labour, with identical technology", for all empirical facts tell a contrary story: the difference between such countries lies in significant gaps in technology and/or labour skill and productivity. And to explain such facts one has to make concrete historical investigations, which – among other things – explain the conditions of work, wage work included.

Let us now look briefly at another Marxisant-minded exposition, in this case by Paul Cooney (2004). Cooney stands for the view that "unequal exchange" cannot be regarded as a primary mechanism in explaining underdevelopment. But, at the same time, it turns out that he both accepts such a concept at its face value and that his image of such an exchange is curiously extensive: it seems that it encompasses every regular transfer of value from "periphery" to "metropolis", especially transfers of money. Methodologically, it is of interest that he wants to transcend international trade as a "standard field", because the more cogent questions are tied to accumulation and the capitalist laws of motion on the level of international economy; these, he finds, are not limited to trade but have to include investments, financial flows and migration (Cooney 2004, 249).

This might count as a textbook example of spontaneism and "economism" in social theory. It should be quite clear that one must seek to analyse composite phenomena through discussions of more simple phenomena. Otherwise, the consequence may be not only a misunderstanding of the totality but also that one shamelessly escapes from the true problems.

For instance, it is fair to expect 1) that accumulation takes place through employment of certain material elements, or physical commodities; accumulation may be based on commodities acquired through import – that is, on the world market. If there is an "unequal exchange" on the world market, it will appear at this point, and it may well even have a decisive influence on accumulation; we do not know about that before we have taken pains to investigate it. Furthermore, 2) it is certainly the case that financial flows take place to initiate investments (primarily from rich to poor countries, but even the other way). Those investments which are basic for economy and development will always, wherever they take place, be investements in material production. It is clear that the eventuality of the products sold on the world market, and at what price, will be of interest (such evaluations will always be in the picture for investments involving transfers on the world market). Also, 3), the question of migration is not at all inessential in relation to commodity trade on the foreign market. The costs that a certain group of migrants have to deal with inside a country, irrespective of the direction of their journey, may well be dependent on the price level of consumer goods, which is often a result of international exchange. Still more important is the fact that an analysis of commodity exchanges may take part in a conceptualization of the very nature of migration. For instance, the class dynamics between the three main groupings inside a developed capitalist society is detrimental to emigration, as we shall see in a moment. But quite the other position may dominate in a non- or semi-capitalist country. In both cases, these will be structures that are pointed out through analyses which take their point of departure from the position of commodity production inside the nation in question.

A further criticism of Cooney's views can be tied to a point inside 3): Cooney criticizes the world market theories not only of Emmanuel but also of Samir Amin, plus the one defended by Ernest Mandel in his *Der Spätkapitalismus* (1972) – counted as a "leftist" classic nowadays. Mandel points out that while Emmanuel and Amin discuss "unequal exchange" as if it rounded off an aggressive competition where different national capitals get their profit rates equalized to an international average rate of profit, he maintains that there does not exist any such movement on the world market.

We shall see that Mandel's thesis is correct and that it is of minor importance that the reason he gives is rather weak – a fact that Cooney does not overlook. It is more important that Cooney actually contends that there exists a tendency to an international average profit rate. He argues from the alleged fact that there exists a movement towards open borders for investments ("foreign direct investments" (FDI)) and that this makes it possible for multinational corporations to establish themselves on a broad front in poor nations, something which in practice will raise the latter's average OCC, leading to a global equalization of OCC.

However, such an eventual equalization has no inner connection to a possible average profit rate, neither nationally nor internationally. Cooney is making his point in a way that makes it easier to argue that the value transfers between spheres, which, as we know, always go from industrial capitals of low OCC to those of high OCC (since there is relatively more variable capital and therefore relatively more of the value-creating substance in "low" branches), are not as important for the "unequal exchange" as Emmanuel contends.

Cooney then considers transfers of value with a background in differences in productivity inside single spheres (branches). Here, too, it is extremely unclear which importance he ascribes to these movements; he then goes on to consider value transfers in the form of repatriation of capitalist surplus and payments of interest on the side of poor countries, etc. With these considerations, he has withdrawn considerably from any sound point of departure in the real commodity circulation on the world market.

The problematic tendency in Cooney's method comes clearly to the fore in his brief remarks on capitalist price formation related to the picture he advocates of the structure of commodity circulation on the world market. The sale of products for individual consumption is not even mentioned in his article, despite the fact that it was just such products, and not exchange directly between capitals, that was the point of departure for the theory of international trade, as launched by Ricardo.

We shall now go back to the structure of Ricardo's analysis to show how the argument fortifies the Marxian analysis of "money or the circulation of commodities" – to the detriment of many a Marxisant viewpoint.

5.6 Ricardo's comparative advantages: scheme and theory

Ricardo was the most significant labour-value theoretician prior to Marx's time. As a parallel to what the latter did in his main work, from 1867, Ricardo, in his *Principles* fifty years earlier insisted that his law of value was necessarily subject to a modification on the world market:

> The same rule which regulates the relative value of commodities in one country, does not regulate the relative value of the commodities exchanged between two or more countries.
>
> (Ricardo 1969, 82)

It is usually said that Ricardo illustrates the point by means of a model of two commodities and two nations – Portugal and England. He presupposes that the Portuguese economy is more advanced than the English and that it produces a given amount of cloth as well as a given amount of wine cheaper and more effectively than the latter. In England, 100 hours are needed to produce the cloth, while the Portuguese need only 90. As regards wine, the production in Portugal is relatively even more effective, producing a given amount in 80 hours, while the English need 120. Schematically, we get Table 5.1, where gold production is added.[14]

As a labour-value theoretician, Ricardo contends that the amount of living labour in each of these industries is adequately expressed in a definite amount of gold. Productivity per labour unit (hour), regardless of where it takes place,

Table 5.1 Ricardo's two commodities and two nations

	England		Portugal		
Cloth	100 hours	50 ounces gold	45 ounces gold	90 hours	Cloth
Wine	120 hours	60 ounces gold	40 ounces gold	80 hours	Wine

is expressed in its producing half an ounce of gold. The concrete work in the clothes industry is qualitatively different from the concrete work in the wine sector, but the two can be made equal to each other under given circumstances. Here, they are identified as labour inside gold production. Thus, it is not correct that Ricardo's theory of comparative costs is based on a two-commodity example. Three commodities are in the picture, albeit one need not postulate anything concerning the geographical production site of gold. Actually, one might coin the term "three-nation model".

If foreign trade is initiated, Portugal will, after some time, be in position to outcompete the English. The latter will acquire both cloth and wine cheaper than before, if they buy imported goods. England will have to sell the whole amount of cloth for 50 ounces of gold to avoid losses. This sale goes on in English pounds, presupposed to have full coverage in gold. On the English market, the Portuguese can sell the same commodity ten per cent cheaper, weakening the profits on English goods. Portugal can also export wine to England on even better terms. England will get a relative deficit on its trade balance, and this has to be (is already) compensated by the English transfer of gold to Portugal. (Marx would probably add "or of silver", since he was eager to underscore that the world market in his time was characterized by bimetallism.) The augmented mass of gold in Portugal would function as a safeguard for all types of currency reserves in the country, so that any Portuguese searching for pounds for buying goods in England is insured against losing wealth through the weaker English currency.

If this situation persists, the proportions between the gold hoards of the two countries will change substantially. The rising mass of gold in Portugal will lead to a rise in price in domestic products, since – given the "gold standard" of the day – a unit of the Portuguese escudo will be less expensive measured in gold hours. Contrariwise, in England commodity prices will sink, since every given commodity, through the price of the pound, will be measured as a lesser share of the total quantity of gold inside the country.

This, in its turn, leads to the terms of trade between the two countries being changed to the advantage of England. English goods get cheaper, while Portuguese get more expensive, independently of where the sale takes place, since prices are strictly dependent on labour time in gold excavation, which, like labour time in the other two branches, is supposed to be constant.

Ricardo thinks that such regular movements have a tendency to change the structure in the inner and outer division of labour of the countries in question – at least to some extent. In this case, the consequence is that the capitalist classes of the two countries will act based on the "comparative advantages". At a certain point, when England is making up its deficit, Portugal will sell cloth at a higher price than the English, while the Portuguese will still have an advantage as regards the price of wine, since the demand advantage was more significant here.

According to Ricardo, the capitalists in the two countries will round off their competition at this level: England will specialize in cloth production, Portugal in wine cultivation. Ricardo's solution consequently has a harmonious aspect to it, but *au fond* his theory is not built on any excessive bourgeois illusions. He was a theoretician prior to the time of bourgeois vulgar economy, with a clear consciousness of class contradictons. In a general sense, his method, and the theory, is acceptable.

Still, some Marxisant writers have criticized Ricardo for holding class contradictions all too far in the background as regards foreign trade. For instance, Anwar Shaikh says that Ricardo leaves the class concept and returns to a concept of the nation as a whole, as soon as he turns to the analysis of the consequences of trade (Shaikh 1979, 216).

It is true that Ricardo rather consistently talks of the nations standing opposite each other in the international exchange, not immediately of the capitalists involved. But this is to some extent justified by the fact that on the world market we are confronted with a circulation movement that is different from the one we meet inside a developed capitalist country. Just as did Marx later, Ricardo held that on the world market the actors do not sell and buy their commodities according to rules created by capital developed on the home market. And, again, just as Marx came to do later, Ricardo makes use of a direct consideration of values, leading prices of commodities back to homogeneous quanta of gold. That is, he relates them to such quanta independently of the composition of the capitals that have produced them. In other cases, in the production for the inner market, this composition was crucial for Ricardo in his study of distribution.

Thus, both Ricardo and Marx abstract from any composition of capital, even from the latter's OCC, on the world market. This must mean that both of them think that here, capital is functioning outside the realm dominated by interspherical competition in the domestic economy.[15]

We have arrived at yet another methodological affinity between Ricardo's and Marx's analyses. The schematical example shows that Ricardo lets commodity prices be measured prior to their circulation. Apparently, he is miles away from letting the commodity prices be measured only when the "exchange" (their buying and selling) takes place. However, when he considers the "natural prices" of commodities on the home market, he presupposes them – rightly – to correspond to what Marx called "prices of production", derived from the specific composition of their capitals. But here – to the contrary and faultily – Ricardo holds that such products, in equilibrium sold at their cost of production plus an average profit, have their prices changed in specific ways by movements in the composition of the gold-production capital.

According to Marx's way of looking at things, this is an error which implies that relative commodity prices, in their internal relation and in their deviation from their values, are determined not only by their specific capital composition but also by the composition of the capital producing their measuring material.

Since this means that the price of the money commodity influences not only the nominal but even the *relative* prices of commodities, it follows that in such a theory, the very phenomenon of price will be defined through itself – which amounts to its not being defined at all. And also, quite as cogently, the concept of (exchange) value must be defined through the concept of (exchange) value. Actually, value is here not defined through extensive time (duration) of labour processes.

Economists pursuing this way of reasoning can therefore at most postulate some third factor as a value substance. If they say the substance is human labour, they can do nothing to substantiate such a claim. In the Marxian model, on the contrary, it goes without saying that to appear at all the value must exist as expressed in something other than itself or of its own substance (and a thing is known only through its appearance). Marx holds that it is expressed in some unique use value, which turns out to be a money material.

Through that expression, the leading thread back to labour as the value substance is once again clear: the concrete labour in one sector (gold) represents the universal abstract labour (which is abstracted from any commodity production, including that of gold, whereby this latter can be priced as well as count as a concrete labour).

When Ricardo allows for world-market commodities to be measured directly by means of the immediate working hours laid down in them (and, therefore, through given, homogeneous gold quantities), this indicates that he has no intention of looking at such commodities as "capitalist" in the first place. "The rule which regulates . . . the relative value of the commodities exchanged between two or more countries" is thus not related to prices of production (to shift to a Marxian term). They do not exist in foreign trade. Consequently, Shaikh's criticism is not valid: Ricardo does not unduly abstract from capitalist class relations, since here they do not – as such – in any way structure the prices in question.

The criticism of Ricardo by Marxisant writers may be correct in some details (from which we shall abstract here), but what is methodically important is that both Ricardo and Marx accept the importance of analysing the world market not through financial superstructures but through the direct functions of materially produced commodities.

5.7 The position of the wage: among determined or undetermined value magnitudes? Marx versus Ricardo

What would be the primary Marxian objection to Ricardo's theory of foreign trade? Probably the fact that Ricardo, in contradistinction to Marx, has no concept of the intensive magnitude of labour time (its degree-magnitude) but only of its role as an extensive magnitude. The examples regarding work hours in the schema above do not allow for differences of intensity. Therefore, examples à la Ricardo, especially since they aim at comparing given quanta of gold to bring into the open the qualities in value-producing labour, will be in danger of underestimating the weight of the differences between the economies of different nations. Marx, on the contrary, draws differences in intensity directly into his examples, which implies that from the outset he is watching out for any effects foreign trade may have on these very differences.

As if to take notice even of non-capitalist delivery to the world market (and to its possible consequence of economically weakening non-capitalist countries), he contends that any capitalist development in any country will lead to a increase over the international average. Therefore, quantities of products of the same kind with identical working times in different nations will have *unequal international values,* with different prices. Since "price" is value expressed in money, it follows that the relative value of money will be lower in the more advanced nation and the nominal wage higher (1976, 702; 1968a, 584).[16] The theory of explanatory priority of the (nominal) wage in relations on the world market will then be refuted.

That Marx chose to use his section on the wage, namely the sixth of *Capital* I,[17] to introduce the reader to his theory of international exchange, which as a whole was planned for a later work, has a certain contingency to it. It seems that for many Marxisant writers, this relative contingency, paired with certain weaknesses in their appropriation of Marxian theory in general, has led to the belief that the wage, from a Marxian position, could be used as an independent variable in the study of international exchange.

But, alas, the only actual connection between this view and the structure of the argument in the latter parts of *Capital* I is that here, Marx puts some weight on showing the fetishism that leads to the rise of the category *Arbeitslohn* (imprecisely translated as "wage".)[18] For this is a fetishism that 1) leads to the illusion that what is paid for is not labour power but concrete labour as such, i.e. that the whole of the worker's actual, floating power during a working day is remunerated. Consequently, 2) it leads to the rise of the enigma of how a capitalist can gain an unpaid surplus from production. A possible result for the disturbed ideologist is 3) that the wage is imagined as a fixed "factor" of production or as an expression of such a "factor", which simply does not need explanation.

Now, if we turn to look at Ricardo's theory in "On Value", the first chapter of his main work from 1817, and especially his section "On an invariable measure of value", we will meet a polemic against the then prevailing theories on the connection between wages and the concept of value:

> Adam Smith, and all the writers who have followed him, have . . . maintained that a rise in the price of labour would be uniformly followed by a rise in the price of all commodities. I hope I have succeeded in showing that there is no grounds for such an opinion, and that only those commodities would rise which had less fixed capital employed upon them than the medium in which price was estimated, and that all those which had more would positively fall in price when wages rose. On the contrary if wages fell, those commodities only would fall which had a less proportion of fixed capital employed on them than the medium in which price was estimated; all those which had more would positively rise in price.
>
> (Ricardo 1969, 29)[19]

In this reasoning, we see the substance of Ricardo's argument against a naïve theory of "factors". The wage, or, for that matter, profit or ground rent, may behave and change according to the inner dynamics of the economy, and, basically, they cannot be taken to be the heart of the matter. Since they are subject to measuring problems, they are also – as was Ricardo's inner conviction – subject to the nature of the substance that forms the measuring entity. In Ricardo's view, this is labour time, or, rather, living labour itself.

The principle of Ricardo's alleged solution has won universal endorsement: the search for an invariable measure is accepted everywhere, even if it is not recognized as being a problem of first-rate importance. That is, theories that accept or underpin a system integrating such a principle are *legio*. Even some Marxists, at least among the self-appointed ones, take this stand.

However, Ricardo's triumph stands on feet of clay. His theory presupposes, rightly, that the gold commodity is used as a medium for estimating commodity prices. So it is. But Ricardo believes that this function is effectuated through *the value form* of the money commodity, i.e. through its exchange value; but this, according to Marx, belongs to the "indescribable . . . confusion over measure of value and standard of price ('standard of value')" which is common "with English writers" (Marx 1976, 192, note; 1968a, 113, note). The level of the *price* of the gold (a form of its exchange value) is, of course, completely irrelevant. What is relevant is the *use* value of gold, i.e. the gold *material*. As a *numéraire*, standard of prices, the gold functions as bars, so to speak, in its world-money form, measuring quantities of gold on itself:

> As measure of value, and as standard of price, money performs two quite different functions. It is the measure of value as the social incarnation of human labour; it is the standard of prices as a quantity of metal with a fixed weight. As the measure of value it serves to convert the values of all the manifold commodities into prices, into imaginary quantities of gold; as the standard of price, it measures those quantities of gold. The measure of values measures commodities considered as values; the standard of price measures on the contrary, quantities of gold by a unit quantity of gold, not the value of one quantity of gold by the weight of another.
>
> (Marx 1976, 192; 1968a, 113)

To do as Ricardo does in "On Value" is simply to define relative prices of every commodity through the concept of price (*in casu*, the genesis of the price of gold) itself, i.e. a blatant self-contradiction, *insofar* as the aim is to define commodity prices as related to their labour values – an operation which indisputably is the same as giving "price" its general definition.

It seems that Ricardo was originally on watch for this problem. In December 1815, while preparing the *Principles*, he wrote in a letter to James Mill:

> I know I shall soon be stopped by the word "price".
>
> (Ricardo, 1815, 348; see Sraffa 1951–1952, xiv)[20]

Ricardo here takes it as a given that a commodity is *exchanged* for gold in the setting of its price.

In his study of *Principles* after 1861, traceable in the *Theorien über den Mehrwert*, Marx criticized Ricardo's text directly:

> While it [the gold] . . . thus represents a relatively unchanged [*unverändertes*] medium, it is absolutely inconceivable how any relative combination inside it between capital fixe and circulant, compared with the commodities, can create a difference. But here we have to do with Ric[ardo']s *false presupposition* that money, in so far as it functions as means of circulation, is exchanged [*ausgetauscht*] commodity against commodities. The commodities are evaluated in it before they circulate.
>
> (Marx 1968e, 198)

This interpretation is correct. In Ricardo, there is, in general, a confusion between immediate exchange and circulation, in the sense that circulation is taken to consist of a series of "commodity metamorphoses" (Marx), formed as barter-like exchanges. We have already seen how Marx criticized this view in his work of 1859.

True, a careful reading of "On Foreign Trade" indicates that Ricardo separates the two movements he admixes on other occasions. But that happens only because on the world market it is evident that the "exchange" involves not one but two currencies, so that this market has no barter structure and necessarily, superficially considered, stands out in comparison to capitalist domestic markets. Here, Ricardo says of the circulation movement:

> The exchange is never ascertained by estimating the comparative value of money in corn, cloth, or any commodity whatever, but by estimating the value of the currency of one country in the currency of another.
>
> (Ricardo 1969, 91)

Here, it seems to be presupposed that the first-mentioned kind of "estimation" is the one to be found inside the national economy. This estimation seems to be thought of by Ricardo as a series of equations between the money-commodity and its partners on the commodity market, while for Marx this estimation is already presupposed as a pre-circulation measuring. In this situation, the question arises as to why Ricardo would rule out that an estimation of the kind that he ascribes to the world market should be administered on the domestic market. It does not solve any problem just to suppose, as Ricardo does, that the estimation can be made the way it is because we have to deal with currencies, because the stipulation of these currencies through each other is a function of measuring – inside each nation – of a given weight of gold against any specific piece of labour time incorporated in any commodity. In the richer nation, a greater mass of commodities will correspond to a given weight of gold than in a poorer country, supposing, for the sake of illustration, that both nations refer to a gold industry that produces a given mass in the same time. But to accomplish such a calculation the commodities inside both nations must have measured their value in gold already – which is precisely the Marxian theory.

Ricardo's view, then, more or less openly admitted, is that every inner capitalist market is economically *undetermined*.[21] Why? Because, as has been contended by his followers – *via* Bortkiewicz's criticism of Marx in 1906–1907 (Bortkiewicz 1906–1907; 1907), vindicated basically by P.M. Sweezy in 1942 (Sweezy 1942) and brought on and on by hundreds of somewhat uncritical Marxisant theoreticians – *if* all industries in a nation (or in an equation set!) have their product prices changed according to composition changes in the gold industry (which produces the medium product), one needs independent variables to make the system "determined", i.e. the capitalist system cannot be presented as a system under self-produced, strict and transparent laws. (See Sandemose 1973, 1976, 2004.)

However, as soon as it is seen that no medium commodity need exist (because an exchange of "commodity against commodities" is not a circulation feature) and that what is needed is simply a concept of abstract human labour time, there is no longer a place for those indeterminacies which Bortkiewicz meant to find; furthermore, there remains, on the original, unshattered Marxian premises, an univocal and rational logical connection between the level of average profits and the amount of *ground rent* which is possible inside the given economy; and, not least, the wage level, which modern Ricardians are so apt to select as their independent variable, can be presented as a variable under the domination of the accumulation of capital. In short, the three central movements of distribution between the main social classes, which Ricardo took to be the main subject of political economy, are united in a logical whole in Marx's version of the theory of value.

5.8 Bourgeois post-Ricardian theory of trade: vulgar theory of classes

One might believe that an analysis like Ricardo's was not liable to be misused in imperialistic directions, but unfortunately that is not so. The still dominant bourgeois theory on international trade, the so-called Heckscher–Ohlin–Samuelson model (Sandemose 2010, 158–159), is clearly untenable, even though it contains a Ricardian point.

The model contends that the commodity a nation would choose to produce in what we might call an "Anglo-Portuguese" situation, i.e. the one that gives the most obvious comparative advantage among others, will be the one that from case to case corresponds most adequately to a production which employs a relatively large part of one of the three "factors of production": land, labour power and capital. A poor country, like Kenya or Gambia, can benefit "comparatively" by exporting a commodity which requires large investment in labour power (and little in land and/or capital), because the country has scarce resources of "capital" or (privately owned) land.

This ideological fantasy includes the product, e.g. peanuts, being sold to countries with plentiful land and capital compared to labour power (i.e. a rich, industrialized country), which can then specialize and sell rare minerals and high-tech products the other way. This mystification, easily unveiled, has formed the ideological background for many a rarity – such as when the IMF in the late 1980s proposed to subsidize nut cultivation in Gambia (peanuts having been made expensive in the rich world), while the same institution, in the name of free trade, worked for abolishing subsidies for corn products (Carney 1994, 185). This de facto sabotaging of any serious trade goes on while bourgeois economists keep insisting that "sooner or later" there will take place an equalization on the world market which – in accordance with Ricardo's theory – will mean that poor countries do produce peanuts and a further, narrower range of agricutral-horticultural products.

It is unnecesssary to go ahead with polemic against such presentations. What is interesting about them is that they are taken seriously at all, and the fact that they are founded precisely on the existence of that interactive totality of the three reciprocally contradictory elements – capital, landed property and wage labour – which was the most important result of the industrial revolution in the West and which contrasts so deeply with the actually existing *unity* of manufacture and agriculture in "third world" countries. At the same time, they clarify that bourgeois theories simply do not observe that inequalities between nations on the world market are always to the advantage of nations of one specific type and always to the disadvantage of nations of specific other types. These theories will want to rid themselves of every serious attempt at type classifications; and the theoretical weapon best adapted to spread the vulgarities that follow is the attempts to lead the focus away from analysis of the world market as a *commodity* market.

The paradigm for these attempts, the Heckscher–Ohlin–Samuelson model, can reasonably be understood as a result of the specific logical difficulties which persisted in the Ricardian model – specifically, its final "indeterminacy", which in itself must have been a nuisance to any theoretician.

Marxian theory is well adapted to expose this viewpoint in the history of economic science, since Marx's preliminary methodological drafts on economic theory, published as the *Grundrisse*, can in great part be seen as a criticism precisely of Ricardo's view of the three-class distribution of wealth. At the time he was writing the *Grundrisse*, Marx was not familiar with Ricardo's theory in every detail; however, his criticism concentrated on the role of the classic triad capital–wage labour–landed property inside modern economic theory at large, and he focused on the more or less hiddden presuppositions of the use of those categories in classical political economy. In certain passages (Marx 1993, 264, 279, 512; 1953, 175, 188, 412), he combined analysis of the frames of the reciprocal action (*Aktion*) between the three respective classes with three themes in particular: 1) the "original accumulation of capital" and its expropriation of countryside population from its property; 2) the falling rate of profit in a developed, accumulating capitalist economy; and 3) the latter resulting in the rising price of land and the functional result of keeping members of the working class away from landed property. He set up the corresponding theorems in his developed price theory in *Capital* I–III.[22]

5.9 Some denser comments on intensity of labour

I shall now attempt to set up a more general scheme for an analysis of intensification of labour.

Marx's theory of international values in fact presupposes the intensive magnitude of labour time – as a phenomenon present in all nations taking part in foreign trade – as the basis of relations on the world market, i.e. partly as condition for the very diversity on that market, partly for the social relations that dictate the condition for entry into that market.

As we saw, the argument for the scale character of international economic relations is, according to Marx, directly dependent on labour intensity. It is the core of the definition of labour as value substance, and the international scale [*Stufenleiter*] depends solely on the difference in intensity (Marx 1976, 702; 1968a, 584). Secondly, according to Marx, there is one relation of intensity that is "even more" important for the modification of the law of value here, namely that "national labour which is more productive also counts as more intensive". All these formulations seem to indicate that in his opinion the situation on the world market tends to *limit* competition between the actors, which is the same as saying that it favours a *status quo* relating to their reciprocal relations.

This is because inside nations there is a competition which, as we saw, tends to sublate differences in intensity. That is precisely the reason we can say that intensity has a priority over productivity as such: it is the uneven ups and downs *in intensity* that steadily reproduce the productivity on higher levels. And this is the competitive mechanism that is not present on the world market, unless submarkets are overfilled with commodities.

On the other hand, if markets *are* overfilled, the reawakening of competition through price wars naturally favours big suppliers, which, at least in the sector for means of production for further development of poor nations, are most central. The more advanced capitalist nations will to some degree function as an obstacle for market entry.

Inside the nation – so to speak, in the trenches where production for world-market strife is made – the concept of intensity has a dual nature. Firstly, it shows how one kind of competition works inside a branch, generating a given socially necessary labour time for a given kind of product. This intraspherical competition is then accompanied by an interspherical one, where what is generated is an average rate of profit. This second kind of competition is only possible in a nation-state with a relatively high population density, an advanced financial-institutional system and a material infrastructure of some capacity. It implies unhampered movement of persons and goods, not least an advanced monetary system. These are conditions for a developed accumulation of capital, and, historically, it has been possible to develop them exclusively inside bourgeois nation-states. So what we are looking at here are the very presuppositions for a world market. There is a historical side to this: the poor nation of today is, as nation, a creature of advanced capitalism in its imperialist and colonialist garment. This represents the second element of the "dual" nature of intensification of labour: the capacity of the world's leading industrial forces to set their stamp on the totality.

The finished and rounded-off form of the nation-state, its capitalist character included, is in turn the society whose *membra disjecta* we meet in Marx's analytical exposition in *Capital*. Through all its chapters, the *national* character of the object is made clear. The *capitalist mode of production* arises inside a nation-state and so does the *capitalist social formation*, when the state of modern landed property is dragged into the ambience through the analyses of the forms of ground rent in *Capital* III.

The first important instance, and perhaps even the basic and dominating one, concerns the analysis in the very first chapter of the value-producing labour. Belonging to a "society" here means belonging to a nation:

> Socially necessary labour-time is the labour-time required to produce any use-value under the conditions of production normal for a given society and with the average degree of skill and intensity of labour prevalent in that society.
>
> (Marx 1976, 129; 1968a, 53)

And Marx proceeds immediately with an example relating to, and limited to, the introduction of power looms to England.

Marx often uses the term "intensification" (and similar ones) of labour with terms like "skill" and "skilled" (and "complicated" labour, etc.). In the *Principles*, we find a similar point: a reader will note that when Ricardo in his chapter on foreign trade analyses the predominance of "manufacture" (and machinery) of one nation compared to another, he is not satisfied with such terms and returns to the *movement of precious metals* to describe the situation:

> Thus, then, it appears that the improvement of a manufacture in any country tends to alter the distribution of the precious metals among the nations of the world: it tends to increase the quantity of commodities at the same time that it raises general prices in the country where the improvement takes place.
>
> (Ricardo 1969, 87)

Here, we are talking of relative nominal prices and of their "general" level in the industrialized nation – which in this example is England. Still, this results from a movement in the real economy, since the relative mass of commodities in comparison with gold is unchanged. So what Ricardo is telling us is that the mass of values is enhanced *pari passu* with the mass of use values – a situation which so far is identical with the one that Marx takes as a result of intensification of labour in England relative to other nations. What happens here is only that Marx, unlike Ricardo, goes further along the causal chain and finds that the enhanced mass of gold imported to England (which he does not mention explicitly here) must result from an enhanced mass of value-producing labour in England.

Marx's "intensity" of labour, however, has another meaning, quite different from "skill". Labour intensity for Marx is an aspect of human labour time itself and is related to Ricardo's example only to the extent that human labour in the abstract has its imagined predicate in gold-producing labour. But it is now necessary to specify this term, which in Marx relates to a concept of labour time in a much more fundamental way than we have noted up to this point.

Intensification is a phenomenon that can appear in relation to every kind of labour, even the most primitive. Still, the most glaring example is the introduction of real machinery on a broad basis after the British factory laws at the end of the 1840s. The reduction of the length of the legal working day forced capitalists to augment value production by condensing it instead – or, more to the point, a capitalist now had to shorten the working day in order to intensify labour, because the strain would otherwise have killed the worker. Under such a condition, one gets "the inversion [*Umschlag*] of extensive magnitude into intensive nagnitude, or magnitude of degree" (Marx 1976, 533; Marx 1968a, 431), i.e. a contradiction inside the concept of labour time itself:

> This compression of a greater mass of labour into a given period now counts for what it really is, namely an increase in the quantity of labour. In addition to the measure of its "extensive magnitude", labour time now acquires a measure of its intensity, or degree of density. The denser hour of the 10-hour working day contains more labour, i.e. expended labour power, than the more porous hour of the 12-hour working day. Thus the product of one of the 10 hours has as much value as the product of $1\frac{1}{5}$ of the 12 hours, or even more.
>
> (Marx 1976, 534; 1968a, 433)

Intensification matures the tendency of capital to be "convert[ing] every improvement in machinery into a more effective means for *soaking up labour-power* [*Aussauger der Arbeitskraft*]" (Marx 1976, 542; 1968a, 440), i.e. for shaping the structure for real subsumption and an average rate of profits.

The upshot is that there is a need for a more precise definition of *time* than was given hitherto in the Marxian corpus. It seems clear that time must itself be seen as the form of human labour, as Marx saw it in the *Grundrisse*, where he called labour "the very temporality of things, their *Zeitlichkeit, als ihre Formung durch die lebendige Zeit*" (1993, 361; 1953, 266).

However, we do not need to allocate any more space to this, since any labour, as a living process, is filled with a certain intensity, so that the possibilities of condensation (and its opposite) must be, or must have been, integrated from the start into the concept of value-producing labour.

First and foremost, we must underscore how intensification of labour is a predominant feature of the work extorted from the subjects in Marx's *real subsumption of labour* under capital. We have already considered this term, and, on the contrary, his term "formal subsumption", i.e. tying the worker to the capital relation simply through the wage, where the capitalist has few material means to subject the free worker. Such a subsumption was the rule until the need for intensification broke through – a fact which also in part explains why capitalism easily could abolish slavery: the free worker had turned himself into a creature bound under the command of a machine independent of him. Society at large could, and can, now fancy itself as a true commonwealth of free mankind, and tacitly abstract from the question of the ownership of the said machine.[23]

5.10　The "integrating parts" of the world market

The commodities produced by this most developed, anonymous capital represent the most advanced entities on the world market. Other entities exist there – generated by value-producing firms or persons belonging to other modes of production. Since we talk about a *market*, all things have an (exchange) value, i.e. they are commodities. But they are commodities produced under qualitatively different circumstances. They can be produced by state-owned companies which only accessorily adopt a value-form, i.e. just to gain a reward on the market; they can be produced by petty-bourgeois artisans, owning their own means of labour; and they can be produced by capitalist or non-capitalist land tenants who simultaneously work in a non-capitalist form, i.e. without wage workers. Among producers of this last kind, there are many who – especially if living in "poor" countries – work under conditions which Marxists often term "simple commodity production".[24]

Different modes of production such as these have, as we saw, a kind of non-dynamic co-existence on the world market, in the sense that they do not appear as functions of their own special background in property relations but simply as entities thrown out from "integrating" *countries*. They appear behind specific masks whose only internal difference lies in the value of their currency.

As an example, let us suppose there existed production of a certain exclusive groundnut in Mali. It is the only one of its kind, and if it hits the world market, it will count as a specific species of commodity, separated from any other nut. Let us say that the production is by nature confined to a small field, which limits the possible number of workers, say to 100. Let us suppose that these workers all have a daily outlet of floating labour power which is identical with any American worker producing stainless steel. In that case, they too, in the course of one day, would bring forward a commodity economically similar to a long ton of stainless steel. Say that this commodity consists of 100 tonnes of groundnuts.

Now, it is not quite improbable that the material part of the long ton and the material part of the 100 tonnes which correspond to the value added of the two commodities would sell for an identical sum on the world market – if, that is, the nuts had been produced in the US, or in a country with a currency of the same strength as the US dollar – for the buyer on the international market exchanges the currency of his own homeland to buy the CFA francs the seller must acquire to buy the Mali labour power, etc. Any currency has its value determined by the intensity and productivity (of all commodity production) inside the whole currency area. In a very poor nation such as Mali, the 100 groundnut workers cannot do much to heighten the average. If the buyers come from a decidedly rich nation, the result is an outsluicing of Mali labour values and their appropration through citizens in nations where the labour outlet is remunerated in a very short and "condensed" time span.

This last point needs specification: as mentioned, it is relatively easy to accept that the productivity of labour in the course of, e.g., four hours of continuous work at a given time with a given technical mode of production is a *measurable* function of a given outlet of force through the human psychophysical system.

Up to this point, the value-producing labour in two completely different branches – for groundnuts and for stainless steel – can meaningfully be compared, as we tried so show. But, on the other hand, and conditioned by the point of departure, we will find that the two processes can only with difficulty be compared if we look at their inherent possibilities to begin a process of *intensification* of labour.

Relatively simple agricultural work, as we may suppose is active in the groundnut field, is relatively more difficult to intensify than machine work. It can be done, as when one adds a net to a fork to stop nuts from rolling back to the ground. Then we have an intensification, as long as the worker keeps his mind on the art of holding the fork stable in a more complicated way than before. Some of the force that was present in the worker in the operation as it was before, but did not need to be activated, now passes into the work process proper and heightens the workers' psychical concentration in the generating of the product. But, evidently, such possibilities are poorer in property relations which de facto forbid mechanization than they are in countries that are integrated in structures of large-scale industry. As we saw above, steady intensification is apparent in the very nature of more advanced technology.

Now it is clear that in the ("Western") home countries of this technology, the "double" kind of competition prevails, so that it takes a relatively short time before inter-branch firms gain intensity advantages and lose them to competitors, resulting in differences in intensity levelling out and presenting us with a new level of productivity of labour. Still, the rise of this productivity by way of intensity, and the fact that productivity changes in poor countries are much more difficult to develop, gives some hints about the relatively high differences of productivity between developed capitalism and pre-capitalist or formal-subsumption-based economies.

Actually, it is against the background of such viewpoints on industrial development that we are best equipped to tackle the question of whether there is an "unequal exchange" hidden in the circulation of commodities-and-currencies on the world market.

Certainly, the answer will be negative: any theory of unequal exchange is ideological and at odds with reasonable presuppositions about the world economy. Commodity production is in every corner of the world committed to labour values. But the integration of this very fact happens only on the world market, whose only possible "integrating parts" are currency-bearing entities: nations or bands of nations. "Value" and "exchange value" are generated inside the entities in question (albeit they are universal categories). Groundnuts from Mali tend to be sold at their value on the world market, without any injustice baked into the operation. The problem is only that the product which is, eventually, exchanged against it from a richer nation may cost just a fraction of the mass of labour inside that nation. The exchange, or, better, the transfer effectuated by the simple circulation, is asymmetrical in the sense that the richer nation accomplishes it with a much lesser outlet of labour and *a fortiori* with a relatively far greater gain of labour than the poorer nation. It is in practice a very difficult question whether or not this weakens the poorer nation relatively. I cannot discuss that here. On the other hand, it is cleat enough that wage differences haves no possible place in the question.

Commodity price levels on the world market are a direct function of their *labour* content relatively to efficiency, intensity and productivity in their homeland; they are thus *values*, and as *prices* they are only modified by the "scale" of the world market. All kinds of commodity production may meet each other here.

5.11 Patrimonial capitalist production

In addition to the types of merchandise production we have just summarized, there is a conspicuous one often underrated and more often simply ignored. What is at stake is a clearly delimited group inside a kind of production which Marx sees as generated from what he calls "formal subsumption" of labour under capital. An important point as regards the genesis of this form is the following quote from *Capital* I:

> [Given that] . . . the working day is already divided into two parts, necessary labour and surplus labour. In order to prolong the surplus labour, the necessary labour is shortened by methods for producing the equivalent of the wage of labour in a shorter time. The production of absolute surplus-value turns exclusively on the length of the working day, whereas the production of relative surplus-value completely revolutionizes the technical processes of labour and the groupings into which society is divided.
>
> It therefore requires a specifically capitalist mode of production, a mode of production which, along with its methods, means and conditions, arises and develops *spontaneously* on the basis of the formal subsumption of labour under capital. This formal subsumption is then replaced by a real subsumption.
>
> It will be sufficient if we merely refer to *certain hybrid forms*, in which although surplus labour is not extorted by direct compulsion from the producer, the producer has not yet become formally subordinate to capital.
>
> (Marx 1976, 645; 1968a, 533)

The "industrial revolution" in the West may be analysed using the *manufacture* system as an essential background.[25] The development of this special form of capitalism in the period ca. 1500–1800 helps to explain the rise of "machinery and large-scale industry". This, however, does not mean that it could explain such a development in the case of other countries or periods; nor does it mean that manufacture must in itself lead to large-scale industry.

It is important not to tie the concept of formal subsumption under capital in production to handicraft work alone. In Marx's exposition in *Capital*, the concept is first introduced immediately after the section comparing manufacture and large-scale industry. Since his picture of manufacture here in the main took its point of departure from a handicraft model which was more in style with the continental situation than with the British one, it is easily done to identify his concept of formal subsumption in production with it.[26]

However, it is just as simple to determine that this would be a misunderstanding. Marx clearly denotes that the formal subsumption emerges when capital "takes over an *existing labour process*, developed from diverse and more archaic modes of production" (Marx 1969, 54). He then proceeds with examples, mentioning "handicrafts, [or] a form of cultivation in agriculture which corresponds to a small, independent peasants' economy". Furthermore, he underscores that such labour, when taken up under the wings of capital, may go through important changes without any revolution in the mode of production, something which would have implied that the subsumption under capital had turned out to be *real*. What he hints at, then, is the possibility of a prolonged period of capitalist production, even independent of the structure of actual manufacture on the European continent between 1500 and 1800.

We now turn to the present-day world market, which brings to light an important difference in the structure of capitalist firms and companies that feed it with commodities.

To understand the difference and its contemporary influence and significance, we have to go the whole way back to those elements of the Western European experience Marx calls "the so-called primitive accumulation", which appeared in and dominated England under the the Tudors (roughly the whole of the sixteenth century). More specifically, as we have seen in the previous chapter, those elements are the expropriation of the country people (*Landvolk*) from all kinds of property of the soil, *and* the crushing of the feudal *Gefolgschaften*. Once more with Steuart and Marx:

> A mass of "free" and unattached proletarians were hurled onto the labour-market by the dissolution of the bands of feudal retainers, who, as Sir James Steuart correctly remarked, "everywhere uselessly filled house and castle".
>
> (Marx 1976, 878; 1968a, 746)

The upshot was that the making of a British working class commenced with the development of expropriation, on the one hand, and, on the other, the breaking down of physical feudal class power. The whole process was initiated by feudal overlords with genes passing back to the upper nobility, formed through the politics of Norman conquerors from 1066 on. Its members could afford to get rid of their lesser peers and lackeys because they were already in a de facto alliance with an upcoming bourgeoisie both on land and in towns, riding the wave of the upcoming wool production and trade. This unique development, while retaining a thin stratum of extremely well-to-do overlords, cleared the political field for the bourgeoisie and made the oncoming bourgeois revolution into a process led by the landed gentry.

An essential difference from the first contry outside of the West to initiate a capitalist industry on a broader scale, Japan, is conspicuous. Industrialization in Japan emerged around 1860 through imperial orders (as a movement against "aliens"), and the practical work was led by a class of strong still-feudal, quasi-capitalist lords, politically supported by huge and resourceful groups of samurai and other feudal retainers.

The notable result was a capitalist industry, i.e. manufacture with wage-labourers, without a radical expulsion of country people from property. The "proletariat" was not truly one consisting of people "owning only their own kids" – *proles*. (Still today, the tying of a large number of the Japanese proletariat by loyalty to the patrimonial working place is conspicuous.) And, on the other hand, the capitalists were not pure "character masks" for anonymous capital, which in the West already from the 1840s had taken the extreme form of share companies – *sociétés anonymes*. On the contrary, the joint-stock company was alien to Japanese society – and so it is still today. That reflects a capitalist industry which has not surpassed the level of formal subsumption of workers under capital.

Expressions like "shares" are misleading in this case, even if they are commonly used. We have before us a system where equities are sold not under the ("Western") presupposition that any one of them gives the possessor the right to handle it as he likes but, on the contrary, under the presupposition that the buyer tacitly accepts a difference of class between them. To illustrate, we bring an empirical table (Table 5.2) by the Japanese economist Takatoshi Ito (1992, 181).

What we see here are six groups of the *zaibatsu* type, in the specific (*keiretsu*) form it assumed after the reforms which followed the Great Depression and the policy promoted by the occupying US regime after 1945.

The numbers are from an investigation published in 1987. The example is relevant here because its motivating principle does not differ in any substantial way from the post-World War II set-up, nor from the earlier *zaibatsu* structure (Mitsui, Mitsubishi and Sumitomo were already leading *zaibatsu* in the Meiji period).

By "interlocked" shares Ito means the quantity par in equities in a firm owned by other firms in the group. Mitsui, e.g., owns 17.10 per cent of the shares in the 24 companies in the business area which then are "members" of Mitsui.

The numbers highlight averages from a definite business area, where, e.g., Mitsubishi steers 29 companies. Let us suppose that among these 29 there is a

Table 5.2 Economic magnitudes in six business groups

Selected zaibatsu (keiretsu)	Number of member firms	Interlocked shares in %, on average	Average of intra-group loans in %
Mitsui	24	17.10	21.94
Mitsubishi	29	27.80	20.17
Sumitomo	20	24.22	24.53
Fuyo	29	15.61	18.20
Sanwa	44	16.47	18.51
Ikkan	47	12.49	11.18

company called Zero, where 27.80 per cent of the "shares" are owned by Mitsubishi: then we know that this fraction is owned by a maximum of 28 other members of the Mitsubishi conglomerate. Also, for the sake of illustration, suppose that 20.17 per cent of the capital inside Zero is brought forward through loans from these 28 members.

In the Japanese "system" (it should be called a placebo system), the above implies that a firm like Zero is steered by a quantity of shares that represents 27.80 per cent of the capital. The corresponding capitalists cooperate tightly and intimately under their umbrella, but their dominance is about more than technical finesse: it has to do with a publicly accepted order of things, though one not strictly accepted judicially.[27] It is based on personal power relations, with no clear boundaries to mafia-like activity, and has a background in Japanese feudalism.

As mentioned, Japan was the first non-Western country that came to be dominated by a capitalist mode of production. Capitalist tendencies were present just as early in Russia, but Japan remains the true proto-example, essentially because of the feudal system, which made the transition smooth, effective and dominant – a parallel to Western Europe.

Another characteristic makes the Japanese case important, namely that Japan remains the only country outside of the West and its offshoots and dominions in Northern America and Oceania where a significant capitalist sector inside the economy is built on feudal relations. In all other such countries, be they in Latin America, Asia or Africa, capitalist economic relations are being built, tentatively, on "Asiatic" forms, i.e. on classical despotic forms where basic economic features are characterized by an inert unity of handicraft-and-manufacture with agriculture – including, most of all, the unity of their respective property forms.

In essence, the form of capitalism that is present in all these patrimonial countries has *cartelization* as a common characteristic. Each and every *keiretsu* (to continue to use this Japanese term) tends to have offshoots in as many branches as possible – all, of course, cooperating tightly according to central plans. The anarchic essence in the system comes to the fore when we realize that there is virtually no interspherical competition in such a "capitalist" system. All *keiretsu* may have shoe producers in their ranks – normally, just a few – so it is natural that there is competition in the shoe branch: the competitors are mainly *keiretsu* offshoots. Usually, there are also non-*keiretsu* firms taking part, but always to a lesser degree. This competition, often fierce, is the main impulse in disciplining the propertyless working class in such a society.

Consequently, intraspherical competition must be taken to be a general phenomenon in the (formal) capitalist structure eventually present in the "third world" countries.

However, interspherical competition, which in real, Western capitalism is the decisive factor in establishing an infrastructure and an active, common cultural society, etc., is not present in the patrimonial "third world" capitalist structure – no more than real subsumption under capital is present. The infrastructure is not capitalistically generated. Its "subsumption" is *formal*, and it might be called "formal capitalism".

The reason is obvious: if this were the case, the different *keiretsu*, the *subjects* of competitive activity, would be competing against themselves interspherically, for they own, at least ideally and in principle, companies which produce material commodities or commodity parts in every sphere. And it is clear that a Mitsui producer of radio components is not allowed to compete against a Mitsui textile producer. On the contrary, each and every *keiretsu* has a centralized system of banking and financial policies to avoid such results.

Such "financial cliques" (a common translation for *keiretsu*) are a common feature in societies with a social and historical background in structures which, in advanced politico-economical thinking, were called "asiatic" – as in the Marxian concepts of "Asiatic mode of production" or "Asiatic social formation". The archetype seems to be – even for somewhat one-sided theoreticians such as Karl Wittfogel – the Indian village system, with its status-work (combining every person with the a specific type of work) and collective possession of agricultural plots.[28]

These are complicated matters, all too intricate to be treated adequately in the present chapter. But perhaps the argument for an "Asiatic" patrimonial tendency in "third world" economies can be made in a simpler way.

According to classic theoreticians, with whom the present writer agrees, the last and fundamental cause of the inert, unchangeable nature of Asian societies, as they appeared at least until recently, is, as already hinted at, the unity between "agriculture and industry", to use Marx's expression. Western dynamic development since the Tudors, Marx argued, was caused by the separation of landed property – the principle of all former modes of possession and dominance – from the property forms that resided in handicrafts and industrial means and products. As regards the classical Indian village (which, according Marx, was a direct original form, even of the Russian village), such a development was unthinkable there.

Marx showed, especially in crucial passages in the first and third volumes of *Capital*, that the bloody acts that helped to break up the feudal structure and separate agriculture from industry to enforce a new capitalist order, are internally reproduced by peaceful economic means inside capitalist society:

1 Real subsumption of workers on capitalist premises, massively rising intensity and productivity of labour, is in the last instance effectuated through a system of private property escalated to a unique level that allows not only for intraspherical but also interspherical competition.
2 This Janus-faced, double-natured competition ensures that commodity prices inside the national economy take the form of Marxian "production prices".
3 This system of capitalist price-setting goes on independently of the pricing of products of agriculture and other practices (viz., excavation), which are partly dependent on the old principles of landed property. These prices orbit around values, not production prices.
4 The differences between these price structures, very important for the social and political relations between classes in any capitalist nation, lose their direct importance on the world market, whose competition – at least in

principle – allows for a set of prices orbiting around "international *values*" defined through the "universal labour".

5 The dynamic which, through the average rate of profits, establishes the industrial price level thereby also establishes it for products from economic acrivity based on landed property. The quantitative difference (between price of production and value) is in each case, *contra* Bortkiewiczian ideas, completely determinate, just like the industrial price level itself.

6 The advanced Janusian competition between industrial capitals leads to an accumulation that tends to be relentless. As a consequence, one gets a "law of the tendential fall of the rate of profits" (Marx 1968c, 221–277).

7 This tendential fall leads to a corresponding fall in the rate of interest.

8 This latter tendency leads to a corresponding rise in the *price* of the soil (which is capitalized ground rent).

9 As a consequence, wage labourers, doomed to an existence based on scarce resources, are excluded from escaping the capitalist system through acquiring landed property.

10 It is therefore shown that the "factors" of traditional and modern mainstream political economy lie at the bottom of a dialectics that forms the capitalist social formation into a self-generating and self-sustaining totality.

Some consequences relating to scientific method should briefly be mentioned here. Firstly, the very idea of an integrated whole in which categories like labour, land and "capital" are present stems from the intellectual and cultural situation developed in post-Napoleonic Europe. But rigid categories did not rise from the ground there; rather, men came to be conscious of their totality and their own place in it. In perceiving "categories", they in fact perceived men with specific interests attracting or repulsing each other – an internecine warfare of the Hobbesian calibre.

The idea, generated in the twentieth century, that a theory of three factors, an ideological construction that Marx labelled the "trinitarian (or Trinity) formula", could solve the problems of another ideological construction, namely political economy in general, is parasitic on this original historical situation.

This means that the "formula", if it is serious at all, should be taken as a model only for an economy on a certain historical stage. It cannot be taken seriously if its fetishized appearance form cannot be understood as a result of an actually realized dialectics between workers, capitalists and landowners. This form, however, is present in Western culture only, and not prior to the days of the Napoleonic *L'Empire des Francais*.

It is quite another matter that the perceived action between the animal spirits inside the categories are absurdistically conceived. What happened in the history of those categories was that an abundance of free labour resulted from the expropriation of land into the possession of a small minority of hands and its transformation to a source of gigantic agricultural incomes. (The vulgar contemporary theory, on the contrary, takes a mass of free labour to be an object of investment when the land is *not* there as an object of investment.) Furthermore, workers were not freed from the psychophysical golden chains tying them to the old land-based economy before capital stood before them as an alien force and reforged those chains: capital did not emerge before the mass of free hands was already there; it was not the result of lone initiatives to turn to capital when the labour was in small supply. And, to be sure, to invest in capital is not to invest in money but to invest money in materials that are withdrawn from the property of the hands which are asked to work, a role these latter could not fill if there was no material in which to invest.

Now, the characteristics and conclusions described above as belonging to a world of "real subsumption" can only to a lesser degree be ascribed to systems based on formal subsumption of capital. The following points are crucial in comparison, and stand out as soon as we focus on those economies:

1   The reduction to formal subsumption of workers excludes interspherical competition and therefore is not compatible with a national market based on production prices.
2   There exists a competition inside branches only, which warrants a price level based directly on labour *values*.
3   While in the Western system capitals in spheres with low composition of capital transfer parts of their value product to capitals in spheres with high composition, this mechanism is not present in "third world" countries. Instead, *keiretsu* and similar organisations are in a position to *lose* money relatively, by selling high-composition products at their values. They are then in position to compensate through undisturbed sales at values in their own low-composition companies.
4   Some consequences of the latter structure are evened out by the markedly export-minded industrial structures in poor countries. On the world market, sale at values – albeit modified by the scale of universal labour – is the rule. There is no reason to suppose that "third world" commodities for export are priced at large deviations from their international values. Consequently, action on the world market favours such industries indirectly, and, on the other hand, they favour the world-market action.
5   This self-destructive dynamic, that takes the drive to foreign trade to be the saviour of the system, is the most essential obstacle to true economic development in the semi-advanced countries in the "third world". This role does *certainly not* belong to interventions from developed imperialistic economies.
6   Compared with relations in the Western system, average national profit rates will tend to fall, since intraspherical competition may lead to a rising organic composition of capital. The capacity to take the economy out of such a sloping development is hampered by the extreme privatization (better: *keiretsu*ization) of financial systems (note the Japanese crisis persisting twenty-five years from 1990).
7   Likewise, there will be a tendency for the rate of interest to fall, and a low rate can plague the economy for very long periods, a condition which perhaps can be sublated only by a war economy.

8 The significance of there being a high price of soil will, however, be diminished by the main basic factor leading to the exclusion of real subsumption in industry, namely the absence of a clearly defined private property of soil.[29]

9 On the other hand, since the system is devoid of a set of production prices, there is no clear econonomically formulated limit to ground rent and the misuse of natural resouces on land, including labour forces of all kinds – traditional and modern.[30] The members of the landowning class therefore make up a viable force in patrimonial capitalism, in distinction from Western countries.

10 For the same reasons, the members of the landowning class and the members of the capitalist class intermingle robustly and significantly. Because of the existence of wage labour and, consequently, of a distinct industrial capitalism, the absolute contradiction between the categories of "capital" and "landed property" is upheld. But the solution of the contradiction is sought in a downplayed rate of capital accumulation. In fact, being a landowner sets an individual in much the same social situation as a factory owner, which proves that the old ideal of unity between manufacture and agriculture remains. But the contradiction between the forms *of property* is of course upheld. A landed property can never be capitalist as such.

Let us discuss these last points a little further. A main issue in our exposition is that capitalist activity in poor countries relies on formal subsumption of the workforce. This means that the wage form, not regular machinery, is the main instrument in enforcing work discipline. In the Western European form of the genesis of capitalism, this leads to a continuous lament from owners on the lack of discipline: "Hence the complaint that the workers lack discipline runs through the whole period of manufacture" (Marx 1976, 490; Marx 1968a, 390). That this is a serious problem in the great majority of manual work processes in patrimonial industry seems clear, although it is to some extent hidden and compensated for by the use of military-like drills vis-à-vis the work-force. It was present to such a degree in Russian industry, before 1917 as well as before 1991 and before 2017, that one could ascribe that country's economic breakdown to it. While the degree of undisciplined work may vary, it is always there, although it can be cured periodically to an astonishing degree when procuction is led by FDI. An analysis of labour productivity tells us a great deal about discipline.[31]

However, the most basic relation when it comes to estimating the degree of subsumption of labour under capital is research-guided intuition into the significance of original property relations in the countryside; for here, in every capitalist nation, the basis from which capital has to accomplish expropriation is present. In Tudor England, the expropriation was radical, and its diverse means, not least the unprecedented rise in the Western European population, made it an enduring success for the whole of Western capitalist order. Nothing keeps people in their place in industrial society more than the forlorn hope of getting back to the old order. The patrimonial capitalism of our time, however, has never been able to dominate the populace in this way. Let us take an example of perhaps the most impressive kind, since it concerns the largest national population presently, which is also, allegedly, the biggest exporter of goods to the world market.

Cindy Fan (2009, passim) writes of the Chinese working class that its country-side is still the basis of safety for village migrants and their families. Firstly, these peasants (i.e. "migration workers") have access to agricultural land; secondly, people have no right to sell this land, and change of use is dependent on "govern-ment authorities". Thirdly, Fan finds that the system of migrant work, rather than loosening the ties with the countryside, has the contrary effect of joining migrant families in the task of conserving rights of use, as a safety valve in the case of industrial slumps. This socially conditioned attraction between wage worker and landed property also has to do with the fact that a right to a housing site is funda-mental to so many Chinese, being a sign that they can marry and form a family, i..e. take part in reconstructing precisely the more fundamental institutions of old. Unfortunately, such an end result may represent a universal tendency in the devel-opment of what are misguidedly called "emerging markets".

5.12 Some perspectives

The most important aim of this chapter was to uncover the nature of a certain theory (and to my mind a vulgar one) of "factors" of production, as employed in the study of international trade, and a need for connecting this theory with more advanced ones soon materialized. I have tried to expose an ideological proximity between what is here called the theory of "factors" and another quite widespread set of viewpoints in so-called "radical" or "heterodox" economics, namely the thesis that the total wage of the working class in a nation in some way – measured in value and/or material use values – must be used as an independent variable in a system that otherwise will appear as undetermined.

David Ricardo, whose theory-building ought to be considered with a higher degree of respect than those mentioned in the previous paragraph, was among the first to open up the possibility of considering the wage in such a way. In practice, it is difficult to see that he actually did so. His clear opinion that the national econ-omy was based on real wages did not lead him to Platonic model building, as might easily have been the case had he seriously adopted a "corn model" in the way he was interpreted by Piero Sraffa.

Also, Ricardo's theory-building, in spite of his extensive use of monetary the-ory, never led him into illusions as to the social power of gold as money, a fetish unveiled by Marx, but which, however, is noticeable among "neo-Ricardians" of the day – directly and indirectly criticized in this chapter. Ricardo's separation between "values" and "riches" (Ricardo 1969, chapter 20), and the clear distinc-tions in his chapter on foreign trade seem persuasive to this effect. However, his confusion of exchange value and use value when it came to the basics of money was disastrous.

Given this, the connection of the contemporary theory of the wage as a variable with Ricardo's influential three-classes distribution theory can scarcely be con-tested. Marx's section on the wage was apparently a carefully selected number of manuscripts originally intended for use in a book specifically on *Die Lohnarbeit*, which would also be accompanied by a book on landed property. Originally, Marx's plan for his main work followed the three-class-divisions treated in the *Grundrisse*. In the section on the wage, and especially in the last pages of chapter 20 of *Capital* I, Marx makes use of his view of the intensity differences to deliver brief comments on the force of Western capital, especially in relation to Russian ways of production. In fact, this is perhaps the only place in *Capital* – with the possible exception of his earlier comment on "manufacturer and boyar [*Fabrikant und Bojar*]", where the uneven economic basis for capitalist entrepreneurship becomes a theme. If we combine this with the fact that Marx later turned his interest to the field of Russian landownership, we may be on the threshold of legitimating a new and fruitful field for economic studies.

Notes

1 For arguments to this effect, see Sandemose 2010a. There, the system of these communities is called "modified Asian social formation". In English studies, "Asiatic" is usually preferred in such connections, because it implies the system's presence outside geographical Asia.

2 During a research visit to Rome in 1984, I had a conversation with Rita di Leo, who pointed out how she had visited factories both in Russia and China, where employees were subsumed under work conditions which no Italian would have tolerated, *neanche per cinque minuti*, but where any single worker, without any ado or notice, could break away from the assembly line, short-cutting production for the sole purpose of getting a smoke. That is private initiative adapted to non-Western standards.

3 Stated and formulated in detail in Sandemose 2010a; see also Sandemose 2012a.

4 All italics added for both editions. Translation amended, for two critical errors: Marx's *bloße Dauer*, here "pure duration", is rendered "same duration" by Fowkes (see the comments later in this chapter, where the concept of intensity is taken up more in detail). Furthermore, Marx's *integrierende Teile*, here "integrating parts", is rendered "integral parts" by Fowkes. Marx's original tells us that the world market, in addition to having *countries* as its "parts", also has its form constructed by an *integrating movement* between countries.

5 A subsidiary point is that globalization, and the increased amount of commodity circulation which follows from it, does not in itself imply any tendency to "escape from gold". Historians of economy have pointed out that it might be right to take present-day globalization as a kind of return to a liberal world order, the *Pax Britannica* and the gold standard prior to World War I (see Harley 2007).

6 My translation. The German original runs: *Die Schwierigkeit liegt nicht darin zu begreifen, daß Geld Ware, sondern wie, warum, wodurch Ware Geld ist* (Marx 1968a, 107). The translation in Marx 1976 has: "The difficulty lies not in comprehending that money is a commodity, but in discovering how, why and by what means a commodity becomes money" (Marx 1976, 186). This translation seems to me erroneous. There is no question in this Marxian text of how money becomes commodity or vice versa, only how the two already *are* each other. For instance, there is no question of which commodity takes the role of money, only of its money-existence, given already, which makes it possible for it to turn into any commodity. So to speak, the commodity is money "by second nature" as soon as it is placed inside a commodity equation. It belongs to the money substance, is an *accidens* of that substance and can here only be understood and comprehended as such.

7 See the title of Section 9, this chapter.

8 Evidently, to make the point in its pure form, and in accordance with the limitations of the exposition in the first volume of *Capital*, he abstracts from production prices and also isolates intraspherical competition.

9 It is of course clear that (e.g.) a US capital can place foreign direct investments (FDI) in China and export commodities from that country, benefiting greatly from an under-valued yuan. However, the FDI itself relies on the dollar and so does the accounting of the final mass of profits.

10 See "Bildung einer allgemeinen Profitrate (Durchschnittsprofitrate) und Verwandlung der Warenwerte in Produktionspreise" (Marx 1968c, 164–181).

11 That is, both interspherical and intraspherical competition are in the picture. For reasons which will appear, even non-capitalist production inside nations will count here – a possibility from which we abstract for the moment.

12 I have made such an attempt in Sandemose 2010.

13 It is worth mentioning that Paul Cooney points out that Samir Amin, who eagerly discusses the theme of "unequal exchange", commits precisely this error (Cooney 2004, 247).

14 The scheme is borrowed from Anwar Shaikh (1980). Shaikh makes comparisons between the theories of Ricardo and Marx, but the exposition is weakened by the fact that he has no clear comprehension of Marx's theory of money.

15 Ricardo did not come as far as to Marx' OCC-concept. Instead, he worked with a com-position between fixed capital on he one hand, and on the other labour plus raw mate-rials. (See especially Ricardo 1969, 19 and 29.) However, in practice, he almost consistently let out the material circulating capital from his concrete reasoning, so that one could actually speak of a ratio of fixed capital to labour.

16 The ignorance of these passages by Marx among mainstream economists, as well as among Marxisants, is conspicuous. An acclaimed article by Anwar Shaikh (Shaikh 1979, 1980) is especially shaking. In this text, which explicitly aims to throw light on Marx's theory of "international values", Marx's presentation in *Capital*, the one we are analysing here, is simply *overlooked*. Instead, Shaikh concentrates on flows of money and credit on the world market. This is remarkable, all the more since Shaikh presup-poses the existence of average profit rates on the world market *and* confuses basic determinations in Marx's theory of value, like the *numéraire* and measure of values.

17 Chapters 19–22 of the volume, of which the last concentrate on "National Differences of Wages".

18 The etymology of the German *Lohn* immediately implies the significance of a reward – and, in addition, a just reward. This is not so with "wage", a word that points to a wager and to the risky existential situation of the worker on a market.

19 For an illuminating graphic exposition of the problems caused by general wage changes as regards the price level, from a traditional viewpoint, see Hofmann 1971, 67 (also Sandemose 1976, 55).

20 This more than any other of Ricardo's reflections be studied by would-be Marxists! Ricardo came very near to the solution but escaped into unclear language of "natural" prices, etc.

21 For a precise formulation of the case, see Garegnani 1972, 17–20 (section IV of chapter 2, whose title is "La difficoltà incontrata da Ricardo riducibilie a quella di una coerente misurazione del capitale"). It sees an irony in the fact that Ricardo's approach to science could in general very well be called a method of "the determined market", *il mercato determinato*, as Gramsci has it (1966, 95), since he insists on thought experiments starting from given market relations.

22 On the functions of absolute rent see Marx 1968a, chapter 25; 1976, chapter 33; and 1968c, chapter 45.

23 The reader may have noticed that with the introduction of the measure of degree, i.e. intensity, another essential and determining socially overarching *measure* has appeared. Simultaneously, the quantitative form of labour no longer appears as successive time but as an entity without extension, which means that we have to deal with the abstract

factors building up the negativity of labour as such. As one can easily establish, this amounts to a Marxian parallel to the Kantian transcendental apperception or, better, the Hegelian double negativity, as it appears in a work context, e.g. in the theory of the bondsman's relation to a lord. The tearing-up of the material is a tearing-up of the tearing-up itself: "The devouring [*das Verzehren*] is not simply sublation of the material [*des Stofflichen*], but devouring of the devouring itself; in the sublation of the material sublation of this sublation and consequently [*daher*] *positing* it" (Marx 1993, 301; 1953, 208, my translation). This "positing" *is* the human thought negating the human physical action and sublating it. But this double negation is, even for the most ardent materialist, outside temporal succession and a point multiplied in itself, i.e. generating succession. In its degree, its punctuality, it has differences in strength, i.e. in intensity, and the real qualifying *measure* of labour quantity is therefore found in it. There is no doubt that this is the *basic measure of* value in the Marxian corpus. The *punctum saliens* is to be found in Hegel's discovery of the dynamic of the category of Measure. In fact, when it is possible for him to operate with several measures, all with some "truth" regarding general logical method, it is because they are developed from one single core of double negativity, a form which consequently lies at bottom of all measures. Our development of that category in Marx now shows that the labour quantity is at bottom a synthesis – and precisely the synthesis which lies at the bottom of the specific human existence. Because of its expropriated form, it is coercively limited to being an *abstract* synthesis, i.e. producing (exchange) *value*. The other forms of value measures, looked at in this book, follow immanently from it and do not transcend the character of being forms of labour.

24 To make explicit earlier hints: this term is scarcely present as such in Marx's corpus. However, it is beyond doubt that he counted its economic precondition – namely that commodity prices in a societal ambience, in large scale and on the average did circle around (labour) values – to be a fact. This is primarily shown in his critique of Ricardo's theory of rent in *Theories of Surplus-Value*: "The transformation of values into [pro-duction] prices is only a result of the development of capitalist production. The original state [*Das ursprüngliche*] is (on the average) that commodities are sold to their values. The deviation from this is hampered in agriculture, through landed property" (Marx 1968e, 330–331). Modern agriculture is thus living proof of conditions that in earlier times were general, and which in modern times are surpassed by the transformation to a new price-structure in the industrial part of the economy.

25 See the stance taken *contra* Robert Brenner and Ellen Meiksins Wood in Sandemose 2012 – and the same tendency in Drapeau 2014, especially 210.

26 For this reasoning, see Sandemose 2010, 177.

27 To the knowledge of this author, Chile is the only nation which has implemented such a law.

28 See Sandemose 2010, chapter 7, section 7, 274–286.

29 While the main viewpoint of this author implies that basic property relations in Russia have *not* changed substantially since 1991, it is evident that the demands for change, and the resulting faction strifes between state, provinces and members of earlier collec-tive farms, have brought to light the critical position in Russia in a way still not clearly brought to the fore in other patrimonial-capitalist structures. See especially Lindsay 2009 and also Pomeranz, 2004.

30 Outside of Japan, where a constructive side-product of the feudal background was a free class of smallholding peasants (see also Marx 1976, 878; 1968a, 745).

31 The Chinese labour force is around 750 million people. The economy as a whole is today highly dependent on foreign investments. Still, such investments have accumu-lated a labour force of only around 24 million. John Whalley and Xian Xin hold that the productivity of labour per FDI firm is *nine times* higher in the latter than in the "indige-neously" manned industry (Whalley and Xin, 2009).

Appendices

Appendix 1: on fixed capital

One might remember that when it comes to exposition in monetary terms, Marx's main example is the following:

I	4000c	+	1000v	+	1000s	
II	......		2000c	+	500v	+ 500s

The introduction of real depreciation implies that the 2000 IIc cannot any longer be realized fully in kind against those material parts of constant capital which II needs and which are incarnated in 2000 I(v + s).[1] On the contrary, large parts of IIc (parts of *fixed* capital) will continue to function in kind. At the same time, a part of the *value* of 2000 IIc will consist of an equivalent for wear and tear on fixed capital, i.e. for the part of the fixed capital that is not to be replaced in kind but only in money-form. We may call this part "d", as does Marx,[2] presupposing it to be = 200 monetary units, a sum which is to be accumulated by the capitalists II in a fund for later renewal of fixed capital. The "exchange ratio" would then be 1800c against 2000(v + s). Schematically:

I	1000v	+	1000s
II	...... 1800c	+	200c(d)

A thousand units on each side of the account can be disposed of immediately: since the wages are paid out *post factum*, the workers I do in fact have 1000 units in ready money – from the last period of production.[3] This money now mediates a realization of commodities of (individual) consumption to a value of 1000, and in this way the capitalists I have cleared the natural material of labour power for the next period.[4] The relation now is

I	1000s		
II	800c	+	200c(d)

An equilibrium exchange is now generally not possible and, certainly, the commodity owners I are not about to make their peers in II a present of 200 in monetary units to manage a painless reproduction. What can actually be exchanged is 800 in commodity values from each department. The result is the situation

| I | .... 200s |
| II | ....200c(d) |

Consequently, as Marx says, "One-tenth of the surplus-value I to be replaced cannot be realised, or converted, from its bodily form of means of production into that of articles of consumption." Thus the 200c(d) are unrealizable too, since they cannot be transformed from their natural form as means of consumption to money-form. Such a transformation would presuppose that II is here operating as a "pure seller" of a commodity, and that he should accumulate the 200 in money-form. Equilibrium, therefore, seems to be impossible, or, rather, the problem consists in finding a source for the excess 200 in money-form; evidently, that is possible only when or if this annual reproduction is seen in its interconnectedness, its continuity:

> On examining annual reproduction, even on a simple scale, i.e., disregarding all accumulation, we do not begin *ab ovo*. The year which we study is one in the course of many; it is not the first year after the birth of capitalist production. The various capitals invested in the manifold lines of production of class II therefore differ in age. . . . a host of fixed capitals expire annually and must be renewed in kind out of the accumulated money-fund.
>
> (Marx 1961, 453)

Department II may consequently be treated as consisting of two parts, (1) and (2):

II(1) with capitals where the fixed part has to be renewed in kind together with its circulating parts, and

II(2) with capitals renewing only their circulating parts in kind, while equivalents for wear and tear are stored up in money funds (in Marx's example, 200c a year) for later renewal of their fixed part.

Beginning thus not *ab ovo* but *in media res*, we see that II(1) can only renew its fixed capital in kind through money funds that are already to be found in II(1) itself, funds accumulated earlier through commodity circulation. As regards the acquisition of this fixed capital, II(1) is operating as a "pure buyer" of commodities from I. There is no mutual exchange of commodities in kind here. II(1), is, then, capable of buying the 200 Is (provided they represent fixed capital) without delivering commodities. With this money, 200, equivalents for commodity sold, they buy the remaining 200c(d) present in commodity-form by II(2), whereupon II(2) has fulfilled its role as a "pure seller" and may deposit 200 in money-form for a later renewal in kind of its own fixed capital. Simple reproduction is painlessly carried through, as regards the value-renewal of capital as well as its renewal in kind.

The condition for such a smooth reproduction is that the loss of value resulting from wear and tear on those fixed capitals that are in steady use is equal to the value of the fixed capital that has terminated its function, represented by the money funds previously accumulated inside II(1). Marx says:

> Such a balance would seem to be a law of reproduction on the same scale. This is equivalent to saying that in class I, which puts out the means of production, the proportional division of labour must remain unchanged, since it produces on the one hand circulating and on the other fixed component parts of the constant capital of Department II.
>
> (Marx 1961, 464–465)

That it is impossible to maintain an equilibrium of this kind has its immediate cause not in the process of value production but in the working process, or, rather, in the transitoriness of use values, which lies beyond human control. The most important instance in the Marxian text is the following one:

> If . . . a greater part of the fixed elements of IIc expires than did the year before, and hence a greater part must be renewed in kind, then that part of the fixed capital which is as yet only on the way to its demise and is to be replaced meanwhile in money until its day of expiry, must shrink in the same proportion, inasmuch as it was assumed that the sum (and the sum of the value) of the fixed part of capital functioning in II remains the same. This however brings with it the following circumstances . . . If the greater part of commodity-capital I consists of elements of the fixed capital of IIc, then a correspondingly smaller portion consists of circulating component parts of IIc, because the total production of I for IIc remains unchanged. . . . On the other hand the total production of class II also retains the same volume. But how is this possible if its raw materials, semi-finished products, and auxiliary materials (i.e., the circulating elements of constant capital II) decrease?
>
> (Marx 1961, 466–467)

Besides, there is already a disproportion between value parts of the wear and tear inside II(2) and the money funds that capitals inside II(1) are using as they buy products from I.

Appendix 2: on gold digging

The gold industry and/or its whole product value I shall call G. Whenever parts of G are treated, they will be called g.

Marx operates with a gold industry with a total magnitude of $20c + 5v + 5s$. However, this does not mean that the wear and tear of circulation equals 30 value units, for, as we have seen, gold is also in use for industrial purposes and naturally in Department II (e.g. by capitalist dentists and jewellers) as well as in Department I (nowadays it is much used, e.g., in couplings and semiconductors).

Gold production itself belongs to Department I, since it is a case of production "of metals generally" (Marx 1961, 466–467). Besides, it would seem that the only reason to place it there is that it is not used exclusvely as an instrument of circulation but also in production.

In view of this fact, one has to begin the analysis of the reproduction of the money material by dividing the existing product value G (in this case a value that is expressed in 30 monetary units) in two portions. Marx indicates a division implying that two fifths of it go to means of production and three fifths to replace the wear and tear of circulation. I shall follow up this proposal, even when it comes to my attempt to reconstruct the content of the text missing from Marx's manuscript. Further, I will make the legitimate supposition that the said proportion is valid not only for the product value G as a whole but also for each of the aggregates (c, v, s) inside this product value.

If we look at the product value of G, namely 20c + 5v + 5s, then it is clear that (5v + 5s) is to be exchanged (according to the logic of the general exchange of I(v + s) against IIc) with elements of IIc, so that workers and capitalists in G get something to consume individually. Under normal circumstances, these (5v + 5s) consist of means of production. But in this case, we know that only (2v + 2s) have such a destination, since (3v + 3s) are supposed to serve as (new) *means of circulation*.

Against this background, we report Marx's view on the exchange process:

I(G)   20c   +   5v   +   5s
II 10c

where 10 IIc are means of consumption whose material nature need not be specified. First, to the exchange of 5v(g) against 5 IIc, Marx says:

> As for the 5v, every gold-producing establishment begins by buying labour-power. This is done not with gold produced by this particular enterprise, but with a portion of the money-supply in the land. The labourers buy with this 5v articles of consumption from II, and that buys with this money means of production from I.
>
> (Marx 1961, 470)[5]

This is particularly important and reminds us of the the mediating role pertaining to the variable capital – both in its function as money capital and in its subsequent function as wage. As we know, this mediating role is intimately connected with the workers' reproduction of the capital relation in its totality. The autonomy of the wage labourer is here expressed by the fact that it is *himself*, and not in any way the capitalist (here: inside Ig) who realizes the first part of the exchange with Department II. The aim of the exchange – seen from the standpoint of G – is that capitalists in II buy those of its means of production that are incarnated in I(v + s)g. But the operation is complicated by the fact that half the amount of these means of production, seen from the value side (and from the value side *only*, since we define the wage labourer as a person who does not own means of production) rests with the workers. In other words, the monetary expression of these means of production, the money 5v(g), has to be transferred to the capitalists before the exchange of I(v + s) against IIc can be accomplished. This transfer implies that the workers in I buy means of consumption from capitalists in II, who thereby get sufficient money to buy the whole product I(v + s) of means of production.

We have seen that II buys means of production for "this [same] money", i.e. with the original v(g). We shall mark this money 5v(g)' to underline that it originates from gold that is already circulating, as Marx contends. The difficulty is that II will not buy all the 5v(g)' but only 2v(g)'. As regards the rest, 3v(g)', it has no use value in the material elements in the constant capital in Department II. Therefore, its components will not circulate back to G, and this last one will, it seems, have problems when it comes to making available sufficient labour power for the next period of production, since the 2v(g)' covers only two fifths of the value of this power.

In the case of any other business, reproduction (be it simple or extended) would have become impossible. That is not the case here, for during one period of production, the aggregate G has had workers employed in the production of a new product value (20c + 5v + 5s)g. The different parts inside this product we distinguish with the mark (g)", since they are produced later than the gold that made up the variable capital that G put into use when we began the analysis of its movement. Now, the point is that from this (newly created) product, which is G's own property, he can simply take the 3v(g)" and pay them directly to its workers as an addition to the 2v(g)' – without bothering about any mediation with Department II. For in the gold production, the value side is, figuratively speaking, identical with the side of use value. The concrete labour and the concrete product that we find there directly represent abstract labour and value respectively in the economic system as a whole. The gold dust that corresponds to the 5v has not been reduced one single atom by the fact that 3v(g)' do not circulate back to G, for those 3 originate in earlier production and circulation. Marx says that

> his labourers have supplied him with 5 in gold, 2 of which he sold and 3 of which he still has, so that he has but to coin them, or turn them into banknotes to have his entire variable capital again directly in his hands in money-form, without the further intervention of II.[6]

The reproduction of the gold material v has consequently been cleared.

But in addition to this (simple) reproduction, there is now an excess quantity of 3 v(g)' inside IIc. Here they have nothing to do, partly because the constant capital II already has the gold it needs for its process of production. Likewise, they have no function in part IIv, since the capitalists II must be presumed to be in possession of sufficient money capital v as a result of sales of means of consumption (products of II itself) to the workers of their own department. The only part where they can come to rest is IIs, since there they cannot disturb the course of social reproduction. Consequently,

[t]his money must be transferred in its entirety from IIc to IIs, no matter whether it exists in necessities of life or articles of luxury, and vice versa corresponding commodity-value must be transferred from IIs to IIc. Result: A portion of the surplus-value is stored up as a money hoard.

(Marx 1961, 471–472)

After this consideration of the variable capital and the materials corresponding to it, we may cross over to the other component of the exchange of G against II, namely the surplus value.

Here, things are much less complicated, because the component to be exchanged already and immediately is in the capitalist's possession, both as value and as use value. The surplus product by definition is a new product – not anything that earlier belonged to circulation in one way or other. The capitalist can throw his commodity, the gold, i.e. Is(g)", directly into circulation, "since gold can buy any commodity" (Marx 1961, 467). In return for II he gets means of consumption to a value of 5 from II, while this latter uses 2s(g)" of materials in its own constant capital (together with 2v(g)'). The rest necessarily must be hoarded in IIs. Marx continues:

We see, then, aside from Ic which we reserve for a later analysis, that even simple reproduction, excluding accumulation proper, namely reproduction on an extended scale, necessarily includes the storing up, or hoarding, of money.

(Marx 1961, 472)

The result is gold (in Department II) to an amount of 6 money units. Of these, 3(v) will be produced in some earlier year and 3(s) during the last year. It follows that the capitalists II taken together consume products corresponding to a value of only 494 a year.

As indicated above, the analysis of the constant capital in gold production poses a "hermeneutic" problem. Marx's manuscript, if it ever existed, is lost. And it seems that for all the years that have passed since the edition of Volume II, only two attempts have been made to reconstruct his thoughts on this theme.[7]

Producers of means of production generally replace their constant capital in kind through mutual commodity exchanges inside the whole of the aggregate Ic (Marx: 4000 Ic). But this is only partly the case for G. As we have seen, it is reasonable analytically to divide each of the G parts in portions. So it must be presumed that the capitals inside the remaining 3980 Ic have a demand of just 8c(g)" as regards gold for industrial purposes, since that amount equals two fifths of the 20cg.

If the principle of mutual exchange between the capitals rules, as Marx for simplicity's sake presupposes on a similar occasion, G consequently would have no possibility of renewing three fifths of its constant capital.[8] But since its product consists of gold that may be thrown directly into circulation and can buy any commodity, the problem is solved, at least as regards G taken in isolation. In the main exchange between the departments, we saw that G could force its way, getting rid of its commodities to Department II ("an offer you can't refuse") simply by coining 3v(g)". In the same manner, G coins the 12c(g)", throws them into circulation and gets back means of production in the form and value of 12 Ic. In this way, it can reconstruct its constant capital materially. Also, replacement cannot be effectuated in any other way here.[9] But, of course, through this operation the rest of Ic has lost material elements to a value of 12, and a corresponding amount of constant capital cannot be reproduced. Thus even if the whole of I(c + v + s)g is now realized, a crisis of production is at hand, since 12 units of the remaining 3980 Ic cannot be reproduced in kind, but only on the value side. Besides, all of the material product I(v + s) has been exchanged against IIc, a fact that means all the surplus value of the capitalists I has been consumed or is present in a form exclusively for individual consumption. Thus, a hoarding (of the 12 units) like the one in Department II is not possible.

As said above, this difficulty can be overcome without disturbing the simple reproduction. Here we proceed with numerical examples: if we add 12 in value to the aggregate Ic, so that it comes to have the original magnitude of 4012, then there is once again present a mass of means of production large enough to reproduce the whole of Ic in kind. Since the value composition of the scheme is 4, and the rate of surplus value is 100 per cent, each of the other aggregates must be increased by (12 : 4 =) 3 units.

The relation between the departments, and their mutual exchange, will be

I   4012c   +   1003v   +   1003s
II   .... 2000c   +   500v   +   500s,
      ...

which, strictly speaking, is the correct version of Marx's general simple reproduction model, expressed in monetary units.

Notes

1 Our focus when concentrating on IIc is the exchange situation between the departments. Like all other constant capital in Department I, worn-out fixed capital inside 4000 Ic is replaced by the product of the same department.
2 "d = *déchet*", as he writes in his exposition (Marx 1961, 455), perhaps in veneration of the great French theoretician Quesnay, whose "Tableau économique", according to Marx, was superior to Ricardian thinking on the subject, since it was based on the circuit of commodity capital.
3 Riccardo Bellofiore's view of the place of variable capital in reproduction seems enigmatic. He explicitly says that according to Marx (no reference is given) the worker is paid prior to production, whereupon he has to "wait after the end of production until he will spend the wage" (Bellofiore 2002, 112).
4 Here it is distinctly seen – precisely as in the analysis of simple reproduction in Volume I – how the whole system is dependent on the mediation of the working class.
5 This is the only place in *Capital* that this author knows of where Marx portrays the exchange between capital and labour in a way that seems impossible to reconcile with his thesis that the worker is everywhere forced to sell (contractually) his labour power and consequently "advances" his commodity and lets it work for the capitalists before

he gets paid. He gives the capitalist a perpetual credit (Marx 1976, 278; 1968, 188) and gets his money when the work is done. That the variable capital can function in this way in the mediation of the whole of the circulation of a capital (G) must, if it is consciously set up by Marx, have to do with the fact that gold as variable capital need not circulate to the worker, since the latter actually excavates the "money" commodity.

6 Marx 1961, 471. Marx remarks (1961, 470) that British diplomats in the US, in a publication from 1879, report home about "gold diggers bringing a considerable amount of natural gold directly to the mint in San Francisco".

7 See Luxemburg 1913, 65–79 (chapter 5, on the circulation of money) and the criticism in Grossmann, 1971 (originally 1932). Luxemburg criticized contradictions in the Marxian scheme, without trying to overcome them through a reconstruction of texts missing in Marx's manuscripts. Grossmann tried to do this but in a decidedly unsatisfactory manner (Sandemose 1977, 2010b).

8 See Marx 1961, chapter 20, section VI: "The constant capital of Department I".

9 This kind of replacement as regards the gold-producing capital is mentioned by Marx in chapter 17 of Volume II, "The Circulation of Surplus-Value" (Marx 1961, 327).

Bibliography

Albritton, R. 1999. *Dialectics and Deconstruction in Political Economy*. New York: Palgrave.

André, Ch. 2016. "Household Debt in OECD Countries: Stylised Facts and Policy Issues", *OECD Economics Department Working Papers*, no. 1277, February.

Arthur, Ch. 2002. "Review of *Dialectics and Deconstruction in Political Economy*", *Historical Materialism*, 10, 1, 251–257.

Balibar, E. 1971 (with Althusser, L.). *Leggere Il Capitale*. Milano: Feltrinelli.

Ball, M. 1977. "Differential Rent and the Role of Landed Property", *International Journal of Urban and Regional Research*, 1, 4, 380–403.

Bell, J. R., 1995. "Dialectics and Economic Theory", in Albritton, R. and T. Sekine (eds.), *A Japanese Approach to Political Economy*. New York: St. Martin's Press.

Bellofiore, R. 2002. "'Transformation' and the Monetary Circuit", in Campbell, Martha and Geert Reuten (eds.), *The Culmination of Capital*. London: Palgrave, 102–127.

Bortkiewicz, L. v. 1906–1907. "Wertrechnung und Preisrechnung im Marxschen System", in *Archiv für Sozialwissenschaft und Sozialpolitik*, volumes 23, 1–50; and 25, 10–51, 445–488. Tübingen: J. C. B. Mohr.

Bortkiewicz, L. v. 1907. "Zur Berichtigung der grundlegenden theoretischen Konstruktion von Marx im dritten Band des Kapital", in *Jahrbücher für Nationalökonomie und Statistik*, volume 89, 319–335. Stuttgart: Fischer.

Bortkiewicz, L. v. 1910. "Die Rodbertus'sche Grundrententheorie und die Marx'sche Lehre von der absoluten Grundrente", *Archiv für die Geschichte des Sozialismus und der Arbeiterbewegung*, 1, 391–434. http://dx.doi.org/10.1515/jbnst-1907-0118.

Bortkiewicz, L. v. 1919. "Zu den Grundrententheorien von Rodbertus und Marx", *Archiv für die Geschichte des Sozialismus und der Arbeiterbewegung*, 8, 248–257.

Campbell, M. 1998. "Money in the Circulation of Capital", in Arthur, Christopher J. and Geert Reuten: *The Circulation of Capital*. London: MacMillan, 129–157.

Carney, J. A. 1994. "Contracting a Food Staple in The Gambia", in Little, Peter D. and Michael J. Watts, *Living under Contract*. Madison: University of Wisconsin Press, 167–187.

Cooney, P. 2004. "Towards an Empirical Measurement of International Transfers of Value", in Freeman, Alan, Andrew Kliman and Julian Wells, *The New Value Controversy and the Foundations of Economics*. London: Edward Elgar, 241–260.

Corbet, Th. 1821. *Observations on Some Verbal Disputes in Political Economy (etc)*. London.

Dickinson, H. D. 1956. "A Comment on Meek's 'Note on the Transformation Problem'", *Economic Journal*, 740–741.

Dobb, M. 1953. *Political Economy and Capitalism*. London: Routledge.

Drapeau, T. 2014. *The Atlantic Roots of Working-Class Internationalism: A Historical Re-Interpretation*. York, Ontario: York University Press.

Economakis, G. E. 2003. "On Absolute Rent: Theoretical Remarks on Marx's Analysis", *Science & Society*, 67, 3, 339–348.

Edel, M. 1973. *Economies and the Environment*. Englewood Cliffs, NJ: Prentice Hall.

Elster, J. 1985. *Making Sense of Marx*. Cambridge: Cambridge University Press.

Emmanuel, A. 1972. *Unequal Exchange: A Study of the Imperialism of Trade*. New York and London: Monthly Review Press.

Engels, F. 1970. *Dialektik der Natur. Marx–Engels Werke*, volume 20. Berlin: Dietz.

Engels, F. 1973 [1872]. "Zur Wohnungsfrage", in *Marx–Engels Werke*, volume 18. Berlin: Dietz, 209–287.

Engels, F. 1973a [1887]. "Vorwort [zur zweiten durchgesehenen Auflage "Zur Wohnungs-frage"]", *Marx–Engels Werke*, volume 18. Berlin: Dietz, 647–655.

Fan, C. 2009. "Flexible Work, Flexible Household: Labour Migration and Rural Families in China", in Lisa Keister (ed), *Work and Organizations in China after Thirty Years of Transition*. Bingley: Emerald, 377–408.

Fine, B. 1979. "On Marx's Theory on Agricultural Rent", *Economy and Society*, 8, 3, 241–278.

Fratini, S. M. 2009. "La rendita assoluta di Marx e le equazioni di prezzo di Sraffa", *Working Paper no. 105,* Collana del Dipartimento di Economia, Università degli Studi Roma Tre.

Fritsch, B. 1968. *Die Geld- und Kredittheorie von Karl Marx*. Frankfurt am Main: Europäische Verlagsanstalt.

Garegnani, P. 1972. A. Giuffrè, ed. *Il capitale nelle teorie della distribuzione*. Milano: Dott.

Gehrke, Ch. 2010. "Rent, as Share of Produce . . .; Not Governed by Proportions", *mimeo*, University of Graz. http://host.uniroma3.it/eventi/sraffaconference2010/abstracts/pp_gehrke.pdf.

Gramsci, A. 1966. *Il materialismo storico*. Roma: Einaudi.

Grossmann, H. 1969. *Marx, die klassische Nationalökonomie und das Problem der Dynamik*. Frankfurt am Main: Europäische Verlagsanstalt.

Grossmann, H. 1971. *Die Goldproduktion im Reproduktionsschema von Marx und Rosa Luxemburg. Archiv sozialistischer Literatur*, volume 20. Frankfurt am Main: Neue Kritik.

Hardt, M. and A. Negri. 2000. *Empire*. London: Harvard University Press.

Harley, K. 2007. "Comments on Factor Prices and Income Distribution in Less Indus-tralised Economies, 1870–1939: Refocusing on the Frontier", *Australian Economic History Review*, 47, 3, November, 238–248.

Hartmann, K. 1970. *Die Marxsche Theorie. Eine philosophische Untersuchung zu den Hauptschriften*. Berlin: Walter de Gruyter.

Harvey, D. 1982 *Limits to Capital*. London: Verso.

Hegel. G. W. F. 1969. *Wissenschaft der Logik*, volume 1. *Theorie Werkausgabe*, volume 5. Franfurt am Main: Suhrkamp.

Hilferding, R. 1968. *Das Finanzkapital*. Frankfurt am Main: Europäische Verlagsanstalt.

Hofmann W. 1971. *Wert- und Preislehre*. Berlin: Duncker & Humblot.

Hossein-zadeh Ismail. 1992. "A New Contribution to an Old Debate: the Case of Marxian Theory of Value and Ground Rent". https://ismaelhossein-zadeh.com/rent-theory/.

Howard, M. C. and J. E. King. 1985. *The Political Economy of Marx*. Harlow: Longman.

Ito, T. 1992. *The Japanese Economy*. London: MIT Press.

Laibman, D. 2012. "The Recurrent Temptations of Anti-Equilibrium", *Science & Society*, 17, 4, 425–429.

Lapides, K. 1992. "Henryk Grossmann and the Debate on the Theoretical Status of Marx's Capital", *Science & Society*, 56, 2, 133–162.

Lapides, K. 1998. *Marx's Wage Theory in Historical Perspective*. Wesport: Praeger.

Lazzarato, M. 2011. *La fabrique de l'homme endetté*. Paris: Éditions Amsterdam.

Lebowitz, M. A. 1993. "The 'Book on Wage-Labor' and Marxist Scholarship", *Science & Society*, 57, 1, 66–73.

Lenin, V. I. 1962. "The Agrarian Programme of Social Democracy in the First Russian Revolution 1905–1907", in *Collected Works*, volume 13. Moscow: Foreign Languages Publishing House, 217–431.

Li, M. 2005. "The Rise of China and the Demise of the Capitalist World Economy", *Science & Society*, 69, 3, 420–448.

Lindsay, I. K. 2009. "A Troubled Path to Private Property Agricultural Land Law in Russia". http://works.bepress.com/ira_lindsay/1.

Lipietz, A. 1985. "A Marxist Approach to Urban Ground Rent", in M. Ball (ed.), *Land Rent, Housing, and the Planning System*. London: Helm, 129–155.

Luxemburg, R. 1913. *Die Akkumulation des Kapitals*. Berlin: Vorwärts.

Malthus, Th. R. 1836. *Principles of Political Economy*. London: Pickering.

Mandel, E. 1972. *Der Spätkapitalismus*. Frankfurt am Main: Suhrkamp.

Marx, K. 1953. *Grundrisse der Kritik der politischen Ökonomie*. Berlin: Dietz.

Marx, K. 1965. *Capital* I. Moscow: Progress Publishers.

Marx, K. 1961. *Capital* II. Moscow: Progress Publishers.

Marx, K. 1966. *Capital* III. Moscow: Progress Publishers.

Marx, K. 1969. *Resultate des unmittelbaren Produktionsprozesses*. Frankfurt am Main: Verlag Neue Kritik. [See *Karl Marx Friedrich Engels Gesamtausgabe*, volume 2, 4.1: K. Marx, *Ökonomische Manuskripte 1863–1867*. Berlin: Dietz, 24–130. Also Marx 1976, 943–1084.]

Marx, K. 1968a. *Das Kapital* I. Frankfurt am Main: Europäische Verlagsanstalt.

Marx, K. 1968b. *Das Kapital* II. Frankfurt am Main: Europäische Verlagsanstalt.

Marx, K. 1968c. *Das Kapital* III. Frankfurt am Main: Europäische Verlagsanstalt.

Marx, K. 1968d. *Theorien über den Mehrwert*, book 1. *Marx–Engels Werke*, volume 26, 1. Frankfurt am Main: Europäische Verlagsanstalt.

Marx, K. 1968e. *Theorien über den Mehrwert*, book 2. *Marx–Engels Werke*, volume 26, 2. Frankfurt am Main: Europäische Verlagsanstalt.

Marx, Karl. 1970. *A Contribution to the Critique of Political Economy*. New York: International Publishers.

Marx, K. 1971. "Das Elend der Philosophie", *Marx–Engels Werke*, volume 4. Berlin: Dietz, 63–182.

Marx, K. 1972. *Zur Kritik der politischen Ökonomie. Marx–Engels Werke*, volume 13. Berlin: Dietz.

Marx, K. 1974. "Letter to Engels, 2 April 1858", *Marx–Engels Werke*, volume 29. Berlin: Dietz, 312.

Marx, K. 1974a. "Letter to Engels, 16 January 1858", *Marx–Engels Werke*, volume 29. Berlin: Dietz, 260.

Marx, K. 1974b. "Letter to Engels, 9 August 1862", *Marx–Engels Werke*, volume 30. Berlin: Dietz, 274.

Marx, Karl. 1976. *Capital. A Critique of Political Economy*, volume 1. Ben Fowkes, trans. London: Penguin.

Marx, K. 1978. *Zur Kritik der politischen Ökonomie (Manuskript 1861–1863). Marx–Engels Werke*, volume 2, 3.3. Dietz: Berlin.

Marx, K. 1980. *Zur Kritik der politischen Ökonomie (Manuskript 1861–1863). Marx–Engels Werke*, volume 2, 3.5. Dietz: Berlin.

Marx, K. 1993. *Grundrisse*. M. Nicolaus, trans. London: Penguin.

Marx, K. 1993a. *Zur Kritik der politischen Ökonomie (Ökonomische Manuskripte 1863–1867. Manuskript 1863–1865 zum 3. Buch des „Kapital"). Marx–Engels Werke*, volume 2, 4.2. Dietz: Berlin.

Marx, K. and F. Engels. 1968. *Die deutsche Ideologie. Marx–Engels Werke*, volume 3. Berlin: Dietz.

MCG Blogs de Economía. 2011. "18. Impact of Trade Deficit on crisis and drop of Industrial production in the USA and 5 European major countries: France, Germany Italy, Spain and UK", 23 August. https://euroamericanassociation.blogspot.co.uk/2011/08/18-industry-and-trade-balance-in-5.html.

Meek, R. 1956. "Some Notes on the Transformation Problem", *Economic Journal*, 66, 94–107.

Meiners R. 1980. *Methodenprobleme bei Marx und ihr Bezug zur Hegelschen Philosophie*. Munich: Minerva.

Morf, O. 1970. *Geschichte und Dialektik in der politischen Ökonomie*. Frankfurt am Main: Europäische Verlagsanstalt.

Moseley, F. 1998. "Marx's Reproduction Schemes and Smith's Dogma", in Arthur, Christopher J. and Geert Reuten, *The Circulation of Capital*. London: MacMillan, 159–185.

Murray, R. 1977–1978. "Value and Theory of Rent", *Capital and Class*, 1, 3, 100–121; and 2, 1, 11–33.

Negishi, T. 1985. *Economic Theories in a Non-Walrasian Tradition*. Cambridge: Cambridge University Press.

Nell, E. J. 1980. (ed.) *Growth, Profits, and Property*. Cambridge: Cambridge University Press.

OECD. 2006. http://www.oecd.org/dataoecd/48/4/37867909.pdf.

Pappe, H. O. 1951. "Wakefield and Marx", *Economic History Review*, 4, 1, August, 88–97.

Park, J. 2014. "Land Rent Theory Revisited", *Science and Society*, 78, 1, 88–109.

Plato. 1963 [380 BC]. *Republic*. Paul Shorey, trans. Princeton, NJ: Princeton University Press.

Pomeranz, W. E. 2004. "Whither Russian Property Rights?" Center for International Private Enterprise, Economic Reform Feature Service.

Postone, M. 2003. *Time, Labour and Social Domination: A Reinterpretation of Marx's Critical Theory*. Cambridge: Cambridge University Press.

Preobrazhensky, E. A. 1965. *The New Economics*. B. Pearce, trans. Oxford: Clarendon Press.

Proudhon, P.-J. 1846. *Système des contradictions économiques ou Philosophie de la misère* [*The System of Economic Contradictions or the Philosophy of Misery*].

Quesnay, F. 1758. *Tableau économique*. Paris.

Ramirez, M. D. 2009. "Marx's Theory of Ground Rent: A Critical Assessment", *Contributions to Political Economy*, 28, 71–91.

Reichelt, H. 1970. *Zur logischen Struktur des Kapitalbegriffs bei Karl Marx*. Frankfurt am Main: Europäische Verlagsanstalt.

Reuten, G. 1998. "The Status of Marx's Reproduction Schemes: Conventional or Dialectical Logic?", in Arthur, Christopher J. and Geert Reuten, *The Circulation of Capital*. London: MacMillan, 187–229.

Ricardo, D. 1969 [1817]. *Principles of Political Economy and Taxation*. London: Dent.

Ricardo, D. 1815. "Letter to James Mill of 30 December", in P. Sraffa & Dobb, M. H. (eds.), *The Works and Correspondence of David Ricardo*, volume 6, 348–349. Cambridge: Cambridge University Press.

Rosenthal 1998. *The Myth of Dialectics: Reinterpreting the Marx–Hegel Relation*. London: Macmillan.

Rosdolsky, R. 1968. *Zur Entstehungsgeschichter der Marxschen "Kapitals" I–II*. Frankfurt am Main: Europäische Verlagsanstalt.

Roxborough, I. 1979. *Theories of Underdevelopment*. London: Macmillan.

Rubel, M. 1965. "Editorial Comments", Pléiade edition of Marx's *Oeuvres*. *Oeuvres: Economie*, volume 1. Paris: Gallimard.

Sandemose, J. 1971. "Om kapitalens reproduksjon", *Kontrast*, 26. Oslo: Pax.

Sandemose, J. 1973. "Transformasjonsproblem og verditeori", in Elster, J. (ed.), *Marx i dag*. Oslo: Gyldendal.

Sandemose, J. 1976. *Ricardo, Marx og Sraffa. Kritikk av den nyricardianske retningen i moderne økonomisk teori*. Copenhagen, Oslo and Lund: Rhodos, Gyldendal, Bo Cavefors.

Sandemose, J. 1977. "Overganger. En studie av Das Kapital". *Kurasje*, Copenhagen: Modtryk, 117–158.

Sandemose, J. 1988. "Apans anatomi" [review, in Swedish], *Häften för Kritiska Studier*, volume 1. Lund, 57–71.

Sandemose, J. 2004. "The Transformation Problem: Wage Form, *Numéraire* and Value Transfer", *International Journal of Political Economy*, 34, 3, 41–58.

Sandemose, J. 2006. "On absolute rent". *Science & Society*, Vol 70, no 3. 360–365.

Sandemose, J. 2006b. "Gold digging. A note on money needed for accumulation", *Science & Society*, 70, 4, 528–541.

Sandemose, J. 2007. *Totalitet og metode. Tre essays om Karl Marx' hovedverk*. Oslo: Spartacus.

Sandemose, J. 2010. "Fundamentals of a Science of Capital and Bourgeois Society: Marxian Notions of Value, Prices, and the Structure of Time", in Paul Zarembka (ed.), *The National Question and the Question of Crisis. Research in Political Economy*, volume 26. Bingley: Emerald Group Publishing Limited, 253–299.

Sandemose, J. 2010a. *Kritikk av globaliseringsteorien*. Oslo: Aschehoug.

Sandemose, J. 2010b. "Golden Howlers. Grossmann's attack on Luxemburg", *Science & Society*, 74, 1, 103–114.

Sandemose, J. 2012. "Manufacture and the Transition from Feudalism to Capitalism", *Science & Society*, 76, 4, 463–494.

Sandemose, J. 2012a. "Religious Sanctions and Economic Results. Transfer of Labour Time on the World Market: Religious Sanctions and Economic Results", *Religions*, 3, 739–762. doi: 10.3390/rel3030739 (*Special Issue: Religion & Globalization*).

Sandemose, J. 2013. "Grundrisse, Capital, and Marxist Scholarship", *Science & Society*, 77, 4, 561–568.

Sandemose, J. 2015. *Historisk materialisme og økonomisk teori*. Larvik: Rødt.

Sandemose, J. 2016. "Notes on the Unity of Logic and Materialism". Macrothink. www.macrothink.org/journal/index.php/jsss/article/view/7857.

Sandleben, G. 2008. "Zu Fragen der Modifikation des Wertgesetzes auf dem Weltmarkt". Berlin. http://www.mxks.de/files/ag/Sandleben.ModifikationDesWertgesetzes.pdf.

Sandleben, G. 2011. *Finanzmarktkrise – Mythos und Wirklichkeit. Wie die ganz reale Wirtschaft die Krise kriegt*. Berlin: Norderstedt.

Schanz, H.-J. 1974. "Skitse til en bestemmelse af overgangen fra II. til III. Kapitalbind", in *Kurasje*, 11. Copenhagen.

Schwarz, W. 1974. "'Das Kapital im allgemeinen' und die 'Konkurrenz' im ökonomischen Werk von Karl Marx. Zu Rosdolskys Fehlinterpretation der Gliederung des 'Kapital'", in *Gesellschaft. Beiträge zur Marxschen Theorie I*. Frankfurt am Main: Suhrkamp Verlag.

Scott, Allen. J. 1976. "Land and Land Rent", *Progress in Geography*, 9, 102–145.

Sekine, T. 1997. *An Outline of the Dialectic of Capital 1–2*. London: Macmillan.

Seton, F. 1957. "The 'Transformation Problem'", *Review of Economic Studies*, 24, 3, 149–160.

Shaikh, A. 1979/1980. "Foreign Trade and the Law of Value", *Science & Society*, 43, 281–302 (Part I)/44, 27–57 (Part II).

Shaikh, A. 1980. "The Laws of International Exchange", in Edward J. Nell (ed.), *Growth, Profits and Property*. Cambridge: Cambridge University Press, 204–236.

Shaikh, A. 2016. *Capitalism. Competition, Conflict, Crises*. Oxford: Oxford University Press.

Sraffa, P. 1930 (ca.). "Anti-Marshall". Sraffa Papers at Wren Library, Cambridge: D 1/13.5.

Sraffa, P. 1951–1952. *The Works and Correspondence of David Ricardo*. Cambridge: Cambridge University Press.

Sraffa, P. 1972. *Production of Commodities by Means of Commodities*. Cambridge: Cambridge University Press.

"The State of Manufacturing in the United States." 2011. *Nationwide State of Manufacturing*. 3 March. http://trade.gov/manufactureamerica/facts/tg_mana_003019.asp.

Steuart, J. 1767. *An Inquiry into the Principles of Political Oeconomy: Being An Essay on the Science of Domestic Policy in Free Nations*.

Sweezy, P. M. 1942. *The Theory of Capitalist Development*. New York: Oxford University Press.

Warnock, Veronica C. and Francis E. Warnock. 2008. "Markets and Housing Finance", *Journal of Housing Economics*, 17, 3, 239–251.

Whalley, J. and Xian Xin. 2009. "China's FDI and Non-FDI Economies and the Sustainability of Future High Chinese Growth", *China Economic Review*. doi: 10.1016j/chieco 2009.11.004.

White, J. D. 1996. *Karl Marx and the Intellectual Origins of Dialectical Materialism*. London: Macmillan.

Wittfogel, Karl A. 1957. *Oriental Despotism. A Comparitive Study of Total Power*. New Haven, CT: Yale University Press.

Wood, E. M. 2002. *The Origin of Capitalism. A Longer View*. London: Verso.

Wygodski, W. S. 1970. *Die Geschichte einer grossen Entdeckung*. Berlin: das europäische buch.

Index

absolute ground rent 22n8, 33, 42–45, 52–56, 59–60, 62, 64, 66–67, 69, 70–71, 73–77, 78–83, 85, 86, 134n22; creative basis for landowners' action 50, 85; definition by Bortkiewicz 71; limited by value magnitude through landowners' consumption pattern 75; may disappear and reappear 78
"absolute poverty" 3
agricultural day-labourers 51, 83
Amin, S. 77, 109, 134n13
André, Ch., 90
antiquity 42n27
appearances, as phenomena 2, 7, 9, 16, 32
Arthur, C. 42
Asian mode of production 79, 95, 128
Asian societies 95, 127–128; Asian village system: Chinese 132, Indian 128, Russian 128
Asiatic social formation 94, 128, 133n1

Balibar, E. 40n8
Ball, M. 81
barrier [*Schranke*] 11, 23n19, 26, 32–34, 36, 60, 70, 73, 85
Bell, J. R. 42
Bellofiore, R. 142
bimetallism 111
Bortkiewicz, L. v. 63, 70–75, 78, 85, 92n2, 93n16, 117, 129, 144
bourgeois society, totality of 34, 39
bourgeois state 22n8, 30, 79, 86, 119
Brenner, R. 135n25
building-places 80
business groups 65n15

Campbell, M. 40n8, 41n17
capital in general 11, 12, 21, 34, 40; its active foundation [*sein schöpferischer Grund*] 48, 51, 85; as *active* middle, as active *medius terminus* 49, 62, 86, 84, 87; being-for-self [*Fürsichsein*] 14, 23n17; circuits of capital 10, 42n23; co-existence of capitals 47, *see also* capital in general: plurality of capitals; as creator of values 83; giving work 83; fictitious 85, 88, 92n8; as measure 13; plurality of capitals 12, 28; as a social totality 8, 21, 26, 39, 42, 46, 83; totality of, 26, 38; totality produced by working class 139; *see also* "the many capitals"
capitalist agriculture 10, 25, 37–38, 42n25, 46, 53–55, 57, 68, 74, 77–78, 85, 87; Harvey's views on 82, 92n6; its separation from industry 128, 135n24
capitalist farmer [*Pächter*] 56
capitalist mode of production 1, 43, 58–60, 63, 68, 80, 87, 89, 94, 96–97, 120, 124–125
capitalist money market 49, 85, 88, 96
capitalist social formation 1, 3, 6, 9, 37, 43, 48, 61–62, 68–69, 72, 78, 83, 85, 87–89, 94, 103, 105, 120, 129
capitalist system 1, 18, 30, 32–33, 62, 74, 86–87, 94, 129–130; its overthrow 91
capitalized rent 8, 50, 80, 82, 85, 96, 129
capitalized surplus value 20, 35
Carney, J. A. 118
cartelization 65n15; Japanese 127; landowners 77–79
character masks 4n3, 7, 9, 22, 22n8, 37, 87, 94, 126
Chatterjee, L. 80
Chile 135n27 (on laws on business-group cartel system)
China 133n2, 134n9; housing site and migration workers 132